DIVORCE

a four letter word

DIVORCE

a four letter word

Peter L. Grieco, Jr.

Michael J. Termini

Mark M. Grieco

PT Publications, Inc.
4360 North Lake Blvd.
Palm Beach Gardens, FL 33410
(407) 624-0455

Library of Congress Cataloging in Publication Data

Grieco, Peter L., 1942-
    Divorce, a four letter word / Peter L. Grieco, Michael J.
Termini, Mark M. Grieco.
        p.   cm.
    Includes biographical references and index.
    ISBN 0-945456-09-3
    1. Divorce--United States--Handbooks, manuals, etc.
I. Termini, Michael J., 1948-   II. Grieco, Mark M., 1964-
III. Title. IV. Title: Divorce, a four letter word.
HQ834.G756   1992
306.89--dc20   92-38163
                                                    CIP

TABLE OF CONTENTS

PREFACE

Divorce is an emotional whirlwind. If your feelings of loss and anger were all that you had to deal with, that would be enough. But, they are not. During a divorce, you are also asked to confront some financial and custodial issues which can affect you for the rest of your life. You are probably going to need lawyers, accountants and therapists to help you sort out the mess. It's a situation fraught with tension and anguish in which you can easily feel out of control.

But divorce doesn't have to be as bad as you have been led to believe. There are ways to predict and prepare.

We know. We've been there and that is why we have written this book. There was nothing out there that covered all the facets of divorce and, most importantly, nothing that provided a method for managing the divorce process. We have worked hard to fill this gap in the literature.

It would be easy to blame the lawyers for the turmoil of divorce, but even they are subject to the cumbersome and arcane laws and regulations surrounding the process of divorce. And, as in any profession, there are good lawyers and bad lawyers. One of the purposes of this book is to help you find those professionals who can aid you. The key is to know what you want them to do. You find that out by gathering information.

This book explains in simple terms what you can do to make the divorce process an easier and less expensive proposition. We do this by providing you with examples, checklists, case studies and guidelines. It has been our experience in the world of business that the difference between managing problems and being managed by them is education. The divorce process is no different.

In almost every divorce, the division of property and assets is the stage when emotions and four-letter words begin to fly about. There is, however, an alternative to this financial and emotional wrangling if both parties are willing to manage the process of their divorce. That alternative is to negotiate in a win/win environment. It's not easy, but we show you how it is possible. Win/win negotiations are in the best interests of both parties. The sooner you can settle questions about the division of property and assets, the less money both of you will need to pay out.

Remember, the money paid to divorce professionals (lawyers, accountants, mediators, appraisers, etc.) belonged to both spouses in the beginning.

We hope that our guide will be helpful to you as you face financial, legal and emotional issues in your divorce. Our book is written from the perspective of the people involved. What are your fears? How and when do you tell your spouse? Will I ever see my children? Who pays? And how much will a lawyer cost?

DIVORCE: a four letter word gives you the whole picture. And by knowing what to expect, we know that you can navigate through these emotionally and financially troubling times.

Peter L. Grieco, Jr.
Michael J. Termini
Mark M. Grieco

ACKNOWLEDGMENTS

Many people have told us their personal stories of what happened during their divorces. We believe that the best thank you we can extend to them is the publication of a book which will help others learn from their experiences.

In addition, we would especially like to thank Emanuel Gerstein of Emanuel Gerstein, Inc., Forensic Accountants, for providing us with the information which appears in the chapter on Forensic Accounting and Gerry B. Rose, director of CLE Publications of The Florida Bar for allowing us to reprint material from their manual, "Florida Dissolution of Marriage." Thanks are also due Mary Ellen Bateman for allowing us to use the Florida Simplified Dissolution of Marriage kit in Appendix B.

A special mention must be reserved for the staff of Pro-Tech which has given us the support, patience and guidance to see us through the process of preparing the manuscript. They are Leslie Boyce, Samra Wilson, Judi Echelson and Joe Becker. Our thanks also go to Kevin Grieco who not only showed his support, but designed the cover of the book as well.

Once again, we want to express our continued appreciation to Steven Marks, a major member of the team, for his editorial assistance in the writing, editing and preparation of this book for publication.

We hope that this book helps you to steer a course toward your future happiness.

To Mary, my best friend and wife, who stood by me through my own divorce process. To my sons, Mark and Kevin, who have now become my cherished friends, and to my ex-wife who inspired this book.

Peter

This book is dedicated to my wife, Susan, for her support and inspiration and to my children — Kelly, Justin, Casey and Brad who have lived through the divorce process and felt its pain.

Mike

To my father for his confidence and support. And many thanks to my mother and brother, Kevin, for always being there.

Mark

Preliminary Notes

This book is not intended to give you legal advice. There is no better protection for you, especially at this time, than in the hiring of a competent attorney. This book is intended to provide you with an introduction to the divorce process. After reading this book, you should feel more comfortable with what is going to be happening in your life, both emotionally and legally, during the next several months. You will not be ready to represent yourself in court after reading this book. There is no way that this book, or any book for that matter, can adequately tell you everything you need to know about how to get a divorce. Additionally, most of the legal materials in this book are based on cases and laws in a specific state. The laws in your state may vary. Again, the only way to protect yourself adequately is to hire a lawyer to look out for your interests.

Chapter 1

So You're Thinking of Divorce

You are reading these words because there is a storm brewing on the horizon of your life or because you are already in the middle of the thunder and lightning. Divorce can roar through your life like a hurricane, leaving a wake of destruction in its path—emotional pain, poor health and economic loss. But it doesn't have to be as bad as you have been led to believe. There are ways to predict and prepare. Just like farmers in their fields or sailors on the ocean, it is possible to board up the barn or batten down the hatches before you lose everything. You will need to learn how to read the signs—not only from your spouse, but in the cumbersome and arcane laws and regulations which lawyers and the courts have woven about the process of divorce. This book is intended to help you manage the process, to help you see through the smoke screens and mirrors put up by the legal community.

Let us make it clear from the start that we do not believe that all lawyers are out to gouge you. As in any profession, there are good people and bad people. In fact, there are lawyers just as upset with the present system as we are. In California at the time of writing this book, some lawyers were lining up behind a bill which would eliminate the need for an attorney when using the court for less complicated divorce procedures. California already allows both parties to a divorce to purchase a kit to do their own filing if the divorce is uncontested and there are no child support or custody issues. The new bill would allow paralegals, law clerks and law students to help people fill out the necessary forms. The bill would even allow for the training of special court assistants to give aid as well. Although primarily aimed at low-income people, the bill could make life easier for everybody if the California bill is made law and used as a model for the rest of the country. Even support payments would be handled by computer software. Punch in the financial figures and out comes a number. Before anybody thinks that this system is too impersonal and that you could still be ground up in the gears of justice, the bill also outlines a procedure for using attorneys if the parties to the divorce want them. It sounds like an excellent idea to us.

The same cautions apply to any accountants you may use in your divorce process. They aren't all out to gouge you and there are good ones and bad ones. Nor do we want to lead you to believe that this book is a substitute for the services of a good lawyer and accountant. In fact, this book should help you to find professionals who can aid you. The key is to know what you want them to do. You find that out by gathering information. The principal purpose of this book is to explain in simple terms the process which nobody tells you about.

Before you start reading about how to manage the process of divorce, let us tell you a little about ourselves and why we decided to co-author this book. First, we all know about divorce from personal experience. In the beginning, Pete Grieco had no idea of how much he didn't know about the process. He thought he had read every book on the subject and, although they were all helpful, he realized that there wasn't one book containing all the information necessary to understand the process of divorce. The books out there tended to keep the subject somewhat confusing. He found himself believing there was some truth to what people were telling him: Divorce proceedings are difficult to understand so you better hire a good lawyer.

Mike Termini and Pete Grieco make their livings as consultants to companies throughout Europe and North America and Mark Grieco is a practicing attorney in Florida. Mike and Pete tell companies how to keep their processes under control. Well, eventually the light bulb went on in their heads. Divorce is a process and the way to manage a process is to know how it is performing at certain points and times. In other words, the goal of managing any process is to make it as predictable as possible. Machines, of course, are a lot more predictable than people about to divorce each other. Still, we found it was possible to keep our heads not only above the water, but to keep our hands securely on the helm. It is possible to weather the storm of divorce. We did and we want to show you how you can. That is why this book was written—to help every woman and man undergoing a divorce comprehend the process in easy-to-understand terms.

Why Do You Want a Divorce?

People want to get a divorce for a whole slew of reasons. Whether you are contemplating divorce because you dislike your spouse, your family hates your spouse, you are in love with another person or because of economic reasons, there is always an underlying emotional reason. After all, at one point (your wedding day!) you told your spouse that you would be in love "for better or for worse, for richer or for poorer, in sickness and in health until death do you part." But then something happened. You may have stopped communicating with each other. You may feel that your spouse is holding you back. You may no longer be able to put up with your spouse's constant criticism. You may not be able to stop criticizing your spouse. You may feel unwanted and/or betrayed. There may be a lack of love, affection and warmth in your marriage or a feeling of just being there for convenience.

Erma Bombeck recently wrote a column about the trials and tribulations of being married in which she cited examples of how love can change to hate in a heartbeat. There's the story of the husband who found his wife in bed with another man and then proceeded, at gunpoint, to bond them together forever with one of those "super" glues. Bombeck tells of another story in which the bride shot her new husband at the reception. Just in the foot, but he sure knew she was angry about something. Then there was the man who was upset because the Thanksgiving turkey wasn't defrosted. He threw it through the windshield of the family car and then made threats that he would use the turkey to assault her.

Marriages can turn sour and whether it is for one of these reasons above or, as is more likely, one of your own, you and your spouse are growing apart. You feel that you would be happier (and that even your spouse would be happier) if you were no longer married. Keep in mind, however, that just because you feel this way doesn't mean that your spouse is hearing or seeing the warning signs.

Justifying a Divorce to Yourself

You aren't a bad person to think and feel that you want a divorce. You know that every marriage has its bumps in the road, but yours has been going over gullies big enough to fit a house into. Your marriage may feel like one of those sinkholes in Florida—the bottom just fell out and now you're being sucked underground. Chances are that you have tried to improve the relationship or make things easier and smoother, but nothing you both do seems to work any more. Maybe you and your spouse have even tried counseling, but even that attempt has ended up as one big shouting match over and over again. Maybe it's time to admit that the perfect match you both dreamed of will just never come to be. Sometimes it takes a very strong person, and a basically good person, to say that the marriage and the hurting is finally over. It is very likely that this is what you are saying to yourself right now: "I'm tired of hurting inside, tired of being hurt and tired of inflicting emotional hurt. I want to start over." There is nothing wrong in feeling this way if you have honestly appraised the situation between you and your spouse and found that there was no chance for a good marriage. Be prepared, however, if you are the one to announce that you want a divorce, to be labeled the "heavy." Although many (not just your spouse) will see you in this light, remember that it just ain't necessarily so.

Affairs—Living with Someone

In many instances, one or both of the spouses have already found somebody who they feel is better able to give them the love, warmth and affection which their spouse can't. In fact, this person may be the one who has awakened you to what you have been missing. The temptation is there to enter into a relationship with that person, even move in, before your divorce is final. Resist the temptation. This doesn't mean you have to become a nun or monk sequestered away in some monastery, but that you should proceed with discretion. Laws for adultery are still on the books in many states even though they are rarely enforced or prosecuted. But, judges still readily award most of the assets to the spouse who has been hurt. In some states, in fact, having an affair can be construed as abandonment. A case can be made that the spouse having the affair is spending marital assets on a third party and that the spouse is entitled to a share of what was spent.

Affairs are touchy. Only recently in Wisconsin, for example, a man accused his wife of having extramarital sex with his friend. The prosecutors did not enforce Wisconsin's adultery law after reaching an agreement with the wife in which she performed 40 hours of community service and attended parental counseling classes. If she had been tried and convicted, she would have faced up to two years in prison and a $10,000 fine. Incidentally, the husband's friend was not charged and the husband, even though he admitted to having an affair, was not charged either because officials could not prove that he had committed adultery in Wisconsin.

Our point in relating this story and many others in this book is to show you just how unfair and plain stupid some laws seem. But this doesn't surprise us. We have always said that "life is not fair." The example above is not an isolated case. The laws are still on the books. That means they can and will be used against you. In fact, just recently in Connecticut, three other people had their spouses arrested for adultery. Prosecutors couldn't remember the last time somebody was arrested for that reason. There were some who were guessing some time in the 1700s.

You probably aren't going to jail for having an affair, but if you go before a judge who has a less than tolerant attitude toward extramarital affairs, you may pay dearly for your pleasure. Keep this in mind whether adultery laws are on the books in your state or not. Divorce is still a four letter word. Which word fits you?

What About Sex?

Your sex life will be questioned during the divorce process. Make no mistake about it, your spouse's attorney will ask you some very private questions. We all remember getting asked all about our sex lives during depositions. It was not a very pleasant situation. In fact, talking about such private matters was very embarrassing. There are times, we are sure, when such questions are justified. But, all too often, lawyers are fishing for something (anything!) which they can then use against you. Going on a fishing expedition seems unfair to us unless there is just cause. Can't the same rules of evidence which prevail in most court cases also prevail in divorce cases?

In Florida, adultery is the only factor specifically listed in the statutes which has a bearing on determining the monetary award to a spouse. If you are the party seeking alimony, your adultery becomes relevant. For example, if your lover is giving you money, the courts will consider that money as income and it will relieve your spouse of some of his or her obligation of support. In other words, you will end up getting a smaller alimony check. In Florida, you need to also be aware of the fact that the time of the adultery has a bearing on the case. One court determined that a husband's adultery after his separation from his wife was irrelevant because it was not related to the cause of the dissolution of the marriage. It would be a wise move on your part to understand how your state statutes address the issue of adultery so that you can judge what actions you should or shouldn't take.

There is another issue relative to adultery that is becoming more of a consideration in the nineties. As put by an attorney friend of Mike Termini, adultery in cases where one partner is infected with AIDS by the unfaithful partner is tantamount to manslaughter in the eyes of the court. With the advent of life-threatening diseases like AIDS, the liberalism of the courts in adultery cases is quickly disappearing. Discretion is definitely in order.

Family Considerations

If you have children, a divorce is more than just leaving your spouse. There are so many factors here—number of children, their ages, etc.—that it is almost impossible to give guidelines. In many marriages, people stay together for the children's sake and so a bad marriage can go on for years and everyone suffers. In retrospect, we feel that perhaps the best course of action was to start the process of divorce once we knew the marriage was going to end. Don't wait; life is very precious and too short.

Certainly, however, part of your eventual happiness will depend upon how well your children's needs are cared for now and in the future. Your children's most immediate needs once they are informed about the divorce are emotional, whether they are eighteen months, eight years or eighteen. It is inevitable that children will wonder what they did or didn't do to keep you and your spouse together. Chances are reasonable that you will receive a lion's share of the blame if you are the one cast as wanting to get out. You will be seen as the abandoner. You will bear the burden of rebuilding your children's trust.

Mike Termini found that the best approach was to have a "family" meeting in which the spouses explained their decision to divorce, and the reasons why, to the children. It's not going to be an easy conversation, Mike warns all of you. In fact, it's going to tear your heart out when you look into the eyes of the children you love so dearly. Talk together, cry together, then try to comfort them as much as you can. Answer their questions and try to work them through the shock. Even if they suspected that trouble was brewing between you and your spouse (and children inevitably do), it is always hard for children to accept the news.

The only course of action here is warmth and a level of honesty appropriate to the maturity level of the child. An eight-year-old does not understand the complexity of human relationships quite as well as an eighteen-year-old. But, just because they don't fully understand at an intellectual level does not mean they don't fully understand at an emotional level. Sometimes, however, it seems that the young ones are better able to cope. You can't hide emotions from a child; they are masters at detecting nuances. In fact, they may have sensed trouble in your marriage long before you or your spouse did. Our advice, then, is not to pretend that there aren't any problems. Your children know; they have been reading both of your faces and reactions for as long as they have been alive. They may have even heard you arguing in the next room. Don't confuse them more by saying one thing and unconsciously showing another.

Emotional issues are important, but they are not the only issues which need to be handled as far as children go. You and your spouse will need to plan some way to take care of their educational and financial needs once your marriage is over. This often takes the form of child support and, in some cases, trust funds to take care of college. These are very complex issues and we will deal with them at length later in the book. Right now, let us just say that you will need to consider them in the divorce process right from the start and that they are part of the obligation you will bear. Remember also that this responsibility extends to loan payments for your children's education which may be the case if you have been married for twenty years or more.

Recently, a number of publications have printed stories about the sorry state of affairs regarding child support. Women who now head a household are finding themselves unable to raise a family without working two jobs, even with child support. But working two jobs means that even more money is needed for child care. It's a vicious circle and not only women get caught in it. There are an increasing number of men, like Mike Termini, with custody of their children who are not getting child support from their ex-wives. Still, approximately 95 percent of the parents who do not pay child support are men and a typical scenario is of an ex-wife and children going from a middle-class existence to collecting welfare checks. There are many proposals for putting an end to this sad situation and we will be discussing them in more detail later in the book.

Money Issues

Every divorce eventually comes down to dividing up assets, and assets mean money. All too often, the division of property and assets stage in the divorce process is full of the emotions and four letter words which we talked about earlier. Lines get drawn. One spouse is looked upon as wanting it all and the other as not willing to share a thing. There is an alternative to this financial and emotional wrangling. One of the first steps that you will be required to take in the divorce process is the completion of a financial affidavit. We will show you what such a form looks like and how to fill it out in the next chapter. You can use this requirement to avoid conflicts later in the process by jointly reviewing your assets with your spouse.

This may be difficult for some whose marriage has entered either the Cold War or something resembling the movie, *War of the Roses*. But every effort should be made, perhaps with a neutral mediator if necessary, to detail each and every asset and to sign a document which can be handed over to your respective attorneys. This list should include all personal items as well, such as furniture, jewelry, silverware, etc. In order to avoid future arguments about value, we suggest that you both prepare this list by naming the item and then assigning each item an appraised or replacement value.

Such moves are in the best interests of both parties to the divorce. The sooner you can settle questions about the division of property and assets, the less money both of you will need to pay out to the lawyers. The only people who make money in a drawn-out divorce battle are the lawyers. Don't let anyone tell you that the husband will pay in the end.

> **Remember, the money paid to lawyers belonged to both spouses in the beginning.**

Another important money issue that we will mention here and discuss in the next chapter is the determination of living expenses for both spouses during the divorce. The principal wage earner can choose to pay for the other spouse or can be ordered by the courts to provide temporary relief in the form of a monthly income. If the latter is the situation you are in, remember that court-ordered relief allows you to claim the expenditure on your yearly tax return.

Staying with a Broken Marriage

You may look at the money and emotional issues above and at your children and decide that divorce is just not an option. We wouldn't presume to talk you out of that decision. You know your financial and emotional positions better than anyone else. However, assuming that the marriage is beyond repair, there is some advice we can provide. Finish reading this book. At least that way you have an accurate idea of what you would be facing if you had chosen the divorce process or if you decide on it in the future. Don't rely only on the horror stories you hear from friends, relatives or fellow workers. It would probably be a good idea to establish a plan where you can work toward a day when you can become independent. If you have not been employed since you were married, try to learn a skill by attending classes. Search for a job or establish a career path. In other words, do what you can to change your financial position now in order to provide for the future. This will help you to make a decision the next time you consider a divorce. Don't despair if you aren't the breadwinner in your marriage and start today to prepare yourself mentally and financially.

One final word: There is a better than average chance that if you are considering divorce so is your spouse. You may have decided "no" and laid the matter to rest in your mind. In the meantime, your spouse has not put his or her doubts aside. He or she has decided "yes" and has begun to prepare for the process of divorce. Where does that leave you? Hanging in the breeze if you are unprepared. Again, even if you have decided "no," you owe it to yourself and to your children to know what a divorce entails in the event that you find yourself in the middle of one, but not by your choice.

So You've Decided on a Divorce

You now have some hint of the pain, trouble and aggravation which will likely accompany the divorce process, but you still want to go ahead. All we can say is to be prepared. By prepared, we don't only mean watch out for curveballs that your spouse may be throwing. We don't only mean be prepared for the spitters and sliders that your spouse's lawyer will be throwing. By prepared, we also mean to watch for the hard, high fastballs that your own lawyers and accountants may try to sneak by you to build their fees. ***Divorce is a "business" in which people sell you their services at a price.*** (Typically, a high price—over $300 per hour!) Although they will act like a friend who is looking out for your best interests, they will be trying to make a profit. They deserve to earn money from the work they perform. But don't forget, you also deserve to get the best service for the lowest total cost. Lowest total cost is the key phrase here, not price. We were recently told a story by a young woman who was stuck with what she felt was an unfair amount of child support because her lawyer didn't object when the judge asked her ex-spouse's lawyer if the amount was fair. A so-so lawyer at half the price may cost you for the next thirty years in unfair support payments or may leave you with far less than the half you thought you were getting. A top-notch lawyer, along with his or her top-shelf prices, may cost less in the long run. There are objectives that must be met in selecting an attorney or accountant. They must clearly know what you expect and you must know exactly what you are being charged for and that they work for *you*. We will discuss this area in much more detail in a later chapter.

While reading the newspapers, we become more and more convinced that divorce brings out more bizarre behavior in people than any other legal action. You need to be prepared for this "craziness" as well. One rule of thumb seems to be that the more money involved (whether it is actually there or just perceived), the crazier it is going to get. While we sit here writing these words, there is a divorce being fought in West Palm Beach between a successful auto dealer and his wife. In the middle of all the proceedings over how much the husband owns and what companies he has interests in, approximately $230,000 worth of jewelry and cash were stolen from his office. The jewelry, but not the money, was later recovered when yet another lawyer handed two duffel bags with the loot over to the police. This lawyer, who is not part of the divorce case for either side, said that somebody contacted him about returning the stolen goods. He won't say who because he contends that it is privileged communication.

Meanwhile, it seems that the husband's lawyers have their suspicions. A maid at the couple's home reportedly saw his wife, daughter and nephew going through the two duffel bags after the theft was alleged to happen. If that seems clear, you haven't heard the latest. The lawyer for the wife says that he doubts that there was a theft at all. He is contending that the husband made up the story as a "red herring" in order to keep attention away from his alleged involvement in a theft during which his wife's wedding ring (worth $1,000,000!!) was stolen. We're still not sure if we understand what's going on here.

Other cases aren't anywhere near as interesting, but they are even crazier. Divorce and murder sometimes go together all too often. There are the more usual murders (if one can call any murder "usual") in which a fight ends up with one enraged spouse going after another. And then there are the murders in which one spouse who feels scorned or unfairly treated acts in the heat of passion. Again as we write this book, there is a murder trial going on in which a woman killed her ex-husband and his new wife. The woman, who is 43 years old, felt that she was unfairly dumped by her million-dollar-a-year lawyer husband for a younger woman after she had helped him to the top. In the heat of passion one night, the defense claims, she shot them both in bed.

Our purpose here is not to scare you. Your divorce doesn't have to be *The War of the Roses.* In most cases, it is decidedly less dramatic than the above examples, but still as "crazy" and painful. IBM, for instance, recently became embroiled in the middle of a battle between ex-spouses. The husband claimed that his ex-wife was getting counseling for their son through IBM's employee assistance program and that this counseling was designed to "brainwash" the child to take sides against his father. The father has sued IBM to release information about the therapy his child is receiving.

Passions run high during a divorce. All we can say is to expect the unexpected because it will probably happen—from irrational behavior to feeling sorry for the spouse you are leaving behind!

You Want a Divorce, Your Spouse Doesn't

So you want a divorce, but your spouse doesn't. Almost every divorce probably goes through some variation of this theme at some point in the process. It's not like you wake up one morning after years of wedded bliss and say, "I think I'll get a divorce today!" As we said earlier, divorces are the result of a long and complicated series of events, emotions and interactions over small and large issues. Undoubtedly, you have either expressed concern about your marriage or even discussed divorce only to decide with your spouse that you would both try one more time.

Finally there comes a time, however, when one of you doesn't want to try anymore. The next step is that you are either going to separate or get a divorce. Separation can sometimes work. We know of one couple who separated for six months before getting back together. That was five years ago and they are still very happily married. Separation taught them a lot. But sooner or later, you will probably have to fish or cut bait. You may meet somebody else that you want to marry; you may wish to make a clean start; you may find it economically advisable to dissolve your marriage. Whatever the reason, you still are in the position of wanting a divorce while your spouse does not. It is extremely important at this point to make a decision which is good for you, and you alone, and not for the benefit of another.

In the final analysis, this state of affairs means there will be a divorce. You both don't have to agree. It will certainly be easier on both of you, but it isn't essential. If this is the case for you, be doubly prepared for a very difficult time. Your spouse may feel that any number of tactics are justified in keeping you in the marriage.

Marriage License vs. Divorce Decree—Cost

A marriage license costs about $100. Obtaining a divorce decree, which is the final decision and agreement between you and your spouse, can cost tens of thousands. One of the unnecessary tragedies of divorce is that the concern over costs is forgotten in the heat of the process. You want to get the divorce over as soon as possible and some settlement issue like who gets ownership of a "figurine" stalls the whole process. This "figurine" becomes the focus of an intense battle over winning at all costs. Ask yourself in a more introspective moment whether your freedom and happiness is worth this type of argument. We think the gentleman we met on a recent flight would vote for freedom. David G. Berkman told us that he looks at the whole process of his divorce and thinks that he just "got paroled from a life sentence after ten years for good behavior." He also went on to tell us that he didn't realize how much he was worth until his ex-wife became a master at accounting.

All this talk about preparation doesn't get you anywhere. What do you need to prepare for? How are you going to handle finances? How will you protect yourself emotionally and economically? Where can you turn for help and who should you avoid? These are questions we had, and we will show you how to handle them in the following chapters.

Chapter 2

Getting Prepared

The first person you need to take care of is yourself during the divorce process. You can best do that by preparing for the process and knowing its effects as well in advance as possible. In this chapter, we are going to start with your role in managing the divorce process and then discuss what you can expect from your spouse. Then, we will briefly discuss how the system often bullies one spouse, particularly the one who is the wage earner. Last of all, we will be covering some tactics you can use while getting prepared to manage the divorce process. We will also be discussing some tactics which, although illegal, may be used against you. In no way do we advocate using illegal activities to get your way, but you must know about these tactics to be fully prepared. We've had too many people tell us that they trusted their spouse until... until he or she cleaned out the bank accounts, took the cat, the dog and the children and headed for Rio de Janeiro.

Your Financial Position

A divorce, when the emotional aspects are taken away, is a process where assets are divided, support payments are decided and custodial rights to children are granted. Even though that definition is easy to say, it doesn't mean that those activities are easy. In fact, our discussion on children requires a separate chapter while the economic aspects of the divorce process are discussed all through this book. For now, however, let's focus on your financial position.

As you contemplate divorce, you will be required to do some financial planning. Part of that planning may include provisions for temporary living, supporting yourself, your children and your soon to be ex-spouse. We know that you are probably thinking that you don't have the money to live separately from your spouse and still pay the household bills. It is best to work out these financial arrangements before you leave the nest. If you leave and decide not to pay, you may be served with a "show cause" order which awards temporary support to your spouse during the divorce proceedings. In short, you will have less ready cash than before and you will need to factor this into how much you need to live on. Typically, one spouse often needs to pay for the maintenance of two households on one paycheck. For months, Pete Grieco lived on a boat because he couldn't afford a separate residence. (During a deposition, his ex-wife's attorney said that it was a luxury to own the boat. Pete's response was to thank God that he had the boat to stay on, or else he would have had no place to live.)

The best way to find out how much money you need is to prepare a financial affidavit which separately lists your expenses and your spouse's. Compare them to your income and show the whole statement to the attorneys and the court. The following forms should help you make a reasonably accurate calculation. You are not compelled to use another form if you don't want to.

ESTIMATED AVERAGE MONTHLY EXPENSES

Household   Amount

	Husband	Wife
Mortgage/rent payments	$ _____	$ _____
Property taxes and insurance	$ _____	$ _____
Electricity	$ _____	$ _____
Water, garbage and sewer	$ _____	$ _____
Telephone	$ _____	$ _____
Repairs/maintenance	$ _____	$ _____
Pest control	$ _____	$ _____
Food and grocery items	$ _____	$ _____
Meals outside home	$ _____	$ _____
Lawn/pool care	$ _____	$ _____
Cable television	$ _____	$ _____
Cleaning service	$ _____	$ _____
Total Household	$ _____	$ _____

Automobile   Amount

	Husband	Wife
Gasoline and oil	$ _____	$ _____
Repairs/maintenance	$ _____	$ _____
Auto tag and license	$ _____	$ _____
Auto insurance	$ _____	$ _____
Total Automobile	$ _____	$ _____

Insurance   Amount

	Husband	Wife
Health insurance	$ _____	$ _____
Major medical	$ _____	$ _____
Total Insurance	$ _____	$ _____

Other expenses not listed above   Amount

	Husband	Wife
Child care	$ _____	$ _____
School expenses (children)	$ _____	$ _____
Laundry/dry cleaning	$ _____	$ _____
Clothing	$ _____	$ _____
Medical/dental/prescriptions	$ _____	$ _____
Beauty parlor/barber	$ _____	$ _____
Cosmetics/toiletries	$ _____	$ _____
Gifts (special holidays)	$ _____	$ _____
Membership dues	$ _____	$ _____
Professional dues	$ _____	$ _____
Entertainment	$ _____	$ _____
Vacations	$ _____	$ _____
Publications	$ _____	$ _____
Church and charities	$ _____	$ _____
Credit cards: VISA	$ _____	$ _____
MasterCard	$ _____	$ _____
Others	$ _____	$ _____
	$ _____	$ _____
Total Other Expenses	$ _____	$ _____

Summary of Monthly Expenses

Amount

	Husband	Wife
Household	$ _____	$ _____
Automobile	$ _____	$ _____
Insurance	$ _____	$ _____
Other expenses	$ _____	$ _____
Creditors	$ _____	$ _____
Total Monthly Expenses	$ _____	$ _____

The expense form above provides you with information on how much it costs to live and does not, repeat, does not include lawyer fees, accountant bills, lost time at work, child support, alimony, moving expenses, setting up a new household expenses and all the other aggravations which are sure to come up. This list will be used in the final calculations of your divorce. Hours can be spent giving depositions (more about them later) as lawyers and accountants go over each and every number.

We suggest, if it is at all possible, that you and your spouse fill out these forms together. Most of the time, it doesn't work this way. The norm is that she fills out her forms and he fills out his and then they both start to battle over where the numbers come from. With both sides expecting to fight each other, lawyers and accountants have a tendency to inflate their client's claims in order either to receive more or pay less spousal and child support. A word of advice: Keep a copy of all the bills paid with household money for the last six months. This will substantiate your numbers with solid facts. Also, and this is hard to say, but you can't trust that your soon to be ex-spouse will put the correct numbers on his or her forms. If you thought you knew this person, you may be wrong when it comes to finances.

Now let's look at your income. This is not the same as your assets which you will list after you have completed the income form. This deals with how much money is earned by each party. Note that this form is a summary and that you will need to prepare more detailed reports to back up what you put down.

AVERAGE GROSS MONTHLY INCOME
(1 Month equals 4.3 Weeks)

	Husband	Wife
Regular Pay or Wages	$ _____	$ _____
Bonuses, commissions, allowances, overtime, tips and similar payments	$ _____	$ _____
Business income from sources such as self-employment, partnership, close corporations and/or independent contracts (gross receipts minus ordinary and necessary expenses required to produce income)	$ _____	$ _____
Disability benefits	$ _____	$ _____
Workers' compensation	$ _____	$ _____
Unemployment compensation	$ _____	$ _____
Pension, retirements or annuity payments	$ _____	$ _____
Social Security benefits	$ _____	$ _____
Spousal support from previous marriage	$ _____	$ _____

Interest and dividends	$ _____	$ _____
Rental income (gross receipts minus ordinary and necessary expenses required to produce income)	$ _____	$ _____
Income from royalties, trust or estates	$ _____	$ _____
Reimbursed expenses and in-kind payments (to the extent that they reduce personal living expenses)	$ _____	$ _____
Gains derived from dealing in property (not including non-recurring gains)	$ _____	$ _____
Itemize any other income of recurring nature	$ _____	$ _____
Total Monthly Income	$ _____	$ _____

Less Deductions

Federal, state and local income taxes (corrected for filing status and actual number of withholding allowances)	$ _____	$ _____
FICA or self-employment tax (annualized)	$ _____	$ _____
Mandatory union dues	$ _____	$ _____
Mandatory retirement contributions	$ _____	$ _____
Health and life insurance payments	$ _____	$ _____
Court ordered support payments for the children actually paid	$ _____	$ _____
Total Deductions	$ _____	$ _____
TOTAL NET MONTHLY INCOME	$ _____	$ _____

Just a little side note here: Why is it that the income list is always shorter than the expenses list? Just once, we'd like to see it the other way around.

The next step is to list all mutual and individual assets. If you have completed a premarriage property identification, most of your work is done. Few people, however, have taken this step believing that it somehow indicates distrust. Whether it does or not, the fact is that your marriage is ending in divorce and once that decision has been made, there is very little trust almost right from the beginning. Many divorces would not be so difficult or bitter if the couple had taken the time to list assets and assign ownership and value. If you have an antique silver tea set that has been in your family since Paul Revere gave it to your great-great-great-great grandparents, we don't think it's exactly fair that your spouse gets the creamer and you get the sugar bowl while you cut the pot down the middle. You should list the tea set as a premarital asset so that the court will rule that it is not community property and you will thus avoid a bitter battle. Whatever action you decide to take, remember that an ounce of prevention is worth a pound of cure.

One case recently brought to our attention by a well-known California lawyer involved a wealthy couple. Both the husband and wife were independently wealthy. In fact, the only property which they owned jointly was an 8,400-square-foot home in Malibu. When it came time to negotiate an equitable settlement on the house, the divorce process came to a standstill. Neither party wanted to give up the house. Each of them indicated that the intrinsic value of the home and its oceanside location far exceeded its market value. As the bitterness grew between the couple, so did the attorneys' fees. Finally, half in desperation and half in jest, one of the attorneys shouted, "Why don't we just cut the house in half and each of you take one half or the other!" The lawyer was taken aback when the couple immediately agreed. And so the literal 50-50 division of this final asset brought the divorce to a conclusion.

ASSETS

	Titled Husband	Titled Wife	Gross Assets
Cash	$ _____	$ _____	$ _____
Stocks and bonds			
IBM	$ _____	$ _____	$ _____
Apple	$ _____	$ _____	$ _____
Bendix	$ _____	$ _____	$ _____
Others	$ _____	$ _____	$ _____
Company stock	$ _____	$ _____	$ _____
Savings accounts	$ _____	$ _____	$ _____
Checking accounts	$ _____	$ _____	$ _____
Pension Plan			
Company plan	$ _____	$ _____	$ _____
IRAs	$ _____	$ _____	$ _____
Personal	$ _____	$ _____	$ _____
Real Property			
Marital residence	$ _____	$ _____	$ _____
Investment property	$ _____	$ _____	$ _____
Company investments	$ _____	$ _____	$ _____
Automobiles			
List cars	$ _____	$ _____	$ _____
	$ _____	$ _____	$ _____
	$ _____	$ _____	$ _____
	$ _____	$ _____	$ _____

Personal Property

Jewelry	$ _____	$ _____	$ _____
Clothing	$ _____	$ _____	$ _____
Art (paintings, statues, etc.)	$ _____	$ _____	$ _____
Insurance policies (cash surrender value)	$ _____	$ _____	$ _____
Computers and peripherals	$ _____	$ _____	$ _____
Television, VCR, stereo	$ _____	$ _____	$ _____
Tools (hand, power and garden)	$ _____	$ _____	$ _____
Athletic equipment	$ _____	$ _____	$ _____
Boats, other recreational vehicles	$ _____	$ _____	$ _____
Airline mileage	$ _____	$ _____	$ _____
Books, records, tapes, CDs	$ _____	$ _____	$ _____
Furniture and appliances	$ _____	$ _____	$ _____

Living room

Couch	$ _____	$ _____	$ _____
Chairs	$ _____	$ _____	$ _____
Tables	$ _____	$ _____	$ _____
Lamps	$ _____	$ _____	$ _____
Bookshelves	$ _____	$ _____	$ _____
Fireplace utensils	$ _____	$ _____	$ _____
Drapery	$ _____	$ _____	$ _____
Carpets	$ _____	$ _____	$ _____
Other	$ _____	$ _____	$ _____

Dining room

Chairs	$ _____	$ _____	$ _____
Table	$ _____	$ _____	$ _____
Lamps	$ _____	$ _____	$ _____
Carpets	$ _____	$ _____	$ _____
Hutch, sideboard	$ _____	$ _____	$ _____
Dinnerware	$ _____	$ _____	$ _____
Silverware	$ _____	$ _____	$ _____
Candlesticks	$ _____	$ _____	$ _____
Tea or coffee sets	$ _____	$ _____	$ _____
Drapery	$ _____	$ _____	$ _____
Chandelier	$ _____	$ _____	$ _____
Other	$ _____	$ _____	$ _____

Kitchen

Cookware	$ _____	$ _____	$ _____
Chairs	$ _____	$ _____	$ _____
Tables	$ _____	$ _____	$ _____
Butcher blocks	$ _____	$ _____	$ _____
Glassware	$ _____	$ _____	$ _____
Plates, knives, forks, etc.	$ _____	$ _____	$ _____
Appliances (major)	$ _____	$ _____	$ _____
Appliances (minor)	$ _____	$ _____	$ _____
Other	$ _____	$ _____	$ _____

Master bedroom

Bed	$ _____	$ _____	$ _____
Dressers	$ _____	$ _____	$ _____
Vanities	$ _____	$ _____	$ _____
Wardrobes	$ _____	$ _____	$ _____
Lamps	$ _____	$ _____	$ _____
Brush sets	$ _____	$ _____	$ _____
Carpets	$ _____	$ _____	$ _____
Drapery	$ _____	$ _____	$ _____
Other	$ _____	$ _____	$ _____

Other bedrooms

Beds	$ _____	$ _____	$ _____
Dressers	$ _____	$ _____	$ _____
Vanities	$ _____	$ _____	$ _____
Wardrobes	$ _____	$ _____	$ _____
Lamps	$ _____	$ _____	$ _____
Carpets	$ _____	$ _____	$ _____
Drapery	$ _____	$ _____	$ _____
Other	$ _____	$ _____	$ _____

Bathroom

Vanities	$ _____	$ _____	$ _____
Lamps	$ _____	$ _____	$ _____
Carpets	$ _____	$ _____	$ _____
Drapery	$ _____	$ _____	$ _____
Personal belongings	$ _____	$ _____	$ _____
Other	$ _____	$ _____	$ _____

LIABILITIES

	Titled Husband	Titled Wife	Gross Liability
Creditors	$ _____	$ _____	$ _____
Mortgages	$ _____	$ _____	$ _____
Credit cards	$ _____	$ _____	$ _____
Condominiums	$ _____	$ _____	$ _____
Car loans	$ _____	$ _____	$ _____
Litigation costs	$ _____	$ _____	$ _____
Loans	$ _____	$ _____	$ _____

GROSS ASSETS	*(less)*	GROSS LIABILITY	*(equals)*	NET + / -
$_____		$_____		$_____

EQUITABLE DISTRIBUTION
50 / 50

HUSBAND	WIFE
$_____	$_____

Before we move on, let's discuss some points about the above list of assets. The most important thing your attorney will want to know about them is whether you hold title to the items individually or jointly. For example, you may have the house in your name (as well as the mortgage), but your spouse may be the one who is residing there. Although you may think it is individually owned, the courts will undoubtedly view the house as joint property under most instances. Additionally, there are often items which are not listed in the present, but which can end up being very important in the future. For example, you may have an invention for which you just received a patent. At some point, you plan to market it. The invention is considered property even though you haven't made one penny from it yet. In fact, you may have already sunk a great deal of money into its development. That doesn't matter to the courts. The invention may make a great deal of money some day and your spouse is entitled to a share. The same is true for insurance. It certainly costs you money now, but most policies have a cash surrender value and your spouse is entitled to a share of that as well.

The financial affidavit is the tool you need to use to determine your net worth. Once you know your net worth, divide it in half. That figure represents each person's share of the assets and liabilities. What's fair is a 50/50 split of the net assets. This does not mean that one spouse gets half of all the assets and leaves all of the liabilities to the other spouse. Net assets is the gross assets minus the gross liabilities. This is the figure to split in half. It is also the most you are worth from a strictly financial standpoint.

And what about your financial position during the divorce process? Can you afford to set up another household? The financial affidavit will provide the court with data on what you can and can't afford. A judge may rule, as in Pete Grieco's case, that you must pay your spouse "x" amount of dollars whether you have the money or not based on the data submitted by both parties.

A tactic used by the lawyer of Pete's ex-wife was to ask for partial support and legal fees from the court. The judge awarded the support to be retroactive and ordered that her attorney be paid "x" dollars, without ever having to show a statement. To this day, Pete says he doesn't know how much her lawyer's bill was, but he does know it was far greater than the bill from his attorney. Pete goes on to say that this was the first time he ever felt like the victim. Paying a fee and not receiving any kind of justification of its size was just too much for him.

At another point, her lawyer stated that he could not represent her without some more money up front. Even though Pete's ex-wife had taken all the cash from the joint accounts and put the money in her name, the judge didn't seem to care at all that Pete didn't have any liquid assets. Not only that, but the judge gave Pete ten days to pay or be in contempt of court. The court didn't care how Pete was going to raise the money.

Your attorney will also be asking you many questions about how you handle your financial matters. Below is a list of some of the important questions you will need to consider:

- **At any time during the marriage did your spouse attend college? _____ If so, when? _____**
  - a. **If answer to above is yes, were you employed during that time? _____**
    If you were employed, state at what and when:
    _____
  - b. **Was your spouse employed during that time? _____**

If your spouse was employed, state at what and
when: _____

c. Did any funds earned by you during the time go
to the support of the family unit while your
spouse was in college? _____ If so, describe:

_____
_____

• There are many factors to be considered by the
court in determining the amount and nature of
alimony and in making "an equitable distribution of
the assets acquired during the marriage." One of the
factors set forth in *F.S.* 61.08(2)(f) is "the contribution of each party to the marriage, including, but not
limited to, services rendered in homemaking, child
care, education, and career building of the other
party." We had attempted to elicit from you, by our
prior questions, some aspects of your contribution to
the marriage. Please describe, in some detail, if
applicable, additional contributions you have made.
The more details you give to us as to each, the better
equipped we will be to be of assistance to you.

_____
_____
_____
_____

• Do you or your spouse receive gifts from any
friends, relations or associates on a regular basis, or
in an amount that seems out of the ordinary? _____
If so, please specify the gifts, by whom and when
given: _____

_____
_____

- Have you seen any large amounts of cash in the home? _____ If so, when, where and how much, and if you know, set forth the source of the cash:

  _____
  _____
  _____

- How frequently have you and your spouse dined out and at what restaurants over the past two (2) years? State the average cost for the two of you and whether you or your spouse entertain friends at these restaurants: _____

  _____
  _____
  _____

- Describe other entertainment activities in which you and your spouse participate, such as theatre, ballet, or opera, setting forth whether you have season tickets and their costs. Do you take guests? If so, how often? _____

  _____
  _____
  _____

- If you and your spouse are members of any country club, yacht club, etc., set forth the cost. Also, state whether you take any lessons at the club and the cost of the same. Do you have use of an unlimited charge? Do you or your spouse entertain friends? If so, how frequently? _____

  _____
  _____
  _____

- Do you, your spouse or your children take any private lessons (i.e., music, sports, art, educational)? _____ If so, please state from whom, for how long, and the cost of the same: _____

  _____
  _____
  _____

- Describe all hobbies or sports you, your spouse or children are involved in and state any expense involved in rental or purchased equipment, materials, etc.: _____

  _____
  _____
  _____
  _____

- Describe all vacations you and your spouse took during the last five years: _____

  _____
  _____

  a. Did your children accompany you? _____
  b. Mode of transportation; 1st class or tourist:
     _____
  c. Average daily cost of room and board:
     _____
  d. Special expenses while on trip, i.e., entertainment, lessons: _____
  e. Travel agent (name and address) _____
     _____
  f. Were any of these gambling junkets? _____

As you can see, these questions are designed to set out the standard of living to which you and your spouse were accustomed. This will be important later when the court determines the amount of alimony which will be paid.

While answering the questions and doing the exercises above, your attorney should also know whether you and your spouse entered into a prenuptial agreement. These agreements set out what your rights are during a divorce and what is (and is not) considered joint property. Be sure to have a copy of this document for your attorney.

The figures and answers you have compiled for the above will be invaluable in proving your case to the courts and avoiding situations like the above. They aren't the only figures you will have to reckon with. The divorce process entails more than just going to court. Your next step is to start assessing just how much the legal part of the process will cost.

Cost Expectations

Lawyer's fees vary greatly and the amount of their fee is not always a reliable indicator of the lawyer's competence. How complicated your case may become is also a factor in how many billable hours a lawyer charges. We have heard of hourly fees from a low of $50 per hour all the way up to $500 per hour. What each of your lawyers charges also depends on his or her status in the community and family court. A lawyer with ten years of experience, for example, will quote an hourly rate of $300. For work done by junior partners in the firm, you will be charged rates somewhere between $125 and $200 per hour. What this boils down to is 33 1/3 hours of advice from the senior partner for every $10,000 you are charged. Not a lot of time for a lot of money. In our experience, that's not nearly enough time to handle a case even to the point of mediation (covered in Chapter 11).

In Pete Grieco's divorce case, for example, his lawyers had logged over 100 hours of work by the time they reached an agreement. Mike Termini came in with over 200 hours in lawyer's fees, 60 hours in psychologist's fees and 30 hours in accountant's fees in a divorce case involving custody of the children. ***Keep in mind that for every dollar you are charged, one more dollar comes out of the pool you and your spouse were going to divide.*** Those missing dollars end up in the coffers of the lawyers and accountants you have both hired. It is to both of your advantages to control the divorce process and not spend money needlessly.

Part of the cost of a divorce will also be reflected as lost earnings. The time spent searching for a new house or apartment, establishing another household, consulting with attorneys, spending time in court or giving depositions is time taken away from earning money. Keep this in mind when you estimate how much the divorce process will cost you. Remember also that there are numerous fees and costs to consider: attorneys, accountants, arbitrators, mediators, doctors, and psychologists for yourself, your spouse and your children.

Private Investigations/TRW Report

Private investigations are rarely the motel room raids of yester-
year, the kind of story you could have read in detective magazines.
Since the advent of no-fault divorce laws, private investigations
today are usually probes of financial matters. Instead of getting a
detective to just trail your spouse to a secret tryst, you now hire an
investigator with accounting or actuarial experience to follow
paper trails. Detectives are still hired, but usually for the unfortunate situation in which one spouse takes the children and leaves
the state or one spouse leaves the state and neglects to support the
children. The use of private investigators can also identify potential witnesses in case you go to trial. They may reveal some data
which your attorney can use to support your case. Private investigators can also be used to prove that nothing out of the ordinary
is going on. Private investigations and TRW reports cost money
and you need to weigh what can be gained from such probes
against how much it will cost you.

Moving Out of the House

Leaving home in some states can be construed as abandonment by
the courts even if you and your spouse both agreed that this was
the way you wanted to handle living arrangements. This is
especially true if there are children involved. Leaving home can
also work against you in another, sometimes unexpected way.
Your spouse may be perfectly content with a separation and may
move slowly on any divorce proceedings. In some cases, this
spouse may even use legal tactics, like court continuances, to
delay the divorce further. In all likelihood, you want the divorce
to proceed as quickly as possible if you have left your home.
Delaying tactics can then be used as leverage. In other words, if
you want a divorce quickly, you better be willing to make some

concessions. Usually, these concessions must be made in your property settlement. When thinking about moving out, also remember that the longer you stay away, the more difficult it will be to go back if your spouse doesn't want you there. The court system tends to see the spouse who moved out as giving up rights. The best advice is to have the separation agreement filed with the court or to have the marital residence deemed partial support to the spouse staying at home.

Another alternative is to remain in your marital home. Some attorneys, in fact, recommend staying in the house in order to maintain your rights of ownership. Other people opt to move in with their new boyfriend or girlfriend. This may seem like a welcome relief but the hurt and anger it can cause your spouse may haunt you when it comes time to settle. Such a living arrangement will also wreak havoc in any plans you make to have your children visit you. Mike Termini says it simply won't happen.

In all likelihood, you will probably need to set up a temporary residence during divorce proceedings. Where you stay is an important consideration. Living with relatives can reduce costs, but it will almost inevitably bring up privacy issues. The first step to take after making your choice is to list all the items you want to bring with you and all the items each child may need if they are moving out with you. This is not only to make the logistics of the move easier. It is highly probable that your spouse will make it extremely difficult for you to return for something you have left behind. For the same reason, you will need to have your mail forwarded or to obtain a post office box. The latter may be a better choice because the chances are good that you will be moving again in the next year or so.

Another word about leaving personal belongings behind. We

know of some situations where one spouse has proceeded to destroy all of the other spouse's possessions. We know of one example where a wife took a pair of scissors and cut in half each of her husband's shirts, suits, sweaters, ties and even his shorts, packed them in a box and left them outside for him to pick up. That's a true 50/50 split! Sounds funny, maybe, but think about what you would feel like if it happened to you. The best way to prevent this situation is to realize that once the lawyers get involved, you will almost certainly be ordered to stay away from your home and not to harass your spouse. Pete remembers eventually getting a court order which told him what he could remove from the family home. That is why we keep telling you that planning ahead is so important. Nobody wants to be placed in this unpleasant situation.

Establishing a Pattern for Money Requirements

If you have moved out of your marital home and you are the principal wage earner, then you will have to make provisions to support your spouse and your children. Be forewarned that these voluntary payments do set a precedent in the eyes of the court. If you are giving your spouse $300 a week, it will be almost impossible to persuade the court at settlement time that you can only afford $100. You will need to prove that your income has been substantially lowered or that your business has hit hard times. What Mike Termini found was that the court cared little about what he was *actually* earning. They were more interested in what his *potential* earnings would be.

Remember, too, that your spending habits will be analyzed as well. It would not look good if you started living the "high life" all of a sudden. You must strike a balance between making voluntary payments which are too small and thus provoking your spouse into retaliating later and making payments which are too large and giving your spouse little incentive to proceed quickly with the divorce proceedings. In any event, you may want to discuss the size of voluntary payments with your lawyer and accountant before acting. It is more financially practical to have partial support established within the court system so that it is tax deductible. Voluntary payments are not tax deductible. They are considered a gift. Remember, too, that child support is *not* tax deductible either. As for the size of the payment, a good rule of thumb is not to deviate too far from what you have spent already to keep the marital home going. You can figure this out yourself by taking your checkbook and recording the amount of each check for a year or two in different categories which pertain to living expenses. If you add these figures up and divide by the number of months, you will have a good idea of what is reasonable payment.

The same holds true for the wage earner who is trying to establish what his or her living expenses will be. If you show that you only need a small amount to live on, you may end up being told by the court to support your spouse at a higher level than you may have already thought fair. Just remember to be honest and fair. The court looks at wages and expenses during the course of the marriage. Don't expect to fool the court by quitting your job six months before you decide to divorce in order to show a lowered income. It just won't fly. Like we will keep telling you throughout this book, most of the dirty tactics are "old hat" now. Still, people do try.

Joint Credit Cards

Once you have made the decision to get a divorce, it is extremely important to secure your credit position. What you want to avoid is having your spouse run up charges just to get even. At the first opportunity, take your name off all of your joint accounts. If the bank or store won't do this, then cancel the account. Depending on how long you have been married, you may have started a number of accounts:

American Express

MasterCard

VISA

Department store cards

Gasoline credit cards

Lines of credit (banks)

Stock market accounts

Video stores

Florist, butcher, etc.

Remember that you are both liable for every joint credit card you own, no matter who makes the charge. Don't listen to the advice of anybody who tells you to go ahead and charge all you want because your spouse will be the one who has to pay. In a recent court case, a judge ruled that the person spending the money would have to pay all of the outstanding bills since the normal pattern of spending for that person had not been followed. This is another one of those tricks that the courts have seen tried many, many times already. You won't fool anybody easily these days.

While on the subject, we should mention that it is also important to establish your own credit history while you are married. By your own, we mean that you should apply for credit in your own name, separate from your spouse. Many people have found it difficult to obtain credit after a divorce. Although this has particularly affected women, men are finding it increasingly difficult as well. For example, a person recently applied for a VISA card with a $1500 limit and was rejected because the alimony payments put that person in an extended position.

Other areas you will need to watch are life insurance, pensions and loan activity. If your spouse can sign for any of these items, then you need to protect them or to get the courts to protect them until a final settlement is made. These protective actions may be difficult for you to undertake and understand. We know that you think that your soon to be ex-spouse wouldn't do that. Wait and see, we say. Remember that you read it here that we warned you. Neither do you want to be looked upon as a "cheap bastard," but remember that this is your money and your investments and you have a right to get your fair share.

We know of one instance where a spouse had a life insurance policy with a $35,000 cash value. That person's spouse forged a signature and borrowed the full amount. Only after the divorce came the realization to our friend that there was no cash available. We strongly recommend changing the signature authority on your credit cards to just your name. It doesn't matter whether you are male or female: *Do It!*

In Mike Termini's case, his ex-wife withdrew the cash value of his life insurance policies. With the cash, she put a new roof on the house, a new driveway, a new central air conditioning system and bought a new refrigerator. None of these items or improvements, in the court's opinion, appreciably increased the value of the home when considering the division of the assets. Mike was later forced to cancel the policies and pay the interest on the loans because he could not afford to repay the notes.

Being Bullied by the System

Sometimes when one spouse is the principal wage earner and the other spouse has had no career during the marriage, the court system seems to automatically assume that the wage earner has to be bullied in order to get them to comply with court orders. Show cause orders, interrogatories and depositions flow in a steady stream from the lawyer of the spouse who has no career. Even when the wage earning spouse has voluntarily offered to award education and training, the courts and lawyers behave as though it's too good to be true. They act like they are sitting at a card table in a saloon in the Old West, looking for aces hidden up your sleeve. We can understand why courts and lawyers act this way. A great many wage earning spouses could care less, it seems, about how their "no-career" spouse makes out in the future. Most shocking are the wage earners who don't care about their children's welfare. We will talk about child custody later in this book.

Like we said, we can understand the court's behavior, but now we can also understand why some wage earning spouses feel bullied. This is more the fault of the legal system than anything else. Bad feelings just seem to escalate during divorce proceedings and lawyers and judges, who see divorces as adversarial, do little to stop this escalation.

The problem is that attorneys have a duty to protect their clients. Attorneys will never recommend a compromise on any financial position until they have total discovery of both spouse's financial positions. The longer it takes to get discovery, the more expensive the divorce will be for both of you in the long run.

Some attorneys aren't satisfied with just protecting their client, but want to turn over each and every pebble. Sometimes, it appears like they are just trying to rack up billable hours on numerous, petty items. Pete Grieco, for example, remembers sending flowers (costing $42.50) to a client whose spouse had recently passed away. His ex-spouse's attorney filed for disclosures from the florist in order to find out who got the flowers. So what, you may think, but let's take a little walk through this example.

These are the legal steps which were taken:

1. Prepare order to produce records.
2. Send copy to other attorney.
3. Have court issue the order.
4. Your attorney then files for the same data.
5. Two attorneys read responses.
6. Clerk files your case.
7. Copies of motion and disclosures sent to you.

Now, let's show you the costs:

1.	1 hour @ $300	=	$ 300
2.	1/4 hour @ $300	=	75
3.	1/2 hour @ $300	=	150
4.	1 hour @ $300	=	300
5.	1 hour @ $300	=	300
6.	1/4 hour @ $200	=	50
7.	1/4 hour @ $200	=	50
	Total	=	$1225

Not too shabby for a $42.50 florist bill. Now do you see why you must manage the process. The most frustrating part of this type of situation is that you have to respond. If you let it slide, chances are very good that your spouse's attorney will see it as weakness and continue with still more hostile actions.

Sticks and Stones

In the last chapter, we mentioned how the spouse who has asked for the divorce is often labeled the "ogre." All of a sudden, it seems to us, somebody who was looked upon as being a good person takes on a whole new image in the eyes of friends and relatives and not an image to be proud of. People who you thought would understand what has happened, shun or avoid you. Your in-laws begin to say things which affect your relationship with your children. We aren't saying that the spouse who left is blameless, but this should be something left to the spouses to discuss. What we are asking is that people try to understand both sides.

Nobody knows exactly what goes on inside your home and most don't ask. They only see the facade often put up by both parties. Nobody knows how unhappy you really are. Allegiances are formed based more on blood, than logic. Often, the spouse who speaks the loudest or in the strongest language, not necessarily the most truthful, gets the sympathy. Few people take the time to consider that perhaps the spouse being dumped on is providing financial support to the family, or that one of the spouses is running up bills to spite the other. No one is aware that communication and the sexual needs of an individual are not being satisfied.

Keep in mind that you will be most vulnerable when going through a divorce. It will be the time when support is needed the most, but typically the time it's least available from those with whom you used to be close. No matter how hard you try during this period in your life, you will feel pain—not once, but several times. You must be mentally prepared for this to absorb the "sticks and stones" and the verbal beatings which may come from your children as well.

Relying on Friends, Relatives and Family

The best way to be mentally prepared is to be in control of the divorce process by knowing what to expect. Again, that is the reason for this book. When we were going through our divorces, there were few guides to show us the process, and very few, if any, members of the legal profession who wanted to tell us what to expect. This book will also help keep the pressure down during a time that is definitely going to be stressful. Anything which prepares you for the ups and downs is a definite plus. Besides information about the divorce process, you can also turn to friends, parents, siblings and other relatives. Even here, however, you need to be prepared for a number of different kinds of reactions. While it's true that people who have been divorced before can give you the benefit of their past experience, it's also true that people who have not been divorced can be more impartial since they have no bitter memories and no axes to grind. Somebody who just helps you heap blame on your spouse may not be helping you in the long run. In effect, you are only holding on to your spouse by continuing to be angry.

Still, you will need emotional support during this period of time. You should find somebody with whom you feel comfortable talking, somebody to whom you vent your feelings, express doubts and desires and go for comfort. One piece of advice that we have found helpful when you do seek out other people is that you make sure to tell your friend or relative that you are only seeking short-term help, maybe just a shoulder to cry on, and that you won't be a long-term burden. This should make people feel more comfortable and willing to lend an ear or extend a hand.

You will find that your present friends and relatives (including parents and siblings) will divide into five basic categories:

1. Loyal friends and relatives—These are the people who side with you during the divorce.

2. Spouse's friends—This group is made up of the people who side with your spouse.

3. Neutrals—They are the people who try not to choose sides and try to keep both you and your spouse as friends.

4. Runaways—This group may not even realize what they are doing, but your divorce threatens them and they are frightened. What you are going through often makes them aware of shortcomings in their own marriages and they begin to avoid you like the plague because you bring up too many uncomfortable feelings.

5. Advisors—These people are the ones who tell you what to do and how you should be dealing with your spouse and the divorce process.

Keep in mind that friends and relatives can help but that often the best help may come from a professional counselor. What you need most during this time is somebody to listen, not to judge. If you have a friend or relative who can provide you with this, then you are fortunate. If you have no such person to turn to, it may be wise to seek the help of a therapist, rather than keep your many conflicting feelings inside.

We would like to put in a quick word here about using a psychological counselor. Even though this is a very emotional time for you, it is important that you keep a tight rein on what your therapist does as well as to make sure that they don't take advantage of you. Anyone can put out a shingle and call themselves a counselor. Be sure that you seek help from someone who has accreditation and credentials. We will discuss counseling in more detail in Chapter 5.

Controlling Your Emotions—Don't Get Physical

There is never an excuse for one spouse to use physical violence against another, except in the extreme and rare case of self-defense. If you have a quick temper, then don't engage in any conversations with your spouse and never meet without attorneys present. Even if you are a relatively calm person, divorces can stir up emotions quicker than a tornado can touch down and wreck a neighborhood. Your spouse knows your "hot" buttons. The best advice we can give is to walk out on any argument where you begin to "see red."

Forget about winning, forget about your pride. One careless act can make your divorce an even worse nightmare. Judges don't look kindly, and rightfully so, on domestic violence. Some states also now make it mandatory that an arrest be made whenever the police are called to a home because of a domestic disturbance. Just remember that violence solves absolutely nothing.

Close to two million wives are beaten by their husbands every year and about one-third of the women who are murdered each year are killed by husbands or boyfriends. If you are a battered spouse, you may be finding it difficult to tell anyone about what is going on. In a divorce case, you should not keep this information to yourself. Let your attorney know. This is especially true if you have evidence such as police reports or hospital visits. An attorney who knows about a history of abuse is in a position to take the necessary steps which will protect you and your children by obtaining a restraining order.

Falling Down on the Job

There are some attorneys who will advise you to start living a more modest lifestyle once you know you are going to be divorced. The rationale is that the courts will not award large alimony or custody settlements when they see that your income is slowly decreasing. The unspoken part of this advice is that you can start making more money once the divorce is final. Be forewarned! The court system may be overworked, understaffed, and a legal maze designed to confuse ordinary people, but its judges and lawyers are not stupid. If you have two jobs and you quit one, the court will be highly suspect of your action. Also, many divorce settlements these days are structured so that support payments reflect the earning power of the individual making the payments. If your income goes up, you pay more. So, as you can see, the strategy often backfires.

If you own your own business, you may have more control over slowing down your earnings. Some people have refused to take on new customers or blamed diminishing company profits on business slow-downs, recessions and depressions. Again, we only mention these tactics because they may be used against you. A good lawyer with the help of a capable accountant should be able to turn up most of these tricks. The same lawyers, of course, could help your spouse find the hiding places you thought couldn't be found. Remember, too, that many laws are not as clear-cut as most people believe, especially laws and regulations about financial affairs. Actions taken by your spouse are open to interpretation and a competent lawyer will be able to convince a judge that your spouse was acting within the law. For example, taking money out of a joint account for necessary expenses (the mortgage, etc.) or because you are afraid your spouse will spend all the money before it can be divided is not looked upon as dishonest as long as you *let the courts know where they are.* The courts are mainly concerned that the money be available at settlement time for division. The best advice is to reach a written agreement on how money owned in common is to be used.

Before we leave this subject, let us tell you about a person who put all his savings into the spouse's name in order to protect his assets. What do you think happened after the paperwork for the divorce was filed? The spouse closed the account and hid the money. Some went to the children to spend (or hide), some was withdrawn as cash (so it couldn't be traced) and some was put into a new account. By the time still more paperwork was filed to object to these actions, the money was for all intents and purposes no longer available. It was still an asset, but no longer liquid as far as both spouses were concerned.

Hiding Assets

The only way you can guard against the above is to know how assets can be hidden. Then, it is your job to see if your spouse has left any hints and to alert your attorney in the event that you uncover something. The list below gives you some suggestions of where to look for hidden assets and what to do either to prevent them from being hidden or to uncover them.

1) Write down a separate inventory of each and every safe-deposit box you and your spouse have. It is advisable to do this in the presence of a neutral witness so that you aren't accused later of taking something out of the box.

2) Locate any deeds, passbooks, stock certificates, bonds, pension plans, tax returns, loan agreements and other financial papers and make photocopies of them. If your spouse later changes information on a form or conveniently "forgets" their existence, you now have proof.

3) If you notice anything missing, note what it is right away and when you last saw it or knew of its location. Give this information to your attorney.

4) If you suspect your spouse of hiding financial deals or the purchase of assets and property, again note what you know and when. Give this information to your attorney.

5) Don't tell your spouse that you are looking for the assets you believe he or she has secreted away. This is like playing poker with your cards on the table. You can't leverage the information you gather if your spouse already knows what you are attempting.

6) Look for a pattern of cash or in-kind transactions. Many people get paid in cash in order to avoid taxes. This is also a way to hide income from spouses. Other salary dodges include deferred wage increases (until after the divorce is final). Remember, too, that bonuses and commissions are often deferred as well.

7) Examine closely any loans your spouse has made to friends or relatives. Their purpose may be to hide assets or income which can be collected later. The same is also true of bank accounts opened in the name of your children and your spouse.

These are only a few of the tricks we have heard about. There are as many others as there are imaginative people who want to hold on to what they consider to be their assets and not property of the marriage.

Honesty

Honesty is the best policy; it's also the cheapest in the long run. If your spouse thinks you have been dishonest, then his or her attorneys will only prolong the case and spend more of your marital assets in an attempt to uncover the hidden ones. What should you do if you know your spouse is being dishonest? That's a difficult question. The temptation will be to get even. If your spouse took the 17th-century dresser and locked it away in a storage room somewhere, you may want to take that Paul Revere silver tea set and temporarily "store" it with your friend who lives on some little island in the middle of nowhere. We would be less than honest ourselves if we didn't inform you that these things happen. What you do is a matter for your own individual consciences. Remember, however, that if your spouse's attorney catches you even in one little lie, he or she will never trust anything you say again. You can be sure that they will check for accuracy every fact you represent as the truth. And the time they spend checking your statements will show up in the bill.

You can, however, avoid much of this hiding by being honest and up front from the beginning. And that even starts with the way you tell your spouse that you want a divorce. Our advice is to take all personal belongings and items which you and your spouse have agreed upon when you leave the nest. The next chapter will show you how it is possible to lay the groundwork for a relatively harmonious divorce process from the very first step.

Chapter 3

Telling Your Spouse

This step, which is usually taken without much thought, may be the most critical one in the divorce process. A divorce will shake a person's sense of emotional balance and self-worth like few other events. In fact, the feelings present during a divorce are often equated with the feelings felt when a loved one dies. That makes sense because a divorce is the death of a relationship with somebody that you probably loved at some time. Think about this when you tell your spouse that you want a divorce. If you leave him or her feeling worthless or pick a time which will hurt the most, you may pay later in the divorce process. By paying, we don't necessarily mean in dollars and cents. Revenge can come in other ways, such as prolonged court battles. It's best to think a little before you act. This chapter will help you see why it is important to control the divorce process even at these early stages.

When is the Right Time?

The question above is like asking yourself when is the best time to have a root canal. Even if you hate the pain that bad tooth is giving you, it's still going to hurt when you decide to have it worked on. Same with the decision to tell your spouse that you want a divorce: even if you can't stand his or her sight, it's still likely to be very unpleasant for you when you eventually tell your spouse you want a divorce. And if it isn't a battle zone, you can be reasonably sure that your spouse is too shocked to react. Don't worry, the fireworks will happen. In fact, even if they don't happen during the divorce process, you may find yourself fighting in the years after the divorce is final. These battles will come as court actions over custody, support payments, harassment and so on. In the long run, you may be better off if you let yourself and your spouse have the conflict now as long as it doesn't escalate into what we saw on the movie screen in *War of the Roses.*

So when is the right time? We can best answer this question by alerting you to some signals which indicate that a marriage is irreparable. Every marriage, of course, has its ups and downs, its good days and bad days. So, it is inevitable that a normal person will, on occasion, think of being single again and seeing a divorce as a way out. That is a normal reaction to the stresses and strains of marriage. But, when you start thinking of divorce daily, and not every now and then as most married people do, then the time has come to start telling your spouse. Other signs are avoiding conversation and each other's presence and staying late at work more and more often. You also need to be able to recognize the warning signs in your spouse in order to protect yourself. For example, are they draining the savings to pay off your bills or canceling the credit cards? In short, if you feel as though you are generally living an unhappy life, the time has come to talk.

A word here about getting a lawyer before you tell your spouse. In theory, that's a great idea. In real life, however, we are rarely this unemotional and logical. Mr. Spock of *Star Trek* fame may do it this way, but you are a human being and most human beings think that pain is temporary. If you wait long enough, if you put on a band-aid, if you try again, the pain will go away. That's what usually happens in a marriage in trouble. You may be hurting so bad or have become so frustrated that you told your spouse that you want out, but after several arguments and crying sessions, you both decide to try again. During these early stages, most people are still hopeful enough that the marriage will work if they only try harder. Therefore, few think of calling in the lawyers. Many times, of course, the statement "I want a divorce" really means that "I want you to know that I'm unhappy." Any lawyer will tell you that a good percentage of people come to them not to seek a divorce, but to frighten their spouse into paying attention to a bad situation.

We know of a situation in which one spouse approached an attorney to see what it would cost to get a divorce and divide the estate. That person was so frightened by what the cost would be, that a decision was made to continue the marriage as the only viable alternative. This course of action is not the cure for the discontent and unhappiness which other family members may feel as a result.

That said, we want to emphasize that every married couple is different. In your case, going to a lawyer may be the best idea. You will certainly need one to advise you of your rights and of the requirements you may need to meet. This is particularly true if there are assets or money that you believe should be protected. Certainly, we think it also would be advisable to contact a lawyer if any abuse was going on or if there were any threats of physical violence. A case can also be made to contact a lawyer first if children are involved. Men, for example, who leave the marital home may be jeopardizing their rights to see their children. Lastly, if you have a good idea that your divorce will be a complicated one, then it may be advisable to speak with a lawyer before you inform your spouse that you want a divorce. One last word of warning: lawyers (as we will say again and again) tend to be adversarial in their approach to divorce cases. That's fine when they are protecting your interests. But, sometimes it is not in your best interest if they advise you to handle informing your spouse as a purely legal maneuver. In other words, it is generally not a good idea to let your lawyer convince you to serve divorce papers without having ever talked to your spouse. Divorce is not a simple legal process. It is a highly emotional one. In fact, we think that one of the best ways to make a divorce simple is to leave the lawyers out until they are absolutely necessary. As Pete Grieco wrote in the negotiation book, *The World of Negotiations: Never Being a Loser* (PT Publications, Palm Beach Gardens, FL), an adversarial approach in divorce ends with you and your spouse losing and the lawyers winning a lot of the money.

Another way to know when it is time to tell your spouse is when you find yourself saying "I want out" more than "I hope we can work things out." Or, when you walk around your house deciding what belongs to you and what personal items you will take when you leave. It's time to tell your spouse when you feel there is no way to retrieve the love you once had which is now buried under a thick layer of pain and bitterness. Certainly it's time when you and your spouse are both talking, even reasonably, about how you just can't stop hurting each other. Another sign that the end may be near is if you or your spouse feel that counseling is either getting you nowhere or you both don't even want to try. Lastly, the time may be right when you feel so uncomfortable about talking to your spouse about the problems between you that you keep stalling or hoping that your spouse will tell you first.

In short, the right time is the time when you determine that your marriage cannot be saved because there is no love, no true communication, no respect for individuality, no equal rights and obligations and no capacity for forgiveness and reconciliation. That's much more easily said than known because the divorce process is rarely the result of one simple reason. Sometimes, of course, people start the divorce process in a hasty manner. Usually, an argument leads to angry words and one spouse announces that he or she can't stand it any more. This can be costly if you are not prepared as we noted earlier. You may feel great for unloading a burden from off your mind, but your pockets could be emptied as well by creating a vengeful spouse.

Reasons for Divorce

To be honest, the following list is anything but complete. As we listened to more and more people, we came to realize that there are really as many reasons as there are couples. The list below also does not indicate how several reasons can combine and the combinations are infinite. Undoubtedly, you will read the reasons below and see that there are several interwoven ones which best explain your situation.

Our purpose here is to get you started thinking about why you want a divorce. This will certainly help you and your spouse when you tell him or her the news. The more honest and direct you are now, the better you will feel later since guilt has a way of coming back again and again to make you question what you have done. Coming up with some concrete reasons and determining which of the reasons below fit your situation will also help you now, since you will gain the feeling that you are not alone. Think of this list, then, as a way of supporting yourself during these emotionally trying times.

We must also point out that the reasons for divorce are different from the grounds for divorce. You may have a thousand reasons why you want to leave your spouse, but the courts really don't have the time to worry about any of them. In Florida, for example, there are only two grounds which allow a person to dissolve a marriage: 1) the marriage is irretrievably broken, and 2) one of the partners is mentally incompetent. All fifty states have instituted the no-fault divorce concept in some form or another, but just because you say a marriage is irretrievably broken does not necessarily make it so. A judge must determine this from the facts submitted by the parties. That is why we have divorce courts. The courts in Florida have recognized everything from abuse to lack of love and companionship to support a finding that a marriage is irretrievably broken. One court even used, as a basis for determining the economic award, the fact that a spouse was a "lifelong nag and intolerable companion" during the marriage.

The principal reasons people get divorced have to do with communication, sex and money. Money definitely shouldn't come as a great surprise. Numerous studies have shown that money is the leading cause of arguments between couples. It makes sense then that money would be a factor in a lot of divorces. How it is a factor depends on the couple. Money can be a wedge between two people because one spouse is spending too much money. In many people's minds what comes to mind is the wife running up charge cards or buying clothes she doesn't need, but that is only one half of the truth. The husband often spends money on acquiring the best and latest sports equipment or the latest electronic gadget. Overspending is not the province of only one gender. Nor is nagging about the other spouse's spending habits. Both sexes complain and the perceived inequality in spending habits is just as divisive as the reality.

Spending beyond a person's means can often be related to alcohol or drug abuse as well. In the case of alcohol, this of course doesn't necessarily mean that half the paycheck goes down the drain at the local liquor store or bar. Alcohol abuse costs money in lost days of work, in more medical bills because of failing health and even in increased car insurance because of frequent accidents. The same is true for drug abuse. The costs of dependency are often hidden, but their effects on a marriage are just as devastating.

Money also makes its presence known in a marriage when one spouse feels that the other is not making as much money as he or she could. This is often related to the overspending situation above because while the responsible spouse budgets carefully, the other spouse spends money like it's growing on trees. Like many of the other reasons we will list here, repeated and ugly arguments over money and budgets probably indicate a much more serious problem underneath. All married couples have fights over money, but a steady marriage can absorb these shocks. If you find that there is no room for agreement or compromise in an argument over money, then chances are good that your marriage may have some serious problems.

Sex is, of course, another prominent reason why people get divorced. Like money, it's never as simple as one spouse leaving the other because of an extramarital affair or because they have fallen in love with somebody else. People also seek divorces because of sexual incompatibility, loss of desire, feeling ignored and being bored. The fact is that marriage is not like those first few weeks or months when you fell in love. That does not mean there is no chance for romance, but many people are not happy with what can turn into a daily routine—have breakfast, rush to work, come home exhausted, eat dinner, watch television and fall asleep. We aren't going to tell you how to spice up your marriage, but we just want to point out that many people seek divorces because their expectation of living like a prince or princess never comes true in quite the way they wanted. Some people feel that the grass is always greener on the other side of the fence. That this lack of romance is often the reason for a marriage splitting is evidenced by the many songs which have been written about men forgetting to bring home roses or women who feel misunderstood.

A third reason why people divorce centers around communication or, we should say, the lack of it. Marriages which are headed for the rocks show a consistent feature—the partners never talk to each other honestly and openly about the problems between them. So much has been said and written on this subject, that we won't bore you with another rehash of the arguments. We will mention, however, that we believe it is just as important for married couples to communicate with each other about what is going right. It is just as important to share joys and dreams. In fact, we think this is a good method for bringing intimacy and romance back into a marriage. It shows both of you that you still care. Divorces happen between people who no longer can care like this.

All of the old jokes about in-laws are around for a reason. Your relationship with your in-laws or your spouse's relationship with your parents and family has a large effect on your marriage. Many divorces are the result of in-laws butting into their son's or daughter's marriage. We can laugh about the mother-in-law who calls up your spouse to see what was served for dinner every night, but this type of meddling can hurt . Nobody wants to be made to feel that they aren't good enough to be married to you. It will be especially damaging to your marriage if you back up your mother and leave your spouse dangling in the wind. That will be seen and felt as an act of betrayal. It is just this sort of situation which can lead to a divorce if it is repeated over and over again. The situation is compounded, of course, if you are living with your in-laws. One other note about in-laws and divorce: if you have married a person of another nationality, religion, race, or ethnic background, the pressure can be intense. The "old country" attitudes die hard. Some in-laws are not ready to accept this country's more liberal attitudes. Being at odds with your in-laws over this situation can break a marriage apart in a very short time, especially if your spouse puts his or her family before you. One public figure had this to say about his in-laws: "We love our laws, not our in-laws."

Your career or your spouse's can also be a reason why you get a divorce. Many people complain that their spouses are married to their jobs and that their careers are more important. The working spouse, in turn, feels misunderstood for all the hard work he or she puts into the job. Unfortunately, this impasse can grow to the point where nothing but a divorce will make the marriage partners happy. A career can also be a reason for divorce when one spouse feels like the other is holding him or her back from advancement or when one spouse objects to moving from state to state in search of greater opportunities.

As much as people may want to avoid speaking about this situation, children can be a reason why a marriage ends in divorce. This comes about when your spouse treats your children as being more important than you. Children should definitely feel like they are important and should be given all the care and attention you can supply, but some people unfortunately use care of children as an excuse to avoid a spouse. That's not only bad for a marriage, but ultimately not the most healthy environment for children.

Change, itself, is often the reason people divorce. You may wake up one morning and hear yourself say that you are no longer married to the person you fell in love with. He or she has changed so much that you don't even know if you like them any more. On the other hand, you may look in the mirror and think about how much you have changed and that your spouse is still the same. Change is inevitable; a good marriage adapts to life's changes. Perhaps one of the most common changes and reasons for divorce centers around what has been called the "empty nest" syndrome. The children have grown up and you and your spouse are indeed a couple again. It's been twenty-five years since you have been alone together and it's not comfortable. The solution in some cases (if you can't work it out together) is to get a divorce.

The last reason we will mention has to do with power. In the old days (about thirty-five years ago!) the power structure in a marriage was clear. Men worked and women kept a home. That usually meant that the man's position was the most powerful. He paid the bills. Today, most married couples would be in poverty if women did not work as well. Indeed, it is more than just having a part-time job. Women want careers as well. There are still men who don't agree with this. Without putting any value judgments on what a person believes, this situation will still cause a great deal of strain in a marriage. Even in marriages where the husband does not object to his wife's career, there can still be a great deal of tension. The woman often feels that she has to be SuperWoman in order to get everything done. When she complains about this role, her husband feels threatened and often reacts with surprise because he believes he was being understanding. If a couple fails to talk about these types of changes, it can result in a divorce.

We know of a couple where one person had an opportunity for a promotion, but it required a move. The other spouse did not want to move and jeopardize their own career, so both decided not to take the promotion after coming up with a number of alternatives which actually provided a better solution.

Some Patterns in the Divorce Process

Like the reasons above, the discussion of patterns below is a general one. You will most likely find that you fit all of these patterns at different times in the process. Again, we present them here so that you can get a handle on what to expect.

> *Seesaw*—First you want a divorce. You tell your spouse. He or she gets upset and you change your mind and decide to try again. It doesn't work out. Your spouse asks for a divorce. You get upset. Both of you decide to work at it again. It doesn't work out. You ask for a divorce. Your spouse gets... Get the picture. We all go through this stage at some point in the divorce process. Even though it seems like you are just putting off the inevitable, you keep hoping that something will change. Some marriages, of course, keep on like this for years, sometimes forever. Nobody wants to make the final decision to leave. Nobody wants to be the "bad guy."

> *Hide-and-seek*—In this pattern, the couple might as well live in different states or countries with a common, but heavily guarded, boundary. Both partners know that the marriage isn't good, but nobody says a word. The major activity in the marriage is figuring out how to avoid each other, and especially topics which may bring up the fact that everything is not going well. Or, one spouse or the other throws his or her self into work so that they don't have to go home. By the time it comes

to getting a divorce (if it ever gets to that point) this cool distance is maintained throughout the process.

Frequent arguers—These couples are almost the exact opposite of the "hide-and-seekers." They argue about everything—the kids, the color of your suit, the temperature, politics, baseball, etc. You name it, they will go to the opposite sides of the ring and come out fighting. In some respects, this may be the best way to handle the process of divorce, if the fighting is fair and about the real emotional issues, instead of the ones we listed above. Often, divorcing couples hide behind the arguments so they don't have to feel the pain or guilt associated with the process.

The Divers—These people just dive into the process. You want a divorce. Fine, you can have the kids six months of the year. We will divide all our assets in half. I'll help you find a job, establish credit, start a career, etc. This sounds great and it is if two reasonably mature adults are involved. If not, all the rushing to agree may come out later in the divorce process (usually around settlement time) or even months or years after the divorce when one or both realize they may have got a legal divorce, but not an emotional one.

We have tried to present the patterns above and the reasons before as fairly as possible, that is, without making any judgments about what is right or wrong. That's because there is no right or wrong. This is a book about the divorce process, not a guide to happy marriages. Whatever the reason is for your divorce or whatever pattern it takes, both are based on feelings. If you are angry and hurt, somebody telling you that you are wrong has failed to recognize what you are feeling. Don't let others do that to you during the divorce process and don't do it to yourself. The feelings you will have cannot be ignored.

Hurt, Anger, Guilt and Shame

The above heading contains the four words for what may be the most unpleasant feelings you will experience during your divorce. You will probably feel every one of them during the divorce process. We don't mean to depress you any more than you may already be, but we have to be honest if you want to be prepared. Furthermore, you will often feel emotions which are mutually opposed at the same time—love and hate, joy and sadness, relief and dread, etc. Emotions are so powerful during this period of time, psychologists tell us, because you feel as if you are a child again and that your parents are abandoning you.

Whatever the deep, psychological reasons, you need to handle these emotions now. In fact, how well you handle them now will largely determine how well both you and your spouse can heal after the divorce. Before you say that you don't care about your spouse, consider this: the better able they are to recover, the happier they will be and the sooner they will forget the pains of the past and move ahead into a new future. The same holds true for you. We think we can say with some confidence that many difficult divorces are the result of people not trying to understand the emotions which the process brings up. What we have described also holds true if you are a man. It's a myth that men don't hurt during a divorce. They may not show it or they may have learned to stuff down their feelings and "act like a man," but pain is pain. And divorces are painful.

It will be difficult for you not to think there was something you did wrong, that you didn't try hard enough, that you were a bad husband or wife. You will also find it difficult to suppress feeling hurt and angry for wrongs committed against you. During this period when you finally decide to tell your spouse, you will probably go through a sequence like the following:

1. **"WHAT A RELIEF!"**—Initially, you will have the feeling that a great load has been taken off your back. All the indecision and guilt evaporates away. You are ready to move on to a better life.

2. **"OH MY GOD! WHAT HAVE I DONE?"**— Probably within a few days, if not hours, you will begin to feel very anxious. Was it the right decision? Will my spouse hate me? Will my children hate me? Will I ever be in love again?

3. **"HOW AM I GOING TO LIVE ALONE?"**—The sudden feeling that you are now going to be alone comes over you like a tidal wave. I've never been really alone before. Am I strong enough? Where do I go when I need help? I've lost everyone—friends and family—what do I do now?

4. **"WHAT WAS WRONG ANYWAY?"**—Fear of what the future holds may send you back into your marriage. It may be especially enticing now because you and your spouse may have regained a sense of intimacy once again, now that you have been open and honest about your feelings.

5. **"I REMEMBER WHAT WAS WRONG!"**—The

little "honeymoon" period described in the step above starts to disappear. You find the same old arguments and hurts surfacing again. You learn that marriages don't get better just because somebody asks for a divorce and you both get scared enough to "try harder this time."

6. **"THIS IS REALLY IT."**—Sometimes, you may have to cycle through steps 1 through 4 several times before you get here. In this last step, at least one of you has accepted the inevitability of the divorce. That will make you feel hurt, anger, guilt and shame once again, but this time you know that you can't be talked out of it.

Now that the divorce is inevitable, it is advisable to just let all your feelings come out. That doesn't mean you should start feeling sorry for yourself. It means being realistic. You hurt, you feel confused. Denying that you do will only bury these feelings, but you can be sure that they will surface again at some time and maybe in another form. Many times the buried feelings make their presence known as an inability to get close enough to another person to fall in love. You are afraid that you will be hurt again. Do yourself a favor. Feel now, so you can be happy later. If the feelings become overwhelming, don't hesitate to get help from friends, family or professionals. You should never be ashamed to want people to listen.

What to Do if Your Spouse Gets Angry?

Feelings can sometimes get so strong that one spouse will start causing damage to personal items of the other spouse. You might find holes punched in your clothes, favorite items broken, tools missing or, in some cases, that your spouse has sold some of your possessions. Our advice, again, is to be sure to take valuables with you when you leave. If you are the spouse who remains in the marital home during the divorce process, you may consider putting items of personal value in storage or keep them with trusted friends or family. Much as we hate to say it, revenge is a factor in the divorce process. If you don't want to fall victim to some nasty scheme or action, then think ahead and protect yourself. For example, we recently heard of a wife who went on a two-day business trip out of state. When she came home, both her husband and the dog were gone. It took almost four months to locate her husband in another state with a new job. That's nasty.

The Friendly Divorce?

It's possible. Certainly, you will increase your chances of having a less bitter divorce if you are in control of the divorce process. As we tried to point out in this chapter, that means from the moment you tell your spouse. Sometimes a divorce will appear friendly to appease the couple's respective families, but the friendliness disappears as soon as lawyers and accountants get involved in discussing money or custody. About the only time we have heard of a friendly divorce is when the partners were not all that emotionally involved from the start, such as a marriage of convenience in which both people marry to accomplish a goal and know beforehand that they will divorce. We recall hearing about a friend's divorce in which one spouse wanted out so badly that he gave up the majority of the assets just to begin a happier life. This is not the norm, but it does occur if both spouses can agree on what assets to divide and how.

Lawyers everywhere will tell you that the easiest divorce is the one in which the couple was married for five years or less, had no children and had few assets to divide. In the next chapter, we will discuss getting a divorce under these circumstances. That doesn't mean that there was no emotional commitment, but that some of the baggage of life's commitments hadn't had time to pile up. Even so-called friendly divorces are laden with emotion, so don't equate "friendly" with unemotional.

In recent years, some divorcing couples have gone to mediators who are trained to help the couple come to a fair and just settlement. We will discuss mediators in a later chapter, but, once again, they will not make a divorce less emotional, perhaps less painful, but not devoid of strong feelings. The one good thing about mediation is that it does remove the adversarial approach of lawyers from the divorce process. Instead of an "I win, you lose" mentality, there is a "win/win" mentality. We will discuss this approach to divorce negotiation in Chapter 11 as well. Right now, however, let's turn our attention to the process of hiring an attorney.

Chapter 4

Hiring an Attorney

There are lots of jokes about lawyers. One goes like this:

> Q: Why didn't the lawyer get bit when he went swimming in shark-infested waters?
>
> A: Professional courtesy.

Here's another one:

> Q: How can you tell when your lawyer is lying to you?
>
> A: Her lips are moving.

There are even nastier ones, but we won't print them here. Our point is not to slam the law profession, even though some of us have had bad experiences with them. Our purpose in this chapter is to help you find and select a good lawyer who is right for you. In fact, much of the unhappiness with lawyers is due to a mismatch in style because you haven't taken enough time during the selection process. You may be a cooperative person and you may have hired a lawyer who can smell blood in the water from a hundred miles away. Your attorney sees it as his or her duty to be aggressive in protecting your rights and maximizing your share of the marital assets. You, however, know your spouse the best and that this type of shark-like behavior will raise his or her hackles. The lawyer may create a problem where there was none to begin with.

The other side of hiring an attorney is knowing what kind is required, what is to be expected and what your needs are. This side, of course, has been a theme right from the beginning of this book. We think that if you know the guidelines, you will be able to make an intelligent choice when it comes to selecting a lawyer. We will discuss these guidelines and expectations in this chapter.

How to Find a Lawyer

After you read some of the suggestions we are going to give you about how to find a lawyer, you may say to yourself, "Fine, but how do I know whether he or she is a good attorney?" The answer to that question will follow in a later section. But, first, you must determine a selection process and know where to look, before you determine what roles you and your lawyer will play in the divorce process. Keep in mind that you may be in that unfortunate group of people who find themselves suddenly served with divorce papers from a spouse who never mentioned that they wanted a divorce. Now, in order to respond to the petition promptly, you find that you need a lawyer fast.

In either case, our first recommendation is that you ask for referrals from the lawyer you currently use for other legal matters. Or, if you don't currently have one, ask a friend who is a lawyer for somebody he or she may recommend. Since the divorce rate exceeds 50 percent, that shouldn't be a difficult task. A word to the wise is needed here. It probably is not a good idea to use a friend of you and your spouse as your lawyer. Their loyalties will most likely be divided and that will almost certainly make matters more complicated. The same reasoning applies to the family lawyer. Even though you and your spouse may trust him or her and believe that you can both work together to effect a friendly divorce, problems will arise. An attorney, in order to be effective, can only have one of you for a client. There is also the potential that the attorney will be opening himself up to a malpractice claim if one of the parties to the divorce is unhappy with the outcome at some future date. In Florida, the representation of both sides to a divorce is considered unethical. Ask for the names of other attorneys and leave it at that.

You can also ask friends and relatives for recommendations, but be wary of any advice you get from them. Every divorce may go through similar steps, but what goes on in those steps can be radically different. What worked for your Uncle Bert or your best friend may not work for you. Friends and family can be helpful, however, in the same way this book will help. They can give you some idea of what to expect from your lawyer. Best of all, they may be able to tell you what to avoid and what mistakes not to make. Remember that what your friends and family see as a lousy lawyer doing a lousy job will be colored by their emotions about the divorce process in general and by the amount of bad feelings which may still exist between them and their spouses. Best advice: Factor in your friends' and family's advice with care.

Contact the local bar association and ask them for a list of lawyers who specialize in marital and family law. Although your local bar will not recommend a particular lawyer, you at least have a list to start with. We know that some people take this list and go to the local court to watch different lawyers in action. Often, you can tell which ones are the most respected from observing how other lawyers and judges treat them. Obviously, you want a lawyer who gets heard and respected. Be advised, however, that not all courts will allow you to observe the proceedings.

Another place to find the names of divorce lawyers is in advertisements which appear in newspapers, magazines or the Yellow Pages. One West Palm Beach attorney, for example, not only advertises in the telephone book but lists his service under Free Advice. People who call up get a telephone message advertising his services. Like any advertising you encounter, there are some lawyers' advertisements which tend to be inflated. They can make a divorce sound less expensive and complicated than it will actually be. On the other hand, it is no longer true that only fly-by-nights and lawyers who are wet behind the ears advertise. These days, it is just as common for respectable law firms to advertise.

Let's just take a minute to talk about the pros and cons of a big law firm. The cons start with cost. The billing rates of the large firm are inflated to cover the high hourly rate of the senior partners as well as the firm's overhead costs (offices, research and support staff, secretarial typing pool). Often, depending upon the financial size of your case, your divorce will be delegated to a junior partner or associate, rather than handled by a senior partner with more significant experience. Do not let this be a concern. As in most major corporations, law firms have a hierarchical structure of management. As your attorney prepares, he or she will consult with a senior partner to gain their insight and experience.

A law firm builds its reputation on winning cases for its clients. Therefore, one of the major reasons for using a small or large firm is their ability to provide you, the client, with the resources necessary to win. So when you look at the total cost involved, you may find it wise to select a firm where you will pay more per hour, but where your case gets resolved quickly and fairly.

When Mike Termini retained an attorney to represent him in his divorce, he selected a well respected divorce attorney known for his track record of winning. This attorney practiced alone, rather than as part of a large firm. Nevertheless, he kept a support staff of two legal assistants (young lawyers) to handle his research and routine filing activities. Without Mike's knowledge, the attorney turned over his case to one of the legal assistants—to cut his teeth on, so to speak.

Whenever Mike requested to see the attorney, he was referred to the legal assistant but was assured that the senior attorney would be handling the hearings and any depositions. When the hearing day finally came, guess who showed up to represent Mike? That's right, the legal assistant. The outcome? Mike lost everything... custody, the house, the car, household belongings. What he was awarded were the debts and obligations of his spouse during the marriage *and* during the separation.

Our advice: Be sure who you are dealing with. Retain a seasoned professional, not a rookie. The cost may be more initially, but the total cost will be far less in the long run.

Another place to find an attorney is at a law clinic. This is certainly a good place to look if you know that your divorce will be an easy one. Law clinics are able to charge fixed rates because they use as many boilerplate forms and paralegals as possible. Again, there is nothing wrong with that if you fit the criteria we described in a previous chapter—married less than five years, no children, minimal assets.

You can also obtain inexpensive or, in some cases, even free legal services from groups like Legal Aid. There are, however, several words of caution about using such agencies. First, they have rules about who they can and cannot represent. For example, Legal Aid will only represent the respondent in a divorce and not a petitioner. This means that if you are the one who wants the divorce, you are going to have to hire a more expensive lawyer. Your spouse, meanwhile, could use the less expensive assistance of a Legal Aid attorney. In addition to this rule, you must meet certain income level requirements. You must also remember that Legal Aid lawyers are often overworked to such an extent that you may, at times, feel like you are being lost in the shuffle. They handle hundreds of cases on a variety of subjects for little or no money. Legal Aid agencies are so overworked, underpaid and under-staffed that some states have even cut back on the number of cases these groups may undertake. Of course, for some people, there is no choice because they can't afford a lawyer. As a result, Legal Aid and similar agencies provide a substantial number of legal services for people in need.

Yet another place to get names of divorce lawyers is at the meetings of divorce or single-parent divorce groups. We give you the same warning here, however, that we gave you about taking the advice of friends and family. Even though a person's experiences and circumstances may sound similar to yours, that does not necessarily mean their lawyer is the one for you. Again, be aware of different styles and of the presence of emotions when a person tells you a lawyer was good or bad.

Good and Bad Lawyers

The first thing you should know about your lawyer is that you can fire him or her anytime you want. Lawyers are legally and ethically required to hand over all material concerning your case to the new lawyer you hired. You, of course, will be required to hold up your end of the contract you made and pay for services already rendered. Nevertheless, you can fire as many lawyers as you want or can pay for, but you need to know that many judges will not look kindly upon your indecision, especially if you make more than one change. There is a tendency to see frequent changes as the client's fault, not the lawyer's. While we are on the subject of other lawyers, it is also legal for you to get a second opinion from another lawyer without firing your present one. Be aware, of course, that your present lawyer will probably not appreciate that you second-guessed him or her. Still, you pay the bill, so you get to call the tune.

We must also warn you here about the practice of "lawyer shopping." When you consult with a lawyer, he or she is ethically barred from representing your spouse. Knowing this, some husbands or wives have been known to consult with a high-powered lawyer with no intention of hiring them. Their only intention is to prevent their spouse from hiring the attorney for themselves. Obviously, this is not something we would recommend. If the court gets wind of this, and they inevitably do, it will not look good for your case. In addition, it will only serve to further upset and alienate your spouse, something you do not want to do if your purpose is to hold down the costs of a divorce.

What are some characteristics of a good divorce lawyer? Here are some that we think are important:

- Able to listen with honest sensitivity to you while you are going through a very emotional time.

- Has ability to be objective and challenge your assumptions if they will end up hurting you. Tell you when you are wrong and why.

- Will inform you of rates, how you will be billed and what you will be billed for, up front.

- Explains all legal terms and forms fully and in language that you understand.

- Communicates with you and keeps you posted about your case at regular intervals.

- Completely versed in marital and family law as it is practiced in your state. Remember, every state is different. Choose your lawyer and the state you file in carefully.

- Knows the value of a win/win style of negotiation.

- Wants a fair judgment for both parties.

- Will reveal their record of when divorces were settled—initial, mediation, trial.

We think divorce lawyers come in three different models as well—sharks, advocates and win/win negotiators. As advocates of win/win negotiation in both our personal and business lives (see

Pete Grieco's book, **The World of Negotiations:** *Never Being a Loser*, PT Publications, Palm Beach Gardens, FL), we obviously favor the last category. But, that doesn't mean an advocate or shark might not work better for you in your situation. Well, maybe not a shark, unless you are able to keep them on a very short leash. The sharks go in for the kill and they don't care who gets hurt. The worst of them just care about their fee and how much they can bill. The longer the case, the more *they* earn.

The advocates are less vicious than the sharks, but they are mainly looking for their client to win and the other side to lose, badly, if possible. Both sharks and advocates build their reputations (and client base) on winning at all costs. You may find yourself literally forced to take actions you personally feel are wrong, just for the sake of winning. Some lawyers will tell you that you must press the attack because it is in your best interest. In reality, it is their interest which is at stake. They don't want you to sue them for missing something. The win/win negotiators, on the other hand, look for both sides to win. They are not afraid to go head-to-head with sharks or advocates, but they will work to persuade them to sit down and start talking, instead of continuing the attack. They will make sure that both sides play fairly.

You don't want a lawyer who launches unwarranted attacks and yet you do want one who knows how to blunt such attacks when your spouse's attorney launches them at you. You don't want a lawyer who won't listen to you when you tell him or her about the best way to approach your spouse in order to negotiate. We think that the best divorce lawyer is ultimately a good negotiator because that is what a divorce eventually comes down to. And we don't mean the type of negotiator who tries to trick or intimidate the other side like the shark who files a motion to upset you into retalitating. A good attorney, like Lewis Kapner of Palm Beach, recommends that you don't be drawn into a battle of paper. It's wasted money. Such tactics usually come back to haunt you, especially if you have children. As you will see in a later chapter, divorces are rarely over just because the judge had entered the final decree. Strong-arm tactics will be remembered when you come to visit your children or when you ask for flexibility in custodial or spousal support matters. Playing fair from the beginning is not only the right thing to do, but is, in our opinion, the smartest thing to do.

Your Attorney's Role

The role of the divorce attorney has changed since no-fault divorces became law in some states. Whereas before your lawyer may have placed an emphasis on proving what a horrible person your spouse was, that same lawyer now puts the emphasis on protecting your rights to custody and assets. Therefore, one of the primary roles of the attorney is to present you with an honest and unbiased idea of what to expect in terms of the results of your divorce. These expectations should be based on his or her legal experience. They should know the type and size of settlements others in your region and position are getting. Equally important, he or she should advise you of your rights during the process and take into consideration what you want.

Furthermore, your attorney should act in your best interests. Early in his divorce process, Pete was told by an attorney selected by his wife that he could not represent both Pete and his soon-to-be ex-spouse. The attorney recommended that he get another attorney to represent him and that the conversation they just had would be off the record. Pete was clear about what he wanted and thought his wife was sure also: a divorce that was quick and fair. He also let it be known that he was willing to split the assets and liabilities (that is, net assets) right down the middle, "50/50." As soon as Pete's wife hired this attorney, he was then forced to hire his own attorney and the dollars started to flow.

Her attorney's mission was first to get as much money as he could for himself, all the time convincing his client that he was acting in her best interest. We don't think it is a lawyer's role to see how many trees can be cut down to process all the paperwork, but to represent the client in the least costly method possible. We believe the goal should be to leave the divorcing couple with as much spendable money as possible in order for both of them to build a future.

We want to add a few words here about the inequities that exist between the sexes and their effect on the divorce process. Two of the authors of this book have been granted a divorce and have been in the field of business for more years than they sometimes care to admit. The other author is afraid to get married because he has seen what we went through. Our former wives were, to a large extent, more naive in the ways of the business and legal world than we were. As a result, their lawyers tended to be given a freer reign with fees and tactics which were designed to get at everything possible. Asking for everything, whether it has a bearing on the case or not, only made more work for our attorneys which, in turn, usually meant more work for our former wives' attorneys. Remember that spouses in a bad marriage don't listen to each other during the marriage, so why would they start after the marriage was ended? And so on and so on.

You can react in two ways to these tactics. You can get upset and refuse to give the information over and make things more difficult and time consuming. Or, if you are an experienced business person, you can cooperate and speed things along. There is no easy solution to this problem. All we can advise you to do is watch over the way your lawyer practices in order to protect yourself from unnecessary procedures which keep adding to the bottom line of the bill.

Although not strictly a role they will play while undertaking your divorce, divorce lawyers are responsible for being informed about the latest trends in spousal support and custody in your region as well. They also must play the role of keeping on top of the latest changes in the law as well as paying attention to the way various judges apply the laws. An added plus is a lawyer who is on top of tax law or who knows of a good tax lawyer. By the way, this portion of the advice you receive is deductible on your tax return.

Your lawyer should also be unemotional in the sense of not getting caught up in your story. If your lawyer is out for revenge, he or she will not be a competent judge of what to do. Their role is to seek a fair settlement. Like we have said already, an unfair settlement in your favor today may inspire your spouse to pursue a number of different legal courses in order to seek redress. Both the divorce and post-divorce periods are very, very emotional times especially for the spouse who didn't want the divorce in the first place. Keep in mind that the man or woman who tells a lawyer to drain every ounce of blood out of their spouse is not coming up with the best strategy. Revenge is not always sweet.

On the other hand, you don't want a pussy cat, either. Your lawyer must help you uncover hidden assets or information needed for your case. They should not hesitate to go to court in order to get the other side to comply. Likewise, a good lawyer will go to court in order to block any arbitrary or harassing legal maneuvers by your spouse's attorney. Your lawyer should also use his or her skills, along with your input, to come up with a number of settlement options from which you can choose. This means that your lawyer must understand the role of a win/win negotiator who is willing to use creative methods in order to secure a fair settlement.

You, too, have a role to play with respect to your attorney. One of your responsibilities is to gather records and documents which your lawyer will need to validate financial data submitted earlier. We firmly believe that if you play an active role in your divorce, rather than a passive one, you will be more satisfied and may even save money and time. Always ask for interpretations of all legal maneuvers which they take on your behalf. On the other hand, let your lawyer handle the law and don't rely on your lawyer to be your therapist or your friend. A good lawyer will be able to recommend professional counseling help for those who are suffering from the emotional strains of the divorce process.

We have included a list of items that your attorney may ask you to prepare. If you are able to gather this information or answer these questions before you see your lawyer, it will save you both time and money. The preparation will also give you a good idea of what you and your spouse will be dividing. We would even suggest that you give your spouse a copy of your preparations so that you are both working from the same data. In this way, you should be able to quickly clear up any areas where there is going to be disagreement. Don't think that this preparation will prevent all disagreement, however. But, if you can agree that you will disagree and then find a way to smooth out the differences, the process of divorce will be much easier.

1. **FINANCIAL AFFIDAVIT.** A copy of this form will be provided by your attorney.

2. **ESTIMATED TAXES.** Collect estimated tax returns; W2, 1099, and K-1 Forms; payroll stubs; and all other evidence of income since the filing of your last return.

3. **INCOME TAX RETURNS.** Include personal, corporate, partnership, joint venture, or other income tax returns, state and federal, including W2, 1099, and K-1 Forms from the date of your marriage to the present year.

4. **PERSONAL PROPERTY TAX RETURNS.** Gather returns filed in Florida or anywhere else from the date of your marriage to the present year.

5. **BANKING INFORMATION.** Include all monthly bank statements, passbooks, check stubs or registers, deposit slips, canceled checks, bank charge notices on personal and business accounts, certificates of deposit, and money management and retirement account records. You should include all records for any account maintained during your marriage by you or your spouse. Therefore, include all bank documents for individual and joint accounts, those in which you acted in the capacity of a guardian or trustee, and any record of an account in which you have a legal or equitable interest.

6. **FINANCIAL STATEMENTS.** Be prepared to furnish financial statements submitted to banks, lending institutions, or any other person or entities, prepared by or on behalf of you or your spouse at any time during the last five years.

7. **LOAN APPLICATIONS.** Collect loan applications and statements of loan accounts for all loans applied for, whether approved or not, for the last five years.

8. **BROKERS' STATEMENTS.** Provide all statements of account from securities and commodities brokers. The records should cover any account or transaction for the last five years.

9. **STOCKS, BONDS, AND MUTUAL FUNDS.** Include certificates or other evidence of ownership held individually, jointly, or as a trustee or guardian.

10. **STOCK OPTIONS.** Gather all records pertaining to stock options held in any corporation or other entity, exercised or not exercised.

11. **PENSION.** Provide documentation of any pension, profit-sharing, deferred compensation, or retirement plan owned by you or your spouse, or by a corporation in which you or your spouse have been an owner or a participant during your marriage. Documentation of any such plan must be given, regardless of whether or not you are fully, partially, or not vested at the present date.

12. **WILLS AND TRUST AGREEMENTS.** Include a copy of any will, or trust agreement executed by you or in which you have a present or contingent interest. Include those in which you are named a beneficiary, trustee, personal representative, or guardian. Be prepared to provide documentation of

those from which benefits have been received, are being received, or will be received, and that are or were in existence during the past five years. Be prepared to send all declarations of trust and minute books for all trusts to which you are a party, including the certificates, if any, indicating such interest and copies of all statements, receipts, disbursements, investments, and other transactions.

13.   **LIFE INSURANCE.** Be prepared to give a copy of any life insurance policy or certificates of life insurance currently in existence, insuring your life or the life of your spouse or the life of any other person in which you are named either as a primary or contingent beneficiary.

14.   **GENERAL INSURANCE.** Include copies of all insurance policies, including, but not limited to, annuities or health, accident, casualty, disability, motor vehicles, or property liability policies, including contents insurance in which you or your spouse are or have been named the insured for the last five years.

15.   **OUTSTANDING DEBTS.** Provide documentation with regard to all personal and business debts owed by you, whether secured or unsecured, including personal loans, or lawsuits now pending in any court. The evidence of indebtedness should indicate the name of the creditors, the date each debt was incurred, the purpose for which it was obtained, whether it is secured or unsecured, the original amount, and the current balance.

16. **OUTSTANDING LOANS AND RECEIV- ABLES.** Include any documents that reflect all personal and business receivables and loans owed to you, whether secured or unsecured, including personal loans, or lawsuits now pending in any court. The documentation should state the name of the debtors, the date each debt was incurred, the original amount, whether it is secured or unse- cured, and the current balance.

17. **CASH RECEIPT BOOKS.** Include all cash receipt books, evidence of budgets, and cash projections with regard to you and your family's financial status.

18. **REAL PROPERTY.** Compile a list of all real property owned by you and your spouse, including an estimate of the value of each property. Send any deeds, closing statements, tax bills, appraisals, mortgages, security agreements, leases, and any documentation with regard to monthly payments and present principal and interest balances. Docu- ment all real property that you or your spouse own as a sole owner, joint owner, fiduciary, trust ben- eficiary, whether vested or contingent, partner, limited partner, shareholder, joint venturer, or mortgagee. Include documentation of any property in which you had such an interest during any of the years of marriage. Provide documentation of the contributions of you and your spouse toward the acquisition of any real property.

19. **SALE AND OPTION AGREEMENTS.** Be

prepared to provide a copy of any sale and option agreement regarding any real estate owned by you or your spouse individually, jointly, through another person or entity, or as either a trustee or guardian.

20. **PERSONAL PROPERTY.** Provide all documents, invoices, contracts, sales receipts, and appraisals with regard to all personal property owned by you or your spouse, individually, jointly, as trustee or guardian, or through another person or entity during your marriage.

21. **MOTOR VEHICLES.** Provide any purchase orders, contracts, financing agreements, invoices, appraisals, lease agreements, registrations, payment books, and titles to all motor vehicles owned by you or your spouse, individually or jointly, at any time during the last five years. Such vehicles include aircraft, boats, automobiles, or any other motor- or engine-propelled vehicle.

22. **CORPORATE INTERESTS.** Gather records indicating any kind of ownership interest in any corporation, whether foreign or domestic, that you or your spouse have held during the past five years.

23. **PARTNERSHIP AND JOINT VENTURE AGREEMENTS.** Gather any partnership and joint venture agreements to which you or your spouse have been a party during the marriage.

24. **EMPLOYMENT.** Be prepared to provide docu-

mentation of employment compensation and expenses during the marriage. Such records include documentation of wages, salaries, bonuses, commissions, raises, promotions, and expense accounts. Include records of compensation owed to you but to be paid at a future date.

25. **FRINGE BENEFITS.** Provide all records evidencing any benefits available to you or your spouse from any business entity. Such benefits include the use of an automobile, company-sponsored travel, entertainment, and reimbursement for educational and living expenses.

26. **EMPLOYMENT CONTRACTS.** Provide any employment contract under which you or your spouse are performing services or under which someone is indebted either to you or your spouse for services already rendered. Include any such contract to which you or your spouse were a party during the past five years. If the contract was oral, provide a written description of its terms.

27. **BUSINESS RECORDS.** If you are self-employed, a partner, or own more than 10% of the outstanding capital stock of any corporation, please be prepared to produce the documents requested in paragraphs (6), (8), (13), (14), (15) and (26) for that entity.

28. **CHARGE ACCOUNTS.** Gather all documentation for any charge account controlled or authorized by you or your spouse. Include documenta-

tion of an account whether it is for your business or personal use. Include all statements and receipts received by either of you in connection with the use of such charge accounts. In addition, provide a list of those businesses where either you or your spouse are or have been authorized to charge purchases to the account of another person or entity, as well as any billing statement from that business. The documentation should cover the last five years.

29. **MEMBERSHIPS.** Be prepared to provide a copy of any membership card or document identifying participation rights in any country club, key club, private club, association, or fraternal group. Include a copy of any monthly statement from such association that has been sent to you during the last five years.

30. **GIFTS.** Include all records pertaining to gifts of any kind made to you or your spouse, from or by you or your spouse to, any person or entity. In addition, send all records of any transfer of personal property, by sale, gift, or otherwise, during the marriage.

31. **CHARITABLE CONTRIBUTIONS.** Compile all receipts, canceled checks, or other tangible evidence of charitable donations made by you or your spouse.

32. **MEDICAL AND DENTAL EXPENSES.** Compile all bills, prescriptions, evaluations, and re-

ceipts with regard to any medical and dental treatment that you or your spouse have received during the past five years.

You need to also be aware of the fact that there are lawyers who are unethical, just as there are in any profession. Remember that once you have found a lawyer, you can always call your state bar association and check to see if there have been any complaints made against your attorney by former clients. Lawyers are bound by high ethical standards. Your lawyer, for example, should only relate to you on a professional level. Many times, in their time of need, clients become attracted to their lawyers. A good lawyer will know that this is a possibility and will never act on those feelings of attraction. If they do, they should not represent you in court because their judgment will probably be clouded by their involvement with you.

One final word on roles. This may be the most important item for you to remember if you want to keep control of the divorce process:

It is your responsibility to ask questions and your lawyer's responsibility to answer them.

Trust, Truth and Liars

Remember, too, that the client/lawyer relationship is built on trust, so always tell your attorney the truth. The worst thing that can happen is that your lawyer gets "surprised" in front of a judge because you didn't tell the whole truth. As far as the judge is concerned, if you will lie to your lawyer, you will lie to the court. If you lose credibility, you lose the case. Period. End of story.

Both Lawyers Win, You Lose

Lawyers are part of an adversarial system and some see it as their responsibility to use whatever legal means possible to defend you and attack your spouse. As we have tried to point out, this is not always the best strategy. The emotional costs are steep, not only for your spouse, but for you, too. Revenge may be sweet for awhile, but nothing can replace the feeling that you have tried to reach an equitable agreement. This is particularly true when children are involved. As we have also tried to point out, this strategy will almost certainly cost you more money. You will not only be spending more money as your lawyer trots in and out of court at $300 an hour, but you run the risk of all sorts of post-divorce legal actions as your spouse attempts to get even. Take it from us, the only people who get rich in this situation are the lawyers. As Pete Grieco says:

> **"Love is grand,**
> **but divorce**
> **is 50 grand ($50,000)!**
> **Or more!"**

Watch out for the lawyer who keeps telling you about how he or she loves to win and that you are going to be celebrating a great victory when your divorce is over. It may be that your lawyer and your ex-spouse's lawyers are the only ones buying the champagne while, all alone, you toast yourself with a beer. When your case is over, all the lawyers ask each other is "Who's next?" Steer clear, as well, of lawyers who seem to foam at the mouth about beating the lawyer on the other side. Remember, this isn't a football game. Although your lawyer may know his or her opponent, their fun in defeating the other lawyer will be at your, and your spouse's, expense. Remember this simple rule:

**The more money the lawyers make,
the less money both you and your ex-spouse
will have after the divorce.**

It is in your best interest to control the process in your case. The reason why we wrote this book is so you will understand the process. If you know what to expect in a divorce, you will not get the wool pulled over your eyes by "legal eagles" who are looking out for themselves first. Also realize that sometimes you shouldn't try to reason with your soon-to-be ex-spouse. It may be that they didn't trust you before, so they certainly aren't going to trust you now. So don't think that you can run the whole show.

Building their Fees

By this point, some people may be accusing us of knocking lawyers too hard. That's not true. We have a great deal of respect for good attorneys, but let's admit it, there are some bad ones out there. Meeting up with a bad one while you are going through a divorce is a nightmare. That's why we have to address the topic of over-billing by attorneys. You enter the process thinking that the hourly fee quoted to you includes everything. It rarely does. Most lawyers charge extra for photocopying, telephone calls, faxes, postage, court fees, investigative fees, accountant fees, tax advice, use of paralegals and legal secretaries and other administrative and office fees.

Many people do not exactly understand why most lawyers ask for a retainer and exactly what it is. (See sample on following pages.) The retainer is a fee charged upon taking your case. It is based on your lawyer's professional standing, on what the market will bear and on the projected difficulty of your divorce. These days, it can typically be as much as $5,000 to $10,000. A retainer is usually refundable if you decide not to go through with the divorce or if you retain another lawyer. Retainers are often a source of confusion. It is not the full fee. Hours spent on the case are credited against the retainer and when the charges exceed the retainer, you are asked to replenish the fund. Your lawyer keeps track of hours worked on your divorce and bills you.

Many lawyers take a retainer in the beginning and then start billing you immediately for all hours and expenses they incur. The retainer, they explain, is used at the end of the divorce proceedings to cover the costs of court hearings which run longer than anticipated. In other words, it is the attorney's way of ensuring that they get paid *before* rendering a service. Our advice is to get a thorough understanding of how the retainer will be applied up front. Remember, it's your money; not just your spouse's money. Spend it wisely.

An attorney should discuss their fee during your first meeting and should offer you a contract to sign. Remember that you can negotiate the fee and its terms. And you can spell out what your attorney can and cannot bill you for. The sample retainer agreement on the following pages gives you an idea of what you can expect.

Mark M. Grieco
Attorney at Law

4360 NORTHLAKE BLVD., SUITE 214
PALM BEACH GARDENS, FLORIDA 33410
(407) 624-0455
FACSIMILE (407) 624-3689

RETAINER AGREEMENT

To:

Date:

I am pleased to represent you in this legal matter. This Agreement explains the terms of my retention.

Fee

The final fee will be determined by my office at the conclusion of this case. This fee will be based on the factors set out in the Code of Professional Responsibility, including: amount involved and result obtained, difficulty of the case, time expended, skill required, reputation and expertise of counsel and time limitations imposed by the client or circumstances. The hourly billing is the minimum fee. Any additional fee shall be based on the aforesaid factors.

Costs

You are responsible for all costs of litigation including, but not limited to, long distance calls, photocopies, fax transmissions, travel expenses, court reporters' fees, court costs (filing fees, subpoena expenses, etc.), fees for experts, and the like. I have your authority to retain experts and advance costs on your behalf and to apply funds from your trust account toward costs and fees.

Retainer: Periodic Payment

As partial payment towards the final fee, you are giving me a retainer of $_____ which will be applied toward that portion of the bill which is based on the hourly rate that I charge for work on the case. My rate is currently $_____ per hour for out of court work and $_____ per hour for in court work. When the initial retainer is substantially depleted, an additional retainer will be required.

Chargeable Time

This hourly rate includes all time spent on the case, including, but not limited to, conferences, research, travel, correspondence, telephone, and court time (portal to portal). Time is recorded in quarter-hour increments. Every court hearing shall be computed at a minimum of one hour. All fees and costs, including the final fee, and expenses are due within ten (10) days of billing and may be applied from the client trust account. Any overdue balance shall be subject to interest charges of 1/2% per month.

Reasonableness of Fee

If at any time you believe the bill is not reasonable, you will notify me in writing within ten (10) days of the date of the billing, and you and I will review the bill. If no notice is received, it is understood that the billing statement is accepted as correct, accurate and reasonable. The reasonableness of any disputed additional fee over and above the minimum fee shall be settled by the Professional Arbitration Committee of the Palm Beach County Bar Association, which will be the final determination of its reasonableness. The minimum hourly billing is not subject to arbitration.

Court-Awarded Fees

Sometimes the Court orders one party to pay some or all of the fees and costs of the other. Any effort to enforce collection is for your benefit and is billable to you notwithstanding the fact that the Court may order the fee paid directly to us. If the other party pays some or all of your fees, it will be credited to your account, but will not limit my fee nor your obligation to pay this fee.

In the event you discharge me as your attorney, or I withdraw, I may nevertheless pursue collection of attorneys' fees, suit money and costs against your adverse party, and you will cooperate in these efforts.

Nonpayment of Fee

In the event of nonpayment, I shall have a lien on all documents, property or money in my possession for all money due me under this Agreement and I shall have a charging lien filed in the amount owed under this Agreement against the results of litigation. In addition, I have the right to file a lien against your real or personal property or to accept a mortgage on your real property. You will pay all attorneys' fees and costs necessitated by nonpayment including charges for my time. If any lawsuit arises out of our attorney/client relationship and I prevail, then you will pay all attorneys' fees and costs.

I thank you for asking me to represent you. I look forward to serving you.

I have read this contract, and understand it and agree to its terms.

_____ _____
Signature   **Date**

Now comes the tricky question of billable hours. Like, when does two minutes equal fifteen minutes? Answer: Whenever you call up your lawyer to ask "a quick question." Solution: If you are going to call, make sure you have at least fifteen minutes worth of questions. Here's another tricky question: How do you know your lawyer actually worked five hours on your case last week? Answer: You don't know for sure, and if you distrust your lawyer on this issue, it may be that you chose a person with whom you can't work. Solution: Manage the process so that you have a good idea of what is going on. Don't be afraid to call up and say, "Don't charge me for this call. I'm looking for an answer that I asked you last month. This is only a follow-up call."

The vast majority of business and legal interactions require a level of trust which may surprise you. It is very true in our business of consulting. We have spent years building our reputation at Pro-Tech. When somebody comes to us for help, we assure them in every way possible that we are going to do the work that we have promised. We deal with any disagreements immediately. The level of trust people have for what we do is essential to us. Our advice is to look for a lawyer who treats his or her clients with the same respect.

The following story we heard does not build trust. An attorney went to court to present motions for four different clients. This attorney billed each of the four clients for two hours of time. The total time spent was less than two hours, consisting of waiting in the court hallway, spending five minutes presenting each motion to the judge and then driving back to the office. That means that the lawyer had eight billable hours for twenty minutes of work! Not bad at $200 an hour.

In the unhappy event that you do feel you have been overcharged, we recommend that you first make your complaint known directly to the lawyer and in writing. If he or she refuses to rectify the problem and you believe you are right, then you have the option of suing or going through whatever grievance procedure your local bar association has put into place. If you have selected a large law firm, the senior partners will typically mediate a client grievance. Stand your ground if you think you are right and back up your case with any agreements you have made with your lawyer. It's probably not a good idea to get in a shouting match, so don't march into the office and start accusing. After all, they are professionals at verbal warfare. Remember, however, that lawyers don't want inquiries made by the local bar association into their billing procedures, nor the bad exposure from being sued in open court. Also be advised that once the bond of trust is broken between you and your lawyer, it will be difficult to repair. It may be best to move on to a different attorney rather than doubting what he or she is doing all the time.

How can you avoid disagreements with your lawyer?

1. **Make it clear that your lawyer works for you.**

2. **Insist on regular billings, fully itemized by activity performed and number of hours and in terms that you understand.**

3. **Put any and all agreements in writing.**

4. **Be sure that the bill states whether discussions were tax related.**

5. **Keep a personal record of calls, visits, dated correspondence and time expended. This will allow for an accurate audit of the attorney's bill.**

We can't emphasize enough the need for you to keep asking questions about fees and billing practices. We have provided you with a list used by an attorney to help him keep track of his case. Look at how many items there are and consider that it doesn't include things like phone calls. As you can see, a lot of time is involved in preparing a case for a client. Also consider that as a client you get copies of everything. Your attorney will charge you for the copies, the postage and the time he or she spends on the telephone when you call with a question about the document you just got in the mail. In addition, try to estimate the best case and worst case scenarios for total fees you may have to pay. Don't stop asking questions until you are completely clear. Billing starts on "*day one*," the day you go to interview your attorney. Below is a checklist showing the types of charges you may be billed for by your attorney for a case from start to finish. Look at it and think of the amount of time and money it will cost you.

Divorce Checklist

File No. _____

Assistant _____
Client _____

OPENING

___ **Send "How We Will Handle our Divorce" (Form 1) and confidential divorce questionnaire (Form 2) with Letter 1**
___ ***Appointment***
___ **Form 2 returned**
___ **Give confidential financial questionnaire (Form 3) and court financial information statement (Furnished Form [FF] 1)**
___ **File folder to client**
___ **Agreement for fee (Letter)**
___ **Deposit received**
___ **File request**
___ **Brilldex**
___ **File open**

PETITION—BASIC

___ **Prepared (Form 4W [for wife] or 4H [for husband])**
___ **Statement (Letter 3)**

__ **Copy to client (Letter 4)**
__ **Client signed**
__ **Filing fee**
__ **Filed (Letter 5 unless requesting Service)**
__ **Conformed**
__ **Client card**
__ *60 days*
__ **Notify client (Letter 6) and send map giving directions to courthouse (Form 5)**
__ **Waiver**

PETITION—COMPLEX

__ **Prepared (Form 6W or 4H)**
__ **Copy to client (Letter 7)**
__ **Client signed**
__ **Filing fee**
__ **Filed (Letter 5 unless requesting Service)**
__ **Temporary Hearing?**
__ **Conformed**
__ **Client card**
__ *60 days*
__ **Notify client (Letter 6 if no hearing or Letter 8 with hearing) and send map (Form 5)**

SERVICE—PERSONAL—(_____) COUNTY

__ **Constable**
__ **Delivered**
__ *Service date*
__ *Answer date*
__ **Notify client (Letter 9)**
__ **Sheriff**
__ **Constable**
__ **Citation received**
__ **Determine filing fee**
__ **Citation and check to office (Letter 10)**
__ *Service date*
__ *Answer date*
__ **Return Received**

__ **Return file (Letter 11)**
__ **Notify client (Letter 9)**
__ **Return unexecuted**

SERVICE—PUBLICATION

__ **Mail returned**
__ **Motion to publish (Form 7)**
__ **Client signed**
__ **Filed (Letter 12)**
__ **Order signed**
__ **Writ from clerk**
__ **Publication fee**
__ **Copy** *to* **Paper (Letter 13)**
__ **Copy** *of* **Paper**
__ **Posting**
__ *Service date*
__ *Answer date*
__ **Statement of facts (Form 8)**
__ **Ad Litem**

WAIVER

__ **Prepared (Form 10)**
__ **To respondent (Letter 15)**
__ **Client copy**
__ **Returned**
__ **Conformed**
__ **Filed (Letter 11)**

ANSWER BY US

__ **Petition received**
__ **Reviewed**
__ *Answer date*
__ **Adverse party information to client card**
__ **Prepared (Form 11 unless includes Crossaction)**
__ **Filed (Letter 11)**
__ **Client copy**
__ **Attorney copy**

ANSWER BY THEM

__ **Received**
__ **Reviewed**
__ **Adverse party information to client card**
__ **Client copy**
__ **Include Crossaction?**

CROSSACTION BY US

__ **Prepared (Form 12)**
__ **Copy to client (Letter 16)**
__ **Client signed**
__ **Conformed**
__ **Filing fee**
__ **Filed (Letter 7 unless requesting Service)**
__ **Service?**
__ **Attorney copy**
__ **Temporary Hearing**
__ *60 days*
__ **Notify client (Letter 8) and send map (Form 5)**

CROSSACTION BY THEM

__ **Received**
__ **Reviewed**
__ **Temporary Hearing?**
__ *Answer date*
__ **Adverse party information to client card**
__ **Client copy (Letter 18)**
__ **Answer prepared (Form 13)**
__ **Conformed**
__ **Filed (Letter 11)**
__ **Client copy**
__ **Attorney copy**

AD LITEM

__ **Required**
__ **Requested**

__ **Appointed**
__ **Answer prepared (Form 9)**
__ **Answer to attorney (Letter 14)**
__ **Answer signed**
__ **Answer filed (Letter 11)**

TEMPORARY HEARING

__ *Hearing set*
__ **If theirs, notify client (Letter 19) and send map (Form 5)**
__ Service—us?
__ *Service date*
__ **Completed court financial information statement (FF 1) signed by client and returned with 3 copies made**
__ **Attend hearing**
__ **Order by us (Form 14)**
__ **Client signed**
__ **To attorney (Letter 20)**
__ **Order by them**
__ **Reviewed**
__ **Client signed**
__ **Filed (Letter 12)**
__ **Order entered**
__ **Conformed**
__ **Complete support form (FF 2)**
__ **Notify probation office (Letter 21 with FF 2)**
__ **Copy to client with instructions for payment of child support (FF 3)**

INVENTORY BY US

__ *Required?*
__ **Prepared (Form 15)**
__ **Client copy (Letter 22)**
__ **Client signed**
__ **Conformed**
__ **Filed (Letter 11)**
__ **Attorney copy**

INVENTORY BY THEM

___ **Required?**
___ **Reviewed**
___ **Filed**
___ **Client copy (Letter 23)**

INTERROGATORIES BY US

___ **Prepared (Form 16)**
___ **Filed (Letter 24)**
___ **Client copy**
___ **Attorney copy**
___ *Answer date*
___ **Motion to compel (Form 17)**
___ **Motion filed (Letter 25)**
___ *Hearing set*
___ **Attend hearing**
___ **Prepare order (Form 18)**
___ **Answers received**
___ **Review answers**
___ **Client copy (Letter 26)**

INTERROGATORIES BY THEM

___ **Received**
___ *Answer date*
___ **Client copy (Letter 27)**
___ *10 days*
___ **Client information received**
___ **Prepare exceptions (Form 19)**
___ *Hearing set*
___ **Attend hearing**
___ **Prepare order (Form 20)**
___ **Prepare answers (Form 21)**
___ **Client signed**
___ **Conformed**
___ **File answers (Letter 11)**

_   **Client copy**
_   **Attorney copy**

DEPOSITION/CLIENT

_   **By agreement?**
_   *Date*
_   **Notice received**
_   **Notify client (Letter 28) and send "Pointers" (Form 22)**
_   **Arrange for reporter**
_   **Attend deposition**
_   **Our copy ordered**
_   **Client copy ordered**
_   **Copy received**
_   **Copy reviewed**
_   **Copy to client**
_   **Reporter paid**

DEPOSITION/ADVERSARY

_   **By agreement?**
_   *Date*
_   **Arrange for reporter**
_   **Prepare notice (Form 23)**
_   **Filed (Letter 11)**
_   **Client copy**
_   **Attorney copy**
_   **Attend deposition**
_   **Our copy ordered**
_   **Client copy ordered**
_   **Copy received**
_   **Copy reviewed**
_   **Copy to client**
_   **Reporter paid**

DEPOSITION/OTHER

_   **By agreement?**
_   *Date*

___ Arrange for reporter
___ Prepare notice (Form 23)
___ File notice (Letter 11)
___ Client copy (Letter 29)
___ Attorney copy
___ Notice received
___ Client copy (Letter 29)
___ Attend deposition
___ Our copy ordered
___ Client copy ordered
___ Copy received
___ Copy reviewed
___ Reporter paid

SETTING REQUEST BY US

___ *Select date*
___ *Docket date*
___ Prepared (FF 4)
___ Filed by 15th
___ Attorney copy by 15th
___ Client copy
___ Notify witnesses (Letter 30)
___ Prepare witness subpoena(s) (FF 5) and attach $1 bill
___ File
___ Service
___ Motion to strike (Form 24)
___ Motion for continuance (Form 25)
___ Pass setting
___ Answer docket

PROPERTY SETTLEMENT AGREEMENT

___ Financial questionnaire (Form 3) returned
___ Agreement prepared (Form 26)
___ Client copy (Letter 32) with copy of Decree
___ Client signed
___ To attorney (Letter 33)
___ Reviewed theirs

___ **Client copy (Letter 32)**
___ **Client signed**
___ **Signed by all**
___ **Conformed**
___ **File with court**
___ **Complete support form (FF 2)**
___ **Notify probation office (Letter 21 with FF 2)**
___ **Order certified copy (Letter 36)**
___ **Certified copy to client**

BUREAU OF VITAL STATISTICS FORMS COMPLETED

___ **White (FF 6)**
___ **Yellow for each child (FF 7)**
___ **Filed**

FINAL HEARING

___ *Set time/date*
___ **Notify client**
___ **Notify attorney**
___ **Attend hearing**

TRANSFER ASSETS

___ **Prepare deed to house (Form 28)**
___ **Sign deeds**
___ **Conformed**
___ **Record deeds (Letter 37)**
___ **Prepare escrow assignment (Letter 38)**
___ **Sign escrow assignment letter**
___ **Mail escrow letter**
___ **Client copies**
___ **Copies to attorney**
___ **Transfer car title (Special Instruction 1)**
___ **Deliver car title**
___ **Transfer securities**
___ **Insurance beneficiary designations**

DISMISS

___ **Prepare motion (Form 29)**
___ **Attorney signed (Letter 39)**
___ **File (Letter 12)**
___ **Client copy**
___ **Attorney copy**
___ **Conformed**
___ **Notify client (Letter 40)**

WITHDRAW

___ **Client authorization**
___ **Substitute attorney?**
___ **Prepare motion (Form 30)**
___ **Client signed**
___ **Signed by all**
___ **Review theirs**
___ **Signed by all**
___ **File with court (Letter 12)**
___ **Deliver to new attorney**
___ **Order entered**
___ **Conformed**

WINDING UP

___ **Work up time records**
___ **Final bill (Letter 41)**
___ **Strip file**
___ **Send items to client (Letter 42)**
___ **Receipt returned**
___ **Fees paid**
___ **Close file**

**(Used with permission of
The Florida Bar: Continuing Legal Education Series,
Florida Dissolution of Marriage.)**

Interviewing an Attorney

Should you shop around for a lawyer? You bet you should. Unless, of course, the only reason you are shopping around is because you are trying to stop your spouse from using those lawyers. A divorce is a major event in your life. It's not like going to the grocery store and taking a box of cereal off the shelf. It's more like going through a pile of peaches and trying to find the one with no blemishes or bruises.

Just as you wouldn't go to the grocery store to buy a week's worth of groceries without a shopping list, so you shouldn't march into an interview without being prepared. The best advice we can give is to prepare documentation about your financial stability and assets as discussed in Chapter Two. And don't forget to write it all down. Avoid trying to recall what you own or else you'll sound like this: "We have this old grandfather clock that Grandpa said was made in 1635. I think it's worth a lot of money." Find out how much it's worth. Put down the clockmaker's name, the year it was made and how much it has been appraised for. This advice applies to everyday living objects as well. Don't say: "We have some nice furniture. You know, a sofa, some beds, an oak dining room table." List them by room and assign a dollar figure to each and every item, including all the assets in each room.

In addition to property and assets, you can also be prepared by starting to think of how custody and support can be handled. You should provide the potential lawyer with an indication of how difficult these two issues might become. This will give him or her a better idea of how long the process will last and how much outside "help" will be needed, such as accountants, appraisers, etc. While doing this, however, don't get overcome by emotion. Don't lead the lawyer to think that your spouse is going to be fighting you tooth and nail, if you honestly feel this is not the case. You also need to be honest in order to determine whether the lawyer can effectively deal with the issues in your case during the divorce proceedings. Remember, too, that if you expect the worse, it very often happens. Less than reputable lawyers will make sure the divorce process is long and expensive, since they concentrate on billable hours. After all, when there is no client, there is no money being earned.

Peter would like to share this story about interviewing a potential lawyer. Peter makes a one hour appointment at $150 an hour with a prominent attorney in Palm Beach for 6 p.m. one evening. He arrives on time and, after being told that the lawyer would be with him shortly, waits for twenty minutes. (It turns out that, unbeknownst to Peter, the meter has already started to run.) When he is finally escorted into the conference room, Pete comes face to face with the most disorganized person he has ever met. There were files piled on tables, on bookshelves and on the floor. You couldn't even walk, Pete said.

The lawyer introduces himself and announces that he has dealt with hundreds of these cases. Next question to Pete is "How much do you earn? I'm expensive and I normally deal with rich women."

The next thing that happens is that the phone rings. The lawyer covers the mouthpiece and tells Pete to keep on talking. Don't worry, he assures Pete, I can listen to two people at once. I do it all the time. (Double billing?) So Pete starts talking to himself. In comes the lawyer's secretary who tells the lawyer that there are two more calls waiting. What happened next Pete says he finds hard to believe. The lawyer starts talking to the other lawyer on the phone about a case, right in front of Pete. The lawyer then asks his colleague how much money from fees has he collected to date and that he would not settle the case unless he got $100 more than the other attorney.

At this point, Pete stands up and tells the lawyer that he doesn't believe they can work together and that he has other attorneys he wants to interview. The lawyer looks at the clock (by now, it's almost 7 p.m.) and tells Pete that he needs a check for the interview. Pete tells him that since he only got fifteen minutes of time, that is all he is going to pay for and that he would send the check by mail when he got a statement. Watch out for this type, Pete says. Whether you are rich or poor, everybody deserves respect. Ironically, this lawyer was recently rated as one of the top ten in Florida.

What should you look for when you go shopping for a lawyer? Certainly, competence is high on the list of things you want. One clear way to know if your lawyer is competent is to find out whether other attorneys respect him or her? Also check with the bar association to see whether their list of recommended lawyers matches yours. Another characteristic which is important is compatibility. By that, we don't mean that your lawyer should put a happy face on every time you walk into the office. Nor do we mean that your lawyer should hold your hand and agree with everything you say. We mean to find a lawyer who can meet your needs. You will have to trust this person with your assets for the next few months (maybe even longer) so you better find one with whom you can work closely and effectively. Above all, you and your attorney should be in exact agreement on your negotiating stance. If you are looking for a win/win solution and your attorney wants to waltz all over the sobbing hulk of your spouse, you are going to have major problems. Attorneys can either start fires or stop them. We will be discussing negotiating settlements in much more detail in Chapter 11.

Cost is another consideration which will come up while lawyer shopping. You will have to pay to interview an attorney for the initial conference. There is no free legal information. The practice of paying for your initial visit discourages the type of "lawyer shopping" which we talked about earlier, but it may be the best money you spend. As for the fees themselves, we have pointed out before that the amount of a lawyer's fees is not always a reliable indicator of competence, or of how well your divorce case will be handled. The high-priced lawyer may charge higher rates and take a longer time with the process. Another lawyer may charge much less, but you are buying a lot more hours of time. Take a look at the following chart:

HOURS	RATE $/HR	TOTAL
10	$100	$ 1,000
200	$100	$20,000
10	$150	$ 1,500
100	$150	$15,000
10	$300	$ 3,000
100	$300	$30,000

One hundred hours at $300 per hour buys you only 12.5 days of time. You can quickly see that you don't get much help for 100 hours of work. So don't let the attorney start firing off a shot for every shot fired by your spouse's attorney. It is not worth the attorney's fees. Pick and choose your battles carefully; select the ones you want to win.

Also remember to find out whether one rate applies to all the work done on your case. It seems unfair and it is extremely expensive to pay top dollar for junior lawyers to do administrative tasks. We recommend that you pay what you can afford and look for the lawyer in your price range who is the most competent and who you trust the most.

Now that you have developed a short list of potential lawyers, set up a conference to discuss your case. What should you ask him or her? Our quick response is to ask any question that *you* want answered. Here are some guidelines which will assist you in coming up with your own list.

QUESTIONS TO ASK
WHEN INTERVIEWING A LAWYER

- How long have you been practicing law?
- What percentage of your practice is divorce cases? What percentage deals with custodial issues?
- How much trial experience do you have? Have you handled cases with a similar level of assets?
- What were the outcomes of similar divorce cases that went to trial?
- How many of your divorce cases have been contested?
- Are you willing to go to court if necessary?
- Will you try to find creative solutions in order to avoid going to court unnecessarily?
- Who will handle the bulk of my case—you or a junior partner? If a junior partner, when can I interview him or her?
- How do you feel about custody rights and support obligations? What are the laws on each in this state?

- How much experience do you have with tax issues?
- How will I be able to contact you? Will it be easy or difficult? Do you return phone calls?
- Based on what I've told you, about how long do you estimate the divorce process to take? Describe the steps in the process.
- What will you expect me to do? What information will I need to obtain or gather?
- What are your hourly rates? Do they differ whether you are in court or in the office? How do your rates compare to your colleagues in the area?
- What is your retainer and how frequently do you require payments?
- Why should I select you? What are your strengths?
- Tell me about your style?
- Have you used mediation as a tool? What were the results?
- What will I pay for phone calls, copies, letters, express mail, etc?
- Who do you consult with when the services of accountants, psychologists, and other professionals are needed? What are their rates?
- How many hours of work do you estimate this case will take?
- Do you bill both clients when you appear in court while handling more than one motion?
- What about temporary alimony? What can I expect to receive/pay?
- Should I leave the house now or should my spouse leave?
- Do I need to cancel my charge cards with my spouse's name on them?
- What is the maximum and minimum I can expect from this case?

If you don't like the hard work of interviewing attorneys and don't really care about controlling the process of your divorce, you could always contact the people who ran this advertisement in the *International Herald Tribune.*

LEGAL SERVICES

DIVORCE - FAST. Las Vegas, Reno or Dominican Republic. (followed by an address and fax number)

That doesn't exactly inspire trust and confidence. We suggest you stick with a more traditional means of getting a divorce.

Confidentiality and Trust

All discussions with your lawyer are confidential, even the initial interview. If your lawyer breaks this rule in any way, get a new one immediately and report him or her to your local bar association. It is not only unethical; it is illegal. The reason why the lawyer-client relationship is privileged is so that there is enough trust in the relationship for the lawyer to defend your interests to the best of his or her ability. Be sure to obtain a retainer agreement which explicitly states services and fees as well as your obligations.

Trust is, of course, a two-way street. If you want honesty, you have to be honest. It is always the best strategy to tell the whole truth and nothing but the truth to your lawyer. That means warts and all, or you risk cutting the legs out from beneath your case. If you lie about assets to your lawyer and your spouse's lawyer uncovers them, this undermines your lawyer's credibility. Most likely, your spouse will know if you are being deceptive in any way. He or she may not be able to prove it, but they can create enough legal harassment to make your life miserable and to make the costs of the divorce skyrocket. You also run the risk of encouraging retaliatory tactics by your spouse, their lawyer or the judge.

Not telling the whole truth also makes it difficult for your lawyer to prepare the best case. If you're hiding something and the other side finds out, your lawyer will not have time to present your side in the best possible light. Let's say you have a very hot temper and break down walls. Your lawyer could present facts which support why this happens, but not if you haven't alerted the lawyer to the problem. We repeat, the worst thing that can happen to your case in court is not to be able to say anything because your lawyer was caught off guard and not being able to rebut because you were being less than truthful.

Truth, Truth, Truth

Remember, too, that if you are caught in a lie or misrepresentation of facts, it will affect how the judge decides on the final settlement including the awarding of custody of the children. Nobody is going to give the benefit of doubt to a less than honest person or an outright liar. And the courts ability to rule on settlements and custody doesn't end with the final decree if they found out later that you lied during the divorce process. You aren't "scot-free" just because the courts didn't discover your hidden assets earlier. The courts still have jurisdiction over your case and can reverse itself in order to correct an act of fraud.

If you don't trust the way your lawyer is handling your case or a certain situation, talk it over with him or her. Don't stew about it and blow up later. You are only hurting yourself in the long run. Lastly, think long and hard if your lawyer tells you to lie. Do you really want such a person defending your interests? What makes you so sure that he or she won't lie to you as well?

Playing by the Book vs. Dirty Tactics

For the same reason you want to avoid lawyers who will encourage you to lie, you also want to avoid a lawyer who advocates using dirty tactics. You may be incredibly angry at your spouse. They may have left you for someone else. They may have taken the children and left town. A good attorney will take all this into consideration when representing you. But, they won't get angry. They should not be encouraging you to go for blood. They should be advising you instead on what to do to protect your interests.

On the other hand, don't make the assumption that all retaliatory tactics are dirty. Some legal maneuvers are designed not to attack, but to prevent attack. For instance, your lawyer may advise you to cancel your joint credit cards. That's not dirty; it's self-protection. In fact, that's playing by the book, although your spouse may not agree with you. Believe us when we say that you will think it is smart if you don't cancel them and find that your spouse has "maxed out" all your cards. Being fair doesn't mean caving in. Be aware that being fair can also be costly if you are voluntarily paying support. It may not be fair if the other spouse decides to prolong the divorce process. Always ask the question of what is fair for each particular action. On the other hand, don't go to the other extreme and make the other side angry so that they will want to get even.

Joint Attorney—Pros and Cons

Whether you would benefit by having a joint attorney depends on the lawyer and on you and your spouse. In most cases, this type of arrangement is not going to work if there are any areas of dispute. And most lawyers will not represent both parties. Your answer to that is probably that if there weren't any areas of dispute, we wouldn't be getting divorced. So I suppose we should say major disputes over settlements, custody, tax issues, property, real estate, etc. Rare is the divorce case that doesn't have some problems in at least one of these areas. Again, it is a matter of degree. If you are talking about who gets the couch and who gets the dining room table, hiring two lawyers will undoubtedly cost more than ten couches or tables. Somewhere, the law of diminishing returns comes into play. How much can you gain (or, not lose) when each of you hire your own attorney?

As long as you both control the process, it will work. It won't work when your spouse's attorney says not to talk to you because it's not in their best interest. Often, the lawyers don't want you to settle issues because that means less money in their pockets. The attorney of Pete's ex-wife drove a $60,000 Mercedes. Pete's attorney drove a Honda. Guess whose bills were bigger? Who had to pay for overhead expenses and fancy offices? The answer is that both you and your spouse will have to pay. Charity begins at home. We think you would be better off splitting the money in half than giving a share to a third party.

What we are saying is that you may be able to do a lot of the negotiating yourself, but it is highly advisable to get an attorney to advise you. He or she will notice any unforeseen legal consequences in your agreement. For instance, you may have worked out a custodial arrangement in which you are jeopardizing your future ability to see your children. Divorce law is complicated. You certainly can handle much of the negotiation if your spouse is willing to deal with you, but you probably don't have the time to learn all you need to know about legal and tax ramifications. We advise you to settle as much of this as possible together in order to avoid legal costs. Lastly, if you use a joint lawyer, it's like asking a dog to have two masters. Have you ever seen a dog who is being teased by its two owners, each of whom is calling for the dog to come to them? The dog runs halfway toward one, then halfway toward the other, then back again and back and forth until the poor thing starts going crazy. Maybe you think this would be a fun thing to do with lawyers or to drive your spouse crazy, but we guarantee you that, in the long run, it's probably going to backfire.

Remember that a lawyer can only have one of you as a client. Therefore, one of you will technically be without representation during the divorce process. The unrepresented spouse will still be able to consult with another attorney but the lawyer who technically does not represent you cannot advise you. There is a lot of trust involved in this type of arrangement.

In one case involving a friend of ours, the divorcing couple decided to use the same attorney. They had divided up a sizable estate and the only remaining detail was to draw up a divorce decree. Based on the recommendation of the couple's accountant, they began working with an attorney on this part of the process. After three or four months, the wife began to question why the decree was taking so long to finalize. Another four months go by and finally the settlement was completed. It didn't resemble, in any way, what the couple had agreed to. When the wife questioned the revised settlement, the attorney explained that the changes were made as a result of new state and local tax laws. Eventually, the wife gave in and the couple signed the decree. They went to court and the divorce was finalized.

About two months later, guess what happens? The husband gets married to the attorney who had handled the divorce case. Need we say more?!

Was this unethical? Yes.

Was it illegal? Yes.

Is it unusual? No.

Our advice: Be careful!!

The "Simple" Divorce

In this chapter, we have covered the beginning legal steps in your divorce process. Unfortunately, divorce is not a simple matter of law and finance. It's an emotional storm, as we have mentioned before. You may very well find yourself in need of some counseling services. Even if you don't, no divorce process occurs without some difficult feelings. The next chapter will focus on how you can deal with these very trying times.

Chapter 5

Counseling

"There are two sides to every divorce ...," said the plaque Pete picked up on a recent business trip to London, "yours and BLOCKHEAD'S!" Well, as you probably guessed, it didn't say "blockhead," but you get the point. Divorces bring out strong feelings in everybody. Some people show them and some people don't, but they are still there. So, when we say there are two sides to every divorce, what we really mean is that there is the legal and financial side which entails filling out forms, visiting lawyers and going to court. Then there is the emotional side in which you must deal with feelings of anger, betrayal, sadness and loneliness. The final decree may end your marriage legally, but it takes more than a piece of paper to end your marriage emotionally.

In this chapter, we are going to address this emotional side of divorce. In fact, many psychological counselors and therapists speak of emotional divorce as being the harder of the two sides. As we have already pointed out, you have or are experiencing a number of emotions, some of which conflict strongly with each other. You can be elated about moving out of a bad situation, but feel dreadful about walking into your new apartment or house. Sometimes, there is nothing so lonely as opening a can of soup by yourself. It can be so lonely that it makes you doubt whether you want to go through with this divorce. We know how you feel. We have been through the experience and we know that one of the best ways to start feeling better is to have somebody tell you that what you are feeling is not crazy, not weak, not abnormal. That's what we hope to show you in this chapter, because controlling this part of the divorce process is just as important as all the other parts.

Dealing with Feelings

The first useful things to know about emotional divorce are the phases you will go through. They are very similar, as we have noted before, to the phases you pass through when you mourn the death of a loved one. The major similarity is that both divorce and death bring about a change in your life. We even encounter such emotional difficulties when introducing change into a business environment. In a recently published book, **People Empowerment:** *Achieving Success from Involvement,* Wayne Douchkoff speaks about the necessity of introducing and implementing change in ways which are cognizant of the needs, desires and feelings of human beings.

Our strong advice in situations like this is not to allow attitudes and feelings to remain suppressed. Understand that people go through the stages noted below when dealing with change in both the personal arena and the workplace. These stages are present in the divorce process as well:

S = SHOCK—"I don't believe this is happening to me."

A = ANGER—"Why me?! What did I do to deserve this?!"

R = REJECTION—"It's not happening. It will go away in a few weeks when he or she gets bored."

A = ACKNOWLEDGMENT—"I guess he or she is serious. I'll have to accept it."

H = HOPE or HELP—"This may really be all right. I can see how I can adjust in the future..."

We all need to recognize these phases and then transition through them in order to accept change.

The Mourning Process in Divorce

In the divorce process, you are mourning the loss of your married life and a person you once loved. Most people go through stages similar to the ones described below.

Stage 1: The first stage is characterized by either numbness and/or denial. Your mind is protesting against the whirlwind of emotions going on in your life. It just can't cope at this point with all of the pain. You are in shock, even if you may have been the one who initiated the

divorce. Many people, as a result, become
withdrawn or extra busy in an effort to avoid
what is happening. Numbness and avoidance
are not necessarily bad. When you are hurt,
the first reaction is to find a safe place so you
can lick your wounds.

Stage 2: During the second stage, you become increasingly aware of what has happened, that you
are indeed getting a divorce. This will undoubtedly bring up feelings of intense anger.
They will come as questions and statements
like the following: "Why is this happening to
me?" "I don't deserve this." "He (she) treated
me so bad." "I never could be my real self."
"I'll never forgive him (her)!" This stage is
also characterized by restlessness and difficulty in concentrating. Sometimes, it feels like
you have a videotape player in your mind that
you just can't turn off. It plays scenes from
your marriage over and over again until you
feel like screaming. All we can say is that,
hard as this stage may be, it is necessary for
you to experience these feelings before you
can finally let go.

Stage 3: In the third stage, you may feel so depressed
and full of despair that you fear you may be
falling apart. From our own experience, we
can say that you will probably experience this
stage and the preceding one at the same time.
In other words, one day you will be running
around angry at the world and the next day

you will feel so down that you don't want to get out of bed.

Stage 4: Finally, your feelings have run their course and you begin to accept that you are no longer married. If you have allowed yourself the full range of your emotions, chances are very good that you can now start to let go and begin adapting to your new life. You will still have days when you feel down or full of anger, but they will pass. Eventually, you will feel good enough about yourself that you will stop hoping horrible disasters will befall your ex-spouse. You may even be able to wish him or her the best. At the very least, you will have put that person behind you so that you can continue with your future. Until you let go of the past, you cannot experience the future.

I'm glad, you might say, to know about these stages. I now know what to expect, but what I really want to know is how long will this mourning process take? That, as they used to say, is the $64,000 question. And the answer is: It depends. It depends on you. Everybody is different and everybody heals at different rates. It is not unreasonable for the mourning process to last up to two years before a person starts to feel like their old self, or maybe even like a new and improved self. There is a direct correlation between mourning and how long the divorce process takes. The more drawn out the divorce, the longer it takes to go through the stages of mourning. Don't worry, however, you will get better. Psychologists do recommend, however, that you think of getting professional help if you find yourself stuck in one of the stages or if you don't feel appreciably better in a couple of years. On the other hand, if you feel debilitating despair during any stage in the process, it is a very sound idea to get help earlier.

Getting Help

Depending on your mental state, there are a number of alternatives available to you if you want help with the emotions brought up by a divorce.

> **Family doctor**—Your family doctor, especially if he or she has been involved in the care of your family for a number of years, can lend guidance during this difficult period or can recommend other sources of help.

> **Psychologists/psychiatrists/marriage counselors**— Some of these other sources are the psychology professionals mentioned here. Since they have received specialized training, they are more expensive than other alternatives although their fees depend on whether they are in private practice or whether they are affiliated with a hospital or clinic. Private therapists are the most expensive with many psychiatrists now charging from $120 to $150 an hour. You may feel, however, that you require a professional who can also prescribe medications to get you through difficult periods. On the other hand, you may be just as satisfied to pay $60 to $90 an hour for a marriage counselor at a local clinic. The choice is yours, just as it was when selecting a lawyer. In fact, the therapist's reputation, just like a lawyer's, is the most important criterion. You should obtain references from a combination of sources, including:

- Friends who have had similar experiences.
- Your family doctor.
- Your attorney (many lawyers keep a list of referrals because they know their clients will be in need of professional support during an emotionally trying time).
- Divorce groups or associations.
- The American Medical Association.

It pays to shop around if you have time. You want to avoid a situation like the one in the following story which we were told. A man who is having an affair with a woman tells his wife that he wants to end their marriage. She suggests counseling in order to try to save their partnership of a number of years. They both go to their church which recommends a counselor. First, the wife goes alone to the counselor and then the husband goes alone. After about two months, they start to go together, although sometimes they still go separately.

There are no problems with the counselor until the husband tells the woman with whom he is having an affair about the counselor. The woman decides she needs help, too, and (guess what?!) she picks the same counselor. The counselor then tries to persuade the couple who is getting marital therapy to bring along the husband's girlfriend next time because he is interested in writing a paper about the triangle. We don't think this is very ethical at all. If you don't agree with something that the therapist suggests, you have two choices. Inform the therapist of your feelings and have him or her explain their reasoning or, if your needs are not met, find another therapist.

Finally, there is an important distinction between psychologists and psychiatrists. Psychologists do not have the same extensive medical background as psychiatrists who are, in fact, medical doctors. In some states, psychologists do not even have to meet any requirements for licensing. Anybody can be one. Keep that in mind at this time when you are entrusting your deepest feelings to someone. Make sure you check into the background and education of any psychological therapist or counselor. At the first sign of any impropriety, go somewhere else and report that person. We have all heard the horror stories about the counselor who makes advances toward a client. The result is a person who is worse off than before. Don't let this happen to you.

Clinics—Clinics, in this context, are public or semi-public institutions, usually nonprofit, whose purpose is to extend psychological services to members of the community who cannot afford private care. Most fees are on a sliding scale which is based on your ability to pay. Like private counselors, there are good clinics and not so good ones. Again, get references and research these institutions as much as possible.

Divorce support groups—Many local hospitals sponsor divorce groups such as "Parents without

Partners" which meet periodically to help people going through a divorce. Such groups are not run by a professional, but are simply a group of people who get together to listen to each other and offer support. For some people, this may be sufficient. Other people may attend such groups in addition to obtaining professional counseling. Whatever the choice, self-run divorce groups are powerful. Knowing that others are experiencing, or have experienced, the same feelings you are having can make you feel less alone and less "crazy." And, for those of us with financial restraints, divorce groups are free. Don't be confused. Group therapy, in which a professional leads and mediates a group of people in the discussion of their problems, is typically not free. Fees vary, but usually fall into the $30 to $60 range for this method of therapy. And who pays for the therapist or the group therapy? As is the case with lawyers, the spouse with the resources to pay often will be responsible for payment of the other spouse's therapy.

Friends and family—Although we have mentioned it before, relying on a family member or friend to act as your counselor can cause more problems than it solves. You can get some terrible advice from people who may look and act as though they are acting in your best interest. All too often, however, these people are going through many of the same feelings which you are experiencing over your divorce. They may also need outside help, especially if the person was close to your ex-spouse and stands to lose him or her as a friend.

Child psychologists—Although we will discuss

children and divorce in much more detail in Chapter 10, we want to note here that children quite obviously suffer emotionally during a divorce as well. And, because they do, some children will need help from professionals who are trained in helping children cope with and understand the turmoil of divorce. This is an area that cannot and should not be overlooked. Besides helping the child, it will also help you to know that your child is getting the help he or she needs to ride this emotional roller coaster. Knowing that they are getting help will put you more at ease which will not only help your emotional health but make it easier for the children as well.

Emotional Losses

The reason that divorce has this emotional impact is because it completely rearranges the pattern of your life. It's like somebody came into your house, replaced all your furniture with new pieces, put the bedroom in the kitchen and the living room in the foyer and then invited you to come back and live. One other thing: When you came back, you were informed that you would have to live in complete darkness for awhile. You are going to stub your toes and scrape your shins many times before you get accustomed to your new arrangement. Married life has a certain pattern to it as does single life, but they are very different. Waking up in the middle of the night with nobody beside you, eating breakfast alone, not hearing your children arguing about whose turn it is to use the bathroom will all be painful. In fact, you may find yourself missing some of the very things which drove you crazy. It seems to be the nature of people that they would rather bear the known than have to face the unknown.

In addition to this interruption in daily patterns, you will be feeling the loss of a person who, for better or worse, played many roles in your life—comrade, confidante, lover, mother or father, provider or homemaker, adviser, social organizer, partner, confessor and so on and so on. You just don't go out and start advertising for one person to do all this for you. Even if you are fortunate enough to have found another person to be your mate, you still will feel the loss during the period when you are getting used to the new love in your life.

Another important loss will be not having your children around if you are the spouse not granted custody. We don't want you to think that your relationship with your children can't be healed. On the contrary, your divorce can be seen as an opportunity to develop a stronger bond. So don't start beating yourself up because you left your children. No doubt you are going to regret certain things you have done or didn't do. You will wish that you had spent more time with them. These feelings of guilt are inevitable. But, if you really want to help your children, move forward and start building that new relationship. A word of caution: Proceed slowly. Take into account that your children are full of intense feelings as well. Respect their need to be angry and hurt. Also, recognize that they will all go through similar stages of adjustment no matter what their ages are. Younger children will usually hold the hurt inside, while older children (beyond their teens) will often try to hurt the parent who they see as responsible for the divorce. Again, we will discuss children and divorce at greater length in Chapter 10. Above all, remember that the whole family is going through the divorce, not just you and your spouse. Don't tell your children that it doesn't concern them because, like it or not, it does.

Yet another loss, which we already mentioned, is the removal of a sexual partner from your life. By sex, we mean more than the physical act, although that is certainly important. We also mean you will lose the care, tenderness and warmth that we all desire from our spouses. Even if you have found another mate and have chosen to live with them, there will be a period when you feel the loss of somebody with whom you have shared your sorrows and joys, your special times together, your romantic evenings. You can't pretend they didn't happen. We should say that you can pretend, but it is not in your best interest to do so. Only by admitting that these feelings exist can you start to let go of them.

In short, you can no longer take for granted all of those things that you once shared with your ex-spouse. Even the loss of your spouse's family will be felt if you were close to the parents or a brother- or sister-in-law. For that matter, you may even have to put up with losing touch with some of your family. Blood is not always as thick as you might suppose. Divorce has a way of making people afraid to be around the person going through the process. Sometimes they act like it's contagious. The same goes for friends. You may lose contact with some of them, either permanently or until you are "cured," that is, successfully divorced and probably remarried. A funny thing happens to friends. Friends that were both of yours become either "his" or "hers." Very few, if any, will continue to see both of you on a regular basis. As you can see, you are not only dividing up property but people as well.

You may even experience the loss of your health. On that same business trip to London, Pete found an article in the *Daily Express* which noted that divorced men and women are more likely to get cancer, die early, suffer from heart disease and experience psychological difficulties. Makes you wonder whether a divorce is worth the trouble. The article also says that you are more likely to get colds, headaches and asthma, as well as feel more fatigued. The bright side to all of this bad news is that you won't get ill if you can let your feelings surface and successfully deal with them effectively. We believe that being *happy* is most important. You have to like yourself first, before you can love another.

What You Will Feel

What are some of these emotions that are going to surface? Let's take a look at the most common ones:

Fear	the feeling that you can't live alone; that you will never find anybody to love you again; that your children will hate you forever; that you are going to be destitute; that your life is ruined . . .
Guilt	the feeling that you have ruined your children's happiness; that you should have tried harder; that your actions or lack of actions have caused great hardship for other people . . .
Self-pity	the feeling that you have been treated unfairly by your spouse, your lawyers, the courts, your friends, and your family; that nobody can understand the trouble you have been through; that you probably deserve everything that is happening to you; that you are never going to recover; that you are worthless . . .
Failure	the feeling that you have some serious

character flaw which changes everything
you touch into a disaster; that you are never
going to amount to anything; that everything
you have done is worth nothing; that you
aren't able to keep a spouse happy . . .

Anger   the feeling that your spouse has treated you
unfairly; that you don't deserve to be in this
mess; that you will get even; that you will
make your children see what your spouse
has done to you; that you will never forgive
your spouse for all of those lost years . . .

The first thing that you must remember is that it is completely normal to have these emotions during the divorce process. It is even normal to be screaming in anger one minute and then sobbing in grief the next. You are in an emotional crisis. There will be times when you feel all alone in the world with nobody to talk to. Believe it! It's real and it will happen to you!

The sooner you face that fact and treat this period as a preliminary phase to a better life, the sooner you will pass through. The best advice we can give to you for dealing with these feelings is to keep in mind why you are going through with your divorce—to free yourself from an unhappy life. You will have to pay an emotional cost for this release and the cost you bear is an avalanche of feelings. But tell yourself that you are worth the effort.

A special word to you men out there: we have feelings, too. Playing tough is not going to make these emotions go away. In other words, you can run, but you can't hide. Remember the British study we mentioned above. Divorced men (as well as women) are more likely to suffer from cancer, heart disease and to die early. Part of the reason is because they stuff their feelings down and end up with ulcers and other medical problems. The stress of not being able to express yourself can literally be a killer. Please take our advice and open yourself up to someone with whom you feel comfortable. If you have no close friends or relatives, get help from a counselor or a priest, minister or rabbi. There are a number of support groups available today as well for both men and women. You aren't weak because you want help.

Standing on Your Own

A loss like divorce will bring up feelings of abandonment. The person you have counted on at one time for love and security is no longer there. Divorce can make you feel like you are two years old and have just been dropped off in the middle of Times Square in New York City to fend for yourself. Professionals agree that on a certain level, we all experience divorce like a child. It feels like a battle for survival and you are all alone in a cold, uncaring world.

This feeling of being abandoned and betrayed seems to be what is behind the loneliness you will feel. After all, being alone to do what you want is not necessarily an unpleasant experience. But being deprived of many of the activities and relationships which used to define who you were is felt at a much deeper level. You will feel to some extent that you no longer fit in. Even though people today no longer look upon a divorced person as though he or she had two heads, it will still be difficult for you to shake the belief that the world is judging you. That's not to say that some people aren't making hasty judgments, but look carefully to see if you are making the same harsh judgments of yourself. If you are, you will only be alienating yourself further from other people's company.

Getting Your Life Started Again

We will say it again: Even though you will feel miserable, angry and abandoned at the beginning, during the middle and at the end of the divorce process, these emotions are the necessary prelude to a happier life. As we have tried to explain in this chapter, you don't suddenly become single because a piece of paper tells you that your marriage is over. Your emotions and memories are not as clear-cut as the legal process of divorce. When all is said and done, the lawyers meet with new clients tomorrow. For us, we are alone when it is over.

You are still married in a very real sense until you can prove to yourself that your happiness depends mostly on what you can do for yourself. It's pep-talk time. Start finding out what you like about yourself. Ask yourself what you were doing in order to keep others happy, but not yourself. Make new patterns and start a process of self-renewal. For example, if you always ate dinner at 5:30 p.m. but you preferred 7:30 p.m., then eat dinner when you want. That may sound trivial, but it is an example of what you need to do to take responsibility for yourself.

At some point, you will need to lay the past to rest (the earlier, the better) and begin to take responsibility for making a new you and a happier life. Don't think of yourself as a victim anymore. The best years are ahead of you, but you have to start making choices by yourself. You will no longer be making choices with somebody else in mind, not for awhile, even if you do plan to get remarried. Look at this time as an opportunity to start over again with a clean slate. Try to look at your divorce in a positive light—a chance for self-renewal, instead of a disaster which has ruined your life.

One word of warning about this kind of pep talk. Merely wishing and then deciding to make your life happier does not mean it will automatically happen, but it's a place to start. What positive thinking does provide you with is an opportunity, a second chance, but only as long as you are honest and understand that your divorce hurts and that it will take time to heal.

To summarize then: You need to prove that you have worth as an individual outside of a marriage. You can achieve that by doing the following:

- Admit where you are and what you feel.

- Don't deny what you are feeling and throw yourself into something else, whether it's work or a new spouse or lover.

- Reach out to others in new ways.

- Don't get stuck in hate or looking inward.

- Find a safe place where you can express all your feelings without anybody making any judgments.

- Ask yourself daily how you feel.

And one last word about sex. Be careful of new relationships and sex. We're not just concerned about AIDS either. In many ways, sexual encounters after your divorce (in which both partners are mindful that it is not forever) can be helpful. But it can also be a mine field of emotions. Remember, you are vulnerable. Often, somebody expects more and then gets hurt. Don't go out to conquer. Be honest. Don't fall for the first man or woman you meet just because they are the same or the exact opposite of your ex-spouse. Don't repeat the same old mistakes. Don't go out looking for somebody to replace the person you left. Here's your chance to truly find out whether a lasting love exists. We suggest making a pro/con list of attributes you like in a person. Do some deep and honest soul-searching so that you can envision what love and success means to you.

A Few Words about Getting Even

Divorce has a way of bringing up the question of whether you want to be right or happy. Our advice is to let go of feelings of hate and revenge, if you want to move on to a happier life. They will poison you and take control of your life. It will also have a lasting effect on your children. Even if they are siding with you, revenge has a way of coming back to haunt you. We admit that getting even can sometimes feel good, but its effects are only temporary. Revenge is like a drug. You're happy until the time comes when you need another fix. And sometimes no amount of revenge is ever enough, but who wants to live their whole life still hooked on the person you were trying to be rid of?

Don't underestimate what we have said in this chapter. A solid understanding of your emotions will put you in the best position to undertake the process of divorce described in the next few chapters.

Chapter 6

The Process of Divorce

This chapter is an overview of the stages you will go through during the legal process of divorce. Before we discuss those stages, let's first look at some strategical considerations you must consider and the feelings which will arise as you go through the legal requirements.

The best strategy is to know what to expect. That is why you are reading this book. You want to have a good idea of what is coming your way so that you're not surprised or blindsided. Only you and your lawyer can devise the tactics which will put your strategy into action since every divorce case is different even if, on the surface, it looks like your case is similar to the case of another couple. The principal reason why this is so is that you know best what you and your spouse want from this divorce. That knowledge is the basis of your strategy.

Strategy

As we have already said a number of times, most of the battle in a divorce is over property and custody. The court has the final say, but it expects you both to have reached some agreement. The judge's job is to resolve what you can't decide. Therefore, the more you can decide together, the better the chances are that you both get what you want and the less money you will spend on legal fees. Court battles are also unpredictable. No judge can know all the desires of the parties in a divorce case. The judge may award the marital home to a spouse who would have preferred the vacation home, higher support payments or a new car in order to have reliable transportation to work. These are the facts that only you and your spouse know. If you communicate these desires to each other, there is a better chance that both of you will walk away feeling as though you were treated fairly.

If you can't decide, a judge will. We know of a case where one judge gave everything one party wanted to the other party. If the wife wanted the Chinese vase, it went to the husband. If the husband wanted the tool set, it went to the wife. This is what can happen if you let your feelings get the best of you and you forget the most important lesson of strategy making—be realistic!

The first step in developing a strategy is to list everything in the house. Then list what you want and rank those items in their order of importance to you. Since you know your spouse best, make a list of what you think he or she would want in order of importance. This exercise will give you a map of the territory. When you eventually get to negotiating (as discussed in Chapter 11), this information will be vital. So be as explicit as you can possibly be now, especially when it comes to custody, visitation rights and property settlement.

We would like to add a few brief notes here about negotiating. Don't lose control of your emotions and reason. That may be very hard to accomplish since you are already angry and in disagreement with your spouse. Nevertheless, you need to be as objective as possible right now. You want a win/win situation because your relationship does not end with divorce, especially if you have children or must provide some type of support payments. And, as long as you are paying alimony, you never lose touch with your ex-spouse.

You will probably find, at first, that some things appear not to be negotiable for you and your spouse. Try to determine what they are. You probably have a number of items which need to be negotiated and you don't want to get caught in a deadlock over some item that takes up all of the time. It may be best to decide that, on this item, you can't decide. If this happens, then be ready to move on to another topic. Set the stage for agreement, not disagreement.

It's also important in devising a strategy to know your spouse's priorities and emotional needs. Is he or she looking to remarry as soon as possible? Does he or she have sentimental attachments to certain pieces of property? Does your spouse have a fear of being brought to court? One of the strongest strategies used is a delay. It is designed to make you concede something in order to make the divorce final or speed the process along. As hinted above, this strategy is often used when one spouse knows the other spouse wishes to remarry immediately after divorce. It is a smart strategy not to give away your timetable and to determine to the best of your ability your spouse's timetable.

Strategy and negotiations depend on your ability to communicate with your soon-to-be ex-spouse, either directly or through your lawyers. We, of course, advocate that you do as much of the negotiation yourself and leave the difficult or unresolvable problems to the courts. Often, however, one of the first things your attorney will advise you is not to talk to your spouse. There are, of course, reasons for this. They don't want you to say anything that will hurt your case or make the other spouse angry. Anger only seems to drive up the costs of a divorce as both sides try to get even. A good suggestion is to write down what you talked about if you do talk with your spouse so that you can remember it later. And, if you agree on something during these talks, have your lawyer send a letter to confirm it. Also, if you do sit down and discuss the process of divorce with your spouse, don't give anything away. And, if you make a concession, always ask for some concession from the other side in return. This isn't merely a way to get what is rightfully yours. There is no negotiation, if you simply give in without asking for something in return.

Be careful of what you communicate to friends and other third parties. A friend may tell your spouse what you are saying. How many times have you said, "Don't say anything about this," only to hear about it later? This information can and will be used against you. Lastly, you must realize that your spouse may use the children against you in divorce proceedings. It's not fair, it's not right, but it does happen. In Chapter 10, we will discuss this at greater length and tell you the story of how one of us, Mike Termini, fought against this tactic and won.

No discussion of strategy is complete without talking about the impact of emotional issues. Divorce negotiation is always difficult because it violates the first rule of negotiating: Don't get emotionally involved! And that is almost impossible since you are dissolving a partnership which was based, at least at one time, on strong emotional ties. The lack of trust and the feeling of being cheated can't help but color the way you see the divorce process. You may want to place all the blame on your ex-spouse and get everything from them that you possibly can. That's not a strategy; that's revenge and it's rarely sweet in divorce cases. Because the more you want to get even, the less you want to reach an equitable settlement which could save you literally thousands of dollars in lawyer fees.

As we mentioned before, even the best strategy can result in some type of court proceedings. If your spouse is not cooperative, then you will certainly find yourself doing battle in a courtroom. For that reason, we are going to walk you through a more or less typical divorce proceeding from discovery and deposition to pretrial maneuvers to the actual trial days. Keep in mind that every state has a different set of laws governing this process, but there are enough similarities to give you a good idea of what to expect.

The Legal Journey

The first step in the legal process of divorce is either getting served with divorce papers or having them delivered to your spouse. In the latter case, you probably have a good idea of what you are going to do next in the legal battle since you have almost certainly contacted and retained a lawyer already. If you are the one receiving the divorce papers, however, you are probably not as well prepared unless you both agree that papers can be served to your attorney. The first thing to do is not to panic. You have, in most cases, at least 30 days to respond. This gives you the time to find a good lawyer and have him or her explain what the divorce papers mean and how you should respond. The following samples of divorce papers will give you some idea of what the initial flurry of legal papers look like. The first sample is the initial complaint or petition to dissolve the marriage.

IN THE CIRCUIT COURT OF THE
FIFTEENTH JUDICIAL COURT,
IN AND FOR PALM BEACH
COUNTY, FLORIDA.

CASE NO. _____

IN RE: THE MARRIAGE OF

_____,
Petitioner/Wife
and

_____,
Respondent/Husband.

PETITION FOR DISSOLUTION OF MARRIAGE

The Wife, _____, through counsel, files her Petition for Dissolution of Marriage, stating as grounds therefore the following:

1. Action for Dissolution. This is an action for dissolution of marriage.

2. Jurisdiction. The Wife has been a resident of the State of Florida for more than six (6) months prior to the filing of this Petition.

3. Marriage. The parties were married to each other on _____, 19__.

4. Irretrievably Broken. The marriage of the parties is irretrievably broken.

5. Children. There were two children of this marriage, both of whom are over the age of 18 years and self-supporting.

6. Marital Assets and Liabilities. During the course of this marriage, the parties acquired certain assets and incurred certain liabilities which need to be considered by the Court and equitably distributed between the parties pursuant to Florida Statute 61.075.

7. (Company #1.) During the course of this marriage, the Husband founded a business referenced in the caption of this paragraph. The business is a marital asset as it was acquired during the marriage with funds accumulated by the Husband through his work effort during this marriage. The Wife seeks an interest equal to the Husband's in this company although she asks that the Husband be required to satisfy the sale of her interest to him through the payment of lump-sum alimony.

8. (Company #2.) During the course of this marriage, the Husband purchased a grocery store with monies earned during the course of this marriage. The company represents a marital asset subject to equitable division. It was founded by the Husband with monies earned during the course of this marriage and represents an asset subject to equitable distribution. The Wife seeks an interest equal to the Husband's in this company although she asks that the Husband be required to satisfy the sale of her interest to him through the payment of lump-sum alimony.

9. Alimony. This is a long-term marriage having begun 20 years ago. The Wife has been a faithful, loving, dutiful and comforting spouse for her husband at all times since the inception of this marriage. She has served the traditional roles, at the Husband's request, of wife, mother, homemaker, housekeeper, maid, confidant and support system for the Husband. She has been available at the Husband's beck and call throughout this marriage; she has worked for him at his request; and she has performed all services requested by him during the course of this marriage to assure that he was provided with a warm, comfortable and relaxed home environment from which he could spring forth in the open labor market to successfully compete and provide this family with a well-earned and luxurious lifestyle. The Wife is unable to support herself in the style to which these parties have become accustomed. She requests that this Court award temporary, rehabilitative, permanent and lump-sum alimony in accordance with the concept of equity that governs procedures of this type.

10. Pension Plan. During the course of this marriage, the Husband has established to the Wife's knowledge and belief, certain pension and/or profit-sharing plans which are subject to equitable division pursuant to the statute and case authority in the State of Florida. The Wife seeks an equitable interest in any and all pension and/or profit-sharing plans including IRA accounts which have been established during the marriage, the extent of that interest being equal to the Husband's in all respects.

11. Automobiles. During the course of this marriage, the parties have acquired numerous automobiles which remain in the possession, custody and control of either or both parties. The Wife seeks an interest in all of said automobiles equal to that of the Husband as they represent marital assets acquired by the parties during marriage through the joint efforts of both.

12. Disposition of Assets. The Wife is in fear that the Husband will dispose of assets belonging to the parties and/or accumulated by the parties during the course of this marriage if the Court fails to order an injunction prohibiting both parties from disposing of any and all assets accumulated during this marriage. She requests that the court enter a temporary

injunction prohibiting the parties from attempting to alienate, secrete or otherwise dispose of any asset accumulated during this marriage which now exists, pending further Order of Court.

13. <u>Attorney's Fees and Costs.</u> The Wife is obligated and the Husband should be required to pay her attorneys a reasonable fee for their services, plus the costs and expenses of this action.

WHEREFORE, the Wife demands this Court enter a Judgment dissolving this marriage, relief consistent with this Petition, and such other and further relief as may be necessary to achieve equity and justice.

_____

(attorney's name and address)
Attorney for Wife

Pleadings, as they are called by lawyers, are very fact specific. They are the initial indication of what the divorce is going to be about. Often the petition, along with the answer and/or the counter claim, will be the only documents in the court file that the judge will review before the final hearing. As a result, these documents need to list the facts of the case in greater detail than in other pleadings.

Certain items must be in the initial complaint for dissolution of marriage: residency, the existence of a valid marriage and grounds for dissolution. The first requirement, residency, gives the court jurisdiction or the authority to hear the case. The second requirement, a valid marriage, is needed because it identifies the item which the court needs to consider—the termination of the marriage. The final requirement, grounds for dissolution, gives the reason for the court to grant the divorce.

The following items are types of specific allegations which may be in a petition for Dissolution of Marriage that your attorney will either draw up or receive:

1. **Agreement between the parties**—This allegation says that you and your spouse have agreed to certain items and sets them out for the court.

2. **Equitable distribution of property**—Asks the court to equitably divide all the marital assets and liabilities. An important note here: equitable does not mean even, it means fair.

3. **Alimony**—This will be discussed in detail later in this book.

4. **Attorney's fees and costs.**

5. **Child support**—This will be discussed in detail later in this book.

6. **Allocation of the marital home.**

7. **Claims for temporary relief**—Here a party will seek to have either temporary benefits or sanctions awarded until such a time as the trial can be held. For example, a wife may seek to have temporary alimony awarded until she can get permanent alimony later, since she is unemployed and must have some income. Or, a wife may seek to obtain an injunction against the husband from spending the money contained in the joint bank accounts.

The next step in the divorce process is that the party who is petitioning for the dissolution of marriage must serve the other party with papers. There are several ways to do this. Instead of going into the details, we are going to make a few points. First, your attorney will take care of this for you by hiring, most likely, a professional process server. Second, the only major problem that can be experienced at this stage are improper service or lack of service. By lack of service, lawyers mean that the other party is avoiding being served with the papers. Serving the papers is the court's way of exercising its power over the other party. That is why some people will seek to avoid being served the papers. This does not mean that the divorce will not proceed. Your lawyer will know what to do to get you a divorce in the event that your spouse cannot be found. This includes a process in which your spouse does not have to be handed the papers.

Now, let's look at serving papers from the other side. You have just been served with papers that are entitled Petition for Dissolution of Marriage. What do you do next? If you don't have a lawyer, get one. If you do have one, he or she has several weeks to respond and can do that with several kinds of documents. First of all, your attorney will most likely file an Answer. This document takes each of the allegations contained in the Petition for Dissolution of Marriage and either admits or denies them. The Answer may also give additional details which explain the reason for the claims of truth or falsity. It can also demand proof of what the other party is claiming. An example of an Answer begins on the next page:

IN THE CIRCUIT COURT OF THE
FIFTEENTH JUDICIAL COURT,
IN AND FOR PALM BEACH
COUNTY, FLORIDA.

CASE NO. _____

IN RE: THE MARRIAGE OF

_____,
Petitioner/Wife
and

_____,
Respondent/Husband.

ANSWER

Respondent/Husband, _____ (hereinafter referred to as
"Husband"), hereby answers the Petitioner/Wife's, _____
(hereinafter referred to as "Wife"), Amended Petition for Dissolution of
Marriage and states:

1. The Husband admits the allegations contained in paragraphs 1, 2, 3,
4 and 6.

2. The Husband hereby admits the portion of paragraph 5 that refers to
the parties' two (2) children that have reached majority. The Husband
denies all other allegations contained in paragraph 5.

3. The Husband only admits the allegations contained in paragraph 7
to the extent that the Husband founded a business known as (Company #1).
The Husband denies all other allegations contained in paragraph 7 and
demands strict proof thereof.

4. The Husband only admits the allegations contained in paragraph 8
insofar as the Husband purchased a fifty percent (50%) interest in (Company #2) during the marriage. The Husband hereby denies all other
allegations contained in paragraph 8 and demands strict proof thereof.

5. The Husband denies the allegations contained in paragraphs 9, 10,
12 and 13 and demands strict proof thereof.

6. The Husband only admits the portion of paragraph 11 wherein during

the course of the marriage the parties had acquired two automobiles. The Husband hereby denies all other allegations contained in paragraph 11 and demands strict proof thereof.

7. The Husband hereby denies all other allegations contained in the Wife's Amended Petition for Dissolution of Marriage not specifically admitted herein.

The Answer may contain several other items as well. For example, the Answer can even deny that the marriage is irretrievably broken and ask that a marriage counselor be appointed. If both sides want a divorce, the lawyer who drafts the Answer will also, in most cases, want to file a Counter-Petition for Dissolution of Marriage. The reason for this is that, if for some reason, the original Petition for Dissolution of Marriage is dismissed, the court can then proceed with the dissolution based on the counterclaim. It also allows the other party to ask the court for protection on matters not already addressed. An example of a Counter-Petition appears on the following pages. If you look at Number 8, you can see that the husband is asking for protection against the wife disposing of the marital assets, just as the wife asked for this protection in the original petition.

IN THE CIRCUIT COURT OF THE
FIFTEENTH JUDICIAL COURT,
IN AND FOR PALM BEACH
COUNTY, FLORIDA.

CASE NO. _____

IN RE: THE MARRIAGE OF

_____,
Petitioner/Wife
and

_____,
Respondent/Husband.

COUNTER-PETITION FOR DISSOLUTION OF MARRIAGE

The Respondent/Husband, _____ (hereinafter referred to as "Husband"), counter-petitions against the Petitioner/Wife, _____ (hereinafter referred to as "Wife"), for Dissolution of Marriage and states as follows:

1. This is an action for dissolution of marriage.

2. The Husband has been a resident of Palm Beach County, Florida for more than six (6) months next preceding the filing of this Counter-Petition.

3. Neither of the parties hereto is a member of the armed forces of the United States or its allies.

4. The Husband was married to the Wife on _____, 19__.

5. The marriage of the parties is irretrievably broken.

6. Two (2) children were born as issue of this marriage. Both children have reached their majority and no new children are contemplated.

7. During the course of this marriage, the parties acquired certain assets and liabilities which need to be equitably distributed between the parties pursuant to Florida Statute 61.075.

8. The Husband is in fear that the Wife will dispose of assets belonging to the parties and/or increase the liabilities of the parties unless this Court orders an injunction prohibiting both parties from disposing of any and all assets of the marriage or increasing any liabilities of the marriage for other than business purposes. He requests that this Court enter a temporary

injunction prohibiting the parties from alienating, secreting or otherwise disposing of any assets accumulated during this marriage.

9. The Husband has retained the services of (name of lawyer) and has agreed to pay the firm a reasonable fee for its services.

WHEREFORE, the Husband prays this Court will grant him the following relief:

A. That the Court take jurisdiction over the subject matter hereof and the parties hereto.

B. That the Court dissolve the marriage of the parties a vinculo matrimonii.

C. That the Court partition the marital home.

D. That the Court make an equitable distribution of the assets of the parties.

E. That the Court make an equitable distribution of the liabilities of the parties.

F. That the Court partition the parties' personal property.

G. That the Court grant such other and further relief as it deems just and proper under the circumstances.

I HEREBY CERTIFY that a true and correct copy of the foregoing has been furnished by mail/fax/hand, this ___ day of _____, 19__ to:

(name and address of wife's lawyer)

(name and address of husband's lawyer)
Attorney for Husband

If a Counter-Petition for Dissolution was filed, it will have to be answered by the other party or with a temporary injunction. They are made for several reasons:

---

1. To protect the spouse or children from abuse.

2. To protect assets.

3. To keep the minor children in the court's jurisdiction.

The court will hold hearings on these matters as soon as possible in order to protect the necessary items or people. But, remember that "quick" for a court of law is not what you and I think of the adjective. In most cases, you won't be in court the next day.

It takes a long time to see a judge. For example, in order to get a half hour in front of many judges requires at least a one-month notice. This amount of time doesn't even include the emergencies and conflicts which come up for the lawyers representing the clients. All of these situations delay the process even further. An example of an emergency is trying to get a hearing to stop your spouse from selling the family car—one month from now will probably be too late.

On the next page is a sample answer to a counter-petition for dissolution of marriage. As you can see, it is very similar to the Answer we covered earlier.

```
IN THE CIRCUIT COURT OF THE
FIFTEENTH JUDICIAL COURT,
IN AND FOR PALM BEACH
COUNTY, FLORIDA.

       CASE NO. _____
```

IN RE: THE MARRIAGE OF

_____,

Petitioner/Wife
and

_____,

Respondent/Husband.

ANSWER TO COUNTER-PETITION FOR DISSOLUTION OF MARRIAGE

In answer to the Counter-Petition for Dissolution of Marriage, the Wife states as follows:

1. The Wife admits the allegations contained in Paragraphs 1 through 7, inclusive.

2. The Wife denies the allegations contained in Paragraph 8 and demands strict proof thereof.

3. The Wife is without knowledge of the allegations contained in Paragraph 9 and demands strict proof thereof.

CERTIFICATE OF SERVICE

I HEREBY CERTIFY that a true copy of the foregoing has been furnished by mail to (name and address of husband's lawyer), this ___ day of _____, 19__.

(name and address of wife's lawyer)
Attorney for Wife

Now the stage is set for more legal maneuverings. As you can see, both sides at this point are in effect trading allegations back and forth. By the way, the attorney's fees for both parties by now is approximately $5,000.

Motions and Countermotions

As mentioned before, there are other papers, such as temporary restraining orders or motions and countermotions, served along with the divorce papers or soon after. These papers are used either to seek some sort of relief or to object to certain statements or requests made in other legal documents.

Financial Disclosures

The next round of legal papers are the requests for financial affidavits and disclosures. In fact, they are required by the parties for hearings which cover such areas as temporary support, alimony and attorney fees. Financial Disclosure Statements are made under oath. They list the discloser's financial assets and liabilities. Even though you can prepare one affidavit for the temporary hearing and one for the final hearing, you should avoid making any misstatements which can be used against you later. Remember that honesty is critical. Tell your attorney the whole truth, and nothing but the truth. Let him or her decide how best to present it. If you surprise your attorney, believe us, it will cost you more than just money.

We showed you how to prepare a financial affidavit in Chapter 2. By this time, it should already be prepared. Although you should strive to be as accurate as possible, you can make reasonable estimates of expenses if you don't have available all the information you need.

Discovery

Discovery describes the method by which you and your lawyers find out the facts of a case. There are two types of discovery—informal and formal. Informal discovery begins with the initial interview with your attorney and continues through subsequent meetings and conversations. In a cooperative divorce, informal discovery also occurs when your spouse and his or her lawyer voluntarily supplies any documentation that you and your lawyer have requested. All too often, however, this information is not forthcoming and you will need to start a formal discovery process, including depositions, interrogatories, hearings and other legal procedures.

Informal discovery also includes the process by which the attorney and the client decide what they are going to look for in a formal discovery. The spouse with less knowledge of the extent of the marital assets will want to work very closely with their attorney to uncover all possible sources of information. Below is a list of items your attorney will be looking for:

1.   Tax returns.

2.   Bank records.

3.   Stock certificates.

4.   Titles to possessions.

5.   Insurance policies.

6.   Inventory of personal property.

7. Charge card documents.

8. Evidence of debts.

9. Information on lawsuits in which parties are involved.

10. Corporations in which parties have an interest.

11. Wills.

12. Lists of gifts given by spouse.

This list is not complete, but it will give you an idea of what to look for during the informal discovery. It will help you ask for the right things during the formal discovery process. You will be playing detective here, especially if you are the spouse who has not been as heavily involved with legal and financial matters. You will need to talk to as many people as possible to see if there is anything your spouse didn't tell you. Maybe there is a second bank account or some stock that you don't know about. Maybe your spouse has been going on trips with his or her lover and spending the money you have both saved. All of this will be important for your attorney to know. You may even consider hiring a private investigator.

Depositions

There are several stages in the formal discovery process. Let's look at them now. On the following page is a sample notice of taking a deposition:

```
IN THE CIRCUIT COURT OF THE
FIFTEENTH JUDICIAL COURT,
IN AND FOR PALM BEACH
COUNTY, FLORIDA.

         CASE NO. _____
```

IN RE: THE MARRIAGE OF

_____,
Petitioner/Wife
and

_____,
Respondent/Husband.

NOTICE OF TAKING DEPOSITION

TO: (husband's lawyer's name and address)

(name of person who will make deposition)

PLEASE TAKE NOTICE that on the ___ day of _____, 19__, beginning at 11:00 a.m. at the

(Name and address of lawyer taking deposition)

the Wife will take the deposition of _____ upon oral examination before the Florida Court Reporting Company, Notary Public, or some other officer authorized by law to take depositions in the State of Florida. The oral examination will continue from day to day until completed. This deposition is being taken for the purpose of discovery, for use at trial, or for such other purposes as are permitted under Florida Rules of Civil Procedure, Sections 1.200, 1.290, 1.310, and 1.390.

KINDLY GOVERN YOURSELVES ACCORDINGLY

I HEREBY CERTIFY that a true copy of the foregoing has been furnished to the above-named addresses by mail, the ___ day of _____, 19__.

(name and address of wife's lawyer)
Attorney for Wife

Depositions are oral questions asked of a party to the divorce or anyone else with knowledge you need to learn in order to find out about the existence and sources of evidence and the whereabouts of witnesses. They are important because your attorney will have an opportunity to assess your spouse's attitudes and answers. But, remember that you will have to give depositions as well. The actual questions and answers are recorded by a stenographer and your answers will be used against you later if there are any discrepancies in your testimony. Your attorney is there to help you answer the questions to the best of your ability. Some advice you will probably be given by your attorney includes the following:

1. **Always be honest.**

2. **Don't volunteer anything.**

3. **Stay calm.**

4. **If you don't understand a question, tell the attorney.**

5. **It's OK to say "I don't know" when you don't know.**

6. **Give your attorney time to object to a question before you answer.**

7. **You can ask to look at documents to help you remember.**

You will be asked questions that cover everything from how your marriage started to how your marriage ended to are you having an affair to details about your job and spending habits. A checklist of items you can be asked appears in Appendix A. As you can see, it is quite extensive and everything is fair game. You should also be aware of the fact that depositions generally take a long time, several hours, and are therefore quite expensive for both sides.

Interrogatories

Interrogatories are the same as depositions except the questions and answers are written instead of oral. Although they can't be as much in depth as depositions, there are still a great many questions that can be asked. A sample set of interrogatories appears below:

> IN THE CIRCUIT COURT OF THE
> FIFTEENTH JUDICIAL COURT,
> IN AND FOR PALM BEACH
> COUNTY, FLORIDA.
>
> CASE NO. _____

IN RE: THE MARRIAGE OF

_____,
Petitioner/Wife
and

_____,
Respondent/Husband.

NOTICE OF PROPOUNDING
INTERROGATORIES TO WIFE

TO: (name and address of wife's lawyer)

The Husband, propounds the attached Interrogatories to the Wife, to be answered on or before _____, 19__ in accordance with Florida Rules of Civil Procedure 1.240.

The undersigned counsel for the Husband certifies that the original and one copy of these Interrogatories were mailed and faxed this __ day of _____, 19__ and copy of the face page filed with the court as provided in Florida Rules of Civil Procedure 1.080 (d).

(name and address of husband's lawyer)

1.   EMPLOYMENT:
    a. State the name and address of your present employer.
    b. State the commencement of your present employment.
    c. Describe your position or job.
    d. State the names and addresses of your employers for the past three years.

2.   INCOME:
    a. State your gross annual earned income, from all sources, for each of the last three years. Identify source and amount from each source.
    b. State when you are paid and indicate for each pay period your gross salary and wages, itemize the deductions from your gross wages and your net salary or wages.
    c. Set forth any additional compensations, including, but not limited to, overtime, bonuses, profit sharing, insurance, expense account, automobile or automobile allowance, which you have received from your employer or anticipate receiving.
    d. State your total annual income in each of the past three years.
    e. Itemize all other income or support payments received.

3.   ASSETS:
    a. Describe by legal description and addresses all real property which you own, or in which you have an interest, setting forth the percentage of your interest in each parcel. For each parcel, state date of purchase, purchase price and present market value.
    b. List the names and addresses of all persons or entities which own an interest with you in the parcels of real property described in the foregoing sub-paragraph and describe each interest.
    c. List all of the items of tangible personal property, including, but not limited to, motor vehicles, furniture, boats, jewelry or art objects which are owned by you or in which you have an interest. State your estimate of value for each item.
    d. List the names and addresses of the persons who own an interest

with you in the items of tangible personal property described in the foregoing sub-paragraphs and describe such interest.

e. List all accounts in which you have deposited money in your name or jointly with another person within the last twelve months.

f. As to the accounts set forth in the foregoing answer, set forth the account numbers, the cash balances and the persons and their addresses who are authorized to withdraw funds in said accounts.

g. List all intangible personal property, including, but not limited to, stocks, bonds and mortgages owned by you or in which you have had an interest within the last two years. State percentage of your interest and the present value of such interest.

h. List the names and addresses of persons or entities indebted to you and the amount of their obligations to you.

i. List all other assets which you own, have an interest in or the use and benefit of, setting forth your interest and the value thereof.

j. Describe in detail, including the cash value, all insurance policies of which you are the owner or beneficiary, including, but not limited to, health, disability and life insurance. As to each policy, list the issuing insurance company and policy number.

4.   LIABILITIES:

a. List all liabilities, debts and other obligations, indicating for each whether it is secured or unsecured and, if secured, the nature of the security, setting forth the payment schedule as to each and the name and address of each creditor.

b. List all credit cards issued to you. Give the balance owed and present minimum monthly payment owed to each of such credit card companies and the account number for each account.

c. As to each creditor, set forth the current status of your payments and total amount of arrearage, if any.

5.   LIVING EXPENSES:

a. Attach a completed Financial Statement.

b. State the amount of money contributed monthly, directly or indirectly, for the support of your spouse or other dependents for past year next preceding the answers to these interrogatories.

6.   MISCELLANEOUS:

a. State your full name, current address, date of birth and social security number.

b. State the condition of your health and the name and address of all health care providers who have examined or treated you within the last 12 months. State the same information for each child, if any.

THE STATE OF FLORIDA   )
                                            .ss.
COUNTY OF   )

BEFORE ME, the undersigned authority, this day personally appeared _____, the _____, who, first being duly sworn by me, says: he has read the attached Answers to Interrogatories and that the same are true and correct to the best of his knowledge.

IN WITNESS WHEREOF, I have hereunto set my hand and seal in the County and State last aforementioned, this ___ day of _____, 19__.

_____
NOTARY PUBLIC, State of Florida
At Large

My Commission Expires:

WE HEREBY CERTIFY that the Original face page hereof as provided in the Florida Rules of Civil Procedure 1.080(d) has been filed with the Clerk's Office, _____ Judicial Court, _____ County, Florida, and a copy has been furnished to (name and address of husband's lawyer), this ___ day of _____, 19__.

There are many more items that can be covered in an interrogatory than are shown here. It is important to realize that both the interrogatories and the depositions are done under oath. Again, your attorney can object to questions which he or she feels are irrelevant or overly broad.

Request to Produce

Interrogatories are often accompanied by a request to produce. This legal paper entitles an attorney to ask you to provide documents which back up your claims as well as provide additional information which may be needed. Below is a list of some of the items which you may be asked to provide:

1. **Tax returns.**

2. **Pay stubs.**

3. **Copies of stock certificates.**

4. **Bank statements.**

5. **Credit card reports.**

6. **Inventory lists.**

7. **Copies of loan papers.**

8. **Current bills.**

9. **Documents reflecting lawsuits in which you are currently involved.**

A sample request to produce is provided on the next page:

IN THE CIRCUIT COURT OF THE
FIFTEENTH JUDICIAL COURT,
IN AND FOR PALM BEACH
COUNTY, FLORIDA.

CASE NO. _____

IN RE: THE MARRIAGE OF

_____,
Petitioner/Wife
and

_____,
Respondent/Husband.

REQUEST FOR PRODUCTION

TO: (lawyer's name and address)

The Husband, pursuant to Fla. R. Civ. P. 1.350, requests the Wife, to produce for examination, inspection and copying the items listed below at Law Office of _____, (address) not later than the ___ day of _____, 19__. Please produce the following items all for the past five years.

SEE EXHIBIT A.

I HEREBY CERTIFY that a true and correct copy of the foregoing has been furnished by mail and fax, this _____ day of _____, 19__ to the above-named addressee.

_____
(lawyer's name and address)

REQUEST FOR PRODUCTION

1. Financial Affidavit: The financial affidavit (Form 1.975) required by Rule 1.611(a) Florida Rules of Civil Procedure.

2. Wages Information: All of your payroll and pension payment stubs and other information furnished to you with or with regard to your pay and other income for the last twenty-four months.

3. Income Tax Returns: Your federal, state and other income tax returns, W-2s, 1099s, K-1s, and the like, for this year and the immediately preceding three years.

4. Estimated Taxes: Your estimated income tax worksheet record of estimated tax payments, declaration vouchers and all amendments thereto for the current year.

5. Financial Statements: All financial statements on your financial condition prepared by you or on your behalf at any time during the last thirty-six months.

6. Banking Information: All monthly bank statements, passbooks, checkbooks, check stubs, check registers, canceled checks and the like, for the last twenty-four months from any banks, savings and loan institutions, credit unions and like institutions, in which an account is, or was, maintained for or by you individually and jointly, and for all such accounts on which you had signature authority.

7. Property Owned: Deeds, title certificates, stocks, bonds, and other securities, notes, mortgages, security arrangements and all other evidences of ownership of all property, real and personal, tangible and intangible, owned by you, individually and jointly.

8. Personal Property Taxes: Your Florida and all other tangible and intangible personal property tax returns for the current year and the immediately preceding two years.

9. Broker's Statements: All statements from all securities and commodities dealers and mutual funds sent to or received by you during the last twenty-four months.

10. Insurance Policies: All insurance policies, including but not limited to, life, annuity, health, accident, casualty, boat, airplane, property, liability and the like, in which you are or are named as an insured or beneficiary or which you own or have an interest in.

11. Debts and Security: All current bills, statements, invoices, notes and the like for items of your indebtedness and all mortgages, security agreements and the like given to secure each of the same.

12. Retirement and Pension and Profit Sharing Plans: All statements of account, correspondence, notifications and the like, received by you during the last twenty-four months, pertaining to any pension plan, profit sharing plan, retirement plan, or like program of which you are or were a participant or member.

13. Contracts: All employment contracts, purchase or sale contracts, real and personal, and all other contracts, agreements and the like entered into by you during the last twenty-four months.

14. Business Information: If you are self-employed or a partner or own more than 10% of the outstanding capital stock of any corporation, then, for each such business, for the current year and the immediately preceding year, produce items numbered 3, 5, 6, 7, 8, 9, 10, 11 and 13 herein. The words "you," "your" or "yourself," and the like above for this item shall mean "such business."

15. Other Papers: All other papers, documents, letters, correspondence, contracts, reports and writings, pertaining to any matter that is or might be involved in this controversy.

Hearings

Often the court is continuously involved in the discovery process. If your attorney objects to something, a hearing will have to be held so that a judge can settle the differences. Hearings can be held on a variety of subjects. A judge also has the option of either issuing a protective order or appointing a master to look at the documents. Hearings may also be held to compel the other side to answer. A sample notice of hearing is shown on the following page:

IN THE CIRCUIT COURT OF THE
FIFTEENTH JUDICIAL COURT,
IN AND FOR PALM BEACH
COUNTY, FLORIDA.

CASE NO. _____

IN RE: THE MARRIAGE OF

_____,

Petitioner/Wife
and

_____,

Respondent/Husband.

NOTICE OF HEARING

TO: (lawyer's name and address)

YOU ARE HEREBY NOTIFED that the undersigned has called up for
hearing the following:

DATE: _____
TIME: _____
PLACE: Palm Beach County Courthouse
              300 North Dixie Highway, Room 441
              West Palm Beach, Florida 33401

JUDGE: _____
MATTER: Wife's Motion to Shorten Time

I HEREBY CERTIFY that a true copy of the foregoing has been
furnished by mail to the above-named addressee, this _____ day of
_____, 19__.

_____
(lawyer's name and address)
Attorney for Wife

When a hearing is held, a judge will make a decision as to which side will prevail. Then the attorneys will draw up an order and the judge will sign it. A sample order appears below:

IN THE CIRCUIT COURT OF THE
FIFTEENTH JUDICIAL COURT,
IN AND FOR PALM BEACH
COUNTY, FLORIDA.

CASE NO. _____

IN RE: THE MARRIAGE OF

_____,
Petitioner/Wife
and

_____,
Respondent/Husband.

ORDER ON WIFE'S MOTION TO COMPEL

THIS MATTER is presented upon the Wife's Motion to Compel certain business documents. Upon consideration,

IT IS THEREUPON ORDERED that said Motion is denied.

DONE AND ORDERED in chambers at West Palm Beach, Florida this _____ day of _____, 19__.

_____
(Judge's name)
Circuit Court Judge

An attorney will often inform you that you do not need to be present when a hearing comes up and that they will contact you afterwards to tell you the outcome. This practice has advantages and disadvantages that must be considered. First, if you have a job which you can't leave, then it is going to be difficult to get off work to attend every hearing. Second, it is true that you don't need to be at every hearing. They can be very short and often center around some small legal points which can be handled solely by your attorney. You are going to need to trust your attorney about how much time he or she actually spent at your hearing. And you will have to trust them that they spent the entire amount of time working on your case and not others as well. Since this is an area of contention between clients and their lawyers, we are going to give you some guidelines here about how to look at your attorney's bill and some suggestions about keeping the bill to a minimum.

1. **As a general rule, keep involved in the case. The more you seem to be keeping tabs on your attorney, the less likely that they will take advantage of you.**

2. **Review your bills and don't be afraid to question the amount of time he or she spent on any activity. If your attorney is continually arguing with you, it may be time to shop for someone else.**

3. **If you have a conversation with your attorney on billing, make sure you are not billed for it. This conversation should be free.**

4. **If you talk about taxes in your conversation, make sure it is reflected in your bill so that you can have the deduction.**

5. **Every time there is a hearing, your attorney will copy you the notice of the hearing (see sample above). These notices will have on them the amount of time which has been set aside for the hearing. If the hearing is short, the attorneys usually have to wait until they are called. Other times, they have to arrive early in order to sign up. Ask your attorney what their billing practice is for these activities.**

6. **If you go to the hearing, keep track of the time.**

We leave you with a few final notes on discovery. You may not want to give a lot of this information to the other side, but discovery is very liberal and very broad. It's show and tell, not hide and seek. If you cooperate, it will be less time consuming, less upsetting and less expensive. Don't forget either that it will not only be you and your spouse who are involved in the discovery process. Everyone from co-workers to friends, relatives and associates can be called in to answer questions about you and your marriage. Just think of the hours that can take and the money it can cost.

This chapter has explored the general outline of the process of divorce. Now let's turn our attention to some specific topics, the first being what to do if you own a business.

Chapter 7

So You Own a Business

Owning your own business can make the divorce process more complicated. Here, as in every facet of divorce, the more you can settle without resorting to lengthy and costly court battles, the better off both you and your spouse will be. Your business is part of your net worth as a couple and, as such, is subject to equitable distribution. On the other hand, many privately owned businesses have a buy/sell agreement in which clauses are inserted to protect the business owners from having a spouse become involved in the business. In some cases, a clause (as shown below) can be inserted in which the spouse relinquishes any rights to the business in case of a divorce.

Agreement made this ____ day of _____, 19___ by and between John Doe and Jim Smith, being all the "shareholders" of the Greenwich Sock Mill, Inc. (hereinafter referred to as the "Corporation").

The shareholders desire and set forth the terms and conditions under which their shares of stock in the Corporation may be transferred. Therefore, it is Agreed that:

I. Involuntary Transfer

If, for reasons other than a Shareholder's death, shares are to be transferred by operation of law to any person other than to the Corporation (such as, but not limited to, decree of divorce, bankruptcy or the appointment of a guardian or conservator), the Corporation shall have the right, within eighty (80) days of the Corporation's receipt of actual notice of the transfer, to notify such transferee of its desire to purchase all the shares so transferred. In such a case, the purchase price shall be determined by the market value of the Corporation's stock as of the most recent meeting of the Corporation.

INTENDING TO BE LEGALLY BOUND, the parties have executed this agreement as of the date first written.

_____

_____

As you can see, determining how much your business is worth can be a critical area. In fact, this is almost always the point where negotiations break down because your spouse does not trust your evaluation of the business or that you have reported it correctly. If a business grosses $3.0 million and nets $100,000, what figure do you think a spouse will use in determining what the business is worth?

Obviously, the best method for reaching a fair settlement is to fairly state the financial status of your business by providing accurate records. Don't exclude anything because if it is discovered later, your whole case is undermined.

There are many different techniques of valuating a business, but they all cover the following areas:

- **Nature of business.**
- **Stock distribution (of ownership).**
- **Chronology of business.**
- **Economic conditions in your particular industry or field.**
- **Financial condition and track record of business.**
- **Book value of any stock.**
- **Value of similar businesses.**
- **Future earnings of your business.**
- **Goodwill.**

Many of these items require the services of a trained expert to determine their true value. This is where hiring a forensic accountant is an intelligent move, whether it is to value your business or the business of your spouse. The evaluation of a business is a complicated matter and two accountants will almost certainly come up with different figures. That is why it can often save or gain you thousands of dollars or more to hire your own forensic accountant.

Look over the business valuations depicted in the two examples which follow. Note the different interpretations and the logic used to come up with their respective numbers. They are a good example of what two different lawyer/accountant teams can come up with during a divorce proceeding.

Valuation Draft drawn up
by Husband's Accounting Firm

We have made a review of the various financial information provided to us regarding The Company as of March 31.

This valuation considers certain factors normally used in determining the value of a business of this type. These factors have included the earnings' capacity of the business as well as the fair market value of the assets and liabilities. We have also taken into account the marketability of the stock, the additional discount normally applied to a minority interest, and the potential and contingent liabilities arising out of the nature of this business inasmuch as it relies heavily on its principals.

The Company was founded in 1984 as a publishing company. The Company has grown from modest sales and revenues in its early years of development to the point in 1987 and 1988 when it matured into a viable going concern. However, in early 1988 it lost a major customer which accounted for nearly $2,000,000 in annual revenues. It has since recovered some of that volume and seems to be leveling out at the $7,000,000 range of annual sales.

Ownership of The Company at December 31 is as follows:

Common Stock ($ .01 par)

Name	Shares
Co-founder	4,500
Co-founder (Husband)	4,500
Officers	700
Total Shares Outstanding	9,700
Authorized and Unissued	300
Total Authorized	10,000

In any valuation we are looking at The Company as a going concern. The value ascribed to the shares of this company, assumed that those shares are salable and that another party, without coercion or restrictions, would pay a certain amount of dollars for those shares, and that the holder of those shares would sell for that price.

Viewing the balance sheet of The Company as of December 31, it is apparent that this company is not one to be valued based on its so-called "book value." Book value may be adjusted either up or down for certain assets which either have greater value, such as real estate or equipment, and may be adjusted downward for a more realizable value for certain assets, such as notes, accounts receivable, or various investments. As we look at The Company as a going concern, there is no reason to lessen the value of any receivable as not being collectible or the value of their investments as being not realizable.

We are, therefore, compelled to use a more favorable and realistic method of valuing The Company which gives credit above and beyond the book value for history, strength, and ability of the firm to earn profits.

This method is referred to as the *capitalization of earnings method*. Under this method, we take the pretax profits of The Company for its most recent years as a nondevelopment stage company.

We have weighted the years to reflect the earnings trends of The Company. Having averaged those adjusted profits before tax, a weighted average adjusted profit before tax is calculated. This amount, $597,814, is then multiplied times a price earnings ratio. A price earnings ratio is the reciprocal of what an investor would want as an average return on his money if he risks capital on such a venture. We believe that an investor in such a business that relies on individual performance of a few people would require a return of at least 20 percent on pretax income.

A 20 percent return translates into a 5 times price earnings ratio. Applying this price earnings ratio to our calculated weighted average adjusted profit before tax, we have a total value of the business of approximately $2,989,000.

Other Elements:

In the case of The Company, we have (1) a minority shareholder. Therefore, the ability to sell that minority interest may be severely limited by the nature of the business and the availability of buyers. (2) We have a company heavily dependent upon two individuals. The loss of any of those individuals will severely impact the value of The Company. The husband's partner is responsible for the majority of the business, therefore, The Company becomes heavily reliant on one person. (3) The loss of any major customer such as occurred in 1988. (4) Inability to find people to train. (5) Non-marketability of the shares.

Therefore, we have ascribed a 40 percent discount for the lack of marketability and minority interest. Discounts for minority interests alone, in our research of valuations and experience in our office, have been as high as 65 to 75 percent. Applying this discount, we arrive at a value per share of $184.89 based on 9,700 issued and outstanding.

We ascribe a value to the husband's 4,500 shares of $832,009.17.

The Accounting Firm has not, as part of its valuation, performed an audit or review of any of the financial information used and, therefore, does not express any opinion or other form of assurance with regard to this information.

This report was prepared at the request of counsel for the husband regarding a pending dissolution proceeding.

We reserve the right to update our review should we become aware or be made aware of additional information that would change our opinion. We also have no requirement nor take any responsibility for updating this report beyond April 1, 1991.

Very truly yours,

The Accounting Firm
of the Husband

The draft valuation above gave the husband's case. The example below shows the response of the wife and her counsel.


```
Response of Wife's Accountant
to Valuation Draft drawn up
by Husband's Accounting Firm

At your request we have reviewed the valuation
report on The Company prepared by the
husband's accounting firm and render herewith
our comments.

The purpose of our engagement was to determine
if the valuation report, as submitted, pre-
sented in our opinion, the fair market value
of the company. In our opinion, it does not
state the fair market value of the company. We
agree with the husband's accountant's observa-
tions as to the appropriate method of valua-
tion and capitalization rate to be used. We
also agree that adjustments are needed to more
properly state the operating cash flow of the
company so it can serve as a basis for valua-
tion. We believe, however, that the adjust-
ments, as recorded in the report, do not bring
the company's cash flow to that of a similar
company operated and directed by non-owner
personnel. In other words, we believe that
certain expenditures of the corporation were
made more because the beneficiaries of the
expenditures were owners than because they
were employees. While this is not an unusual
condition in an entrepreneurial setting, in
order to properly value the business according
to the standards of an arms length valuation,
it is necessary to identify these items and to
adjust for them.
```

During the fiscal year in question, the corporation paid $200 per month to one of the shareholders as rent for the company's use of a condominium. Since the shareholder was presumably living in the condominium and the office's general operations were conducted at a separate location, it appears to me that any business use of the apartment, for which a non-owner employee would be reimbursed, would be minimal. It is my belief that the entire amount of this rent should be added back to determine net income for valuation purposes. In addition to this rent, the company appears to be paying $800 per month for its old, and still vacant, warehouse building. While there may be good business justification to paying this rent, I believe it should be added back since I doubt that an unrelated landlord would be treated in this fashion.

My inspection of the automobile expenses disclosed that the company was paying the operating and maintenance costs for the company vehicles. This must also be added back in to properly value the corporation.

If we assume that these vehicles were driven 12,000 miles per year each, a number which approximates the national average, and that the cost per mile is $0.34 which is the approximate cost per mile announced by the major rental fleet operators, then the amount to be added back to income would be $8,160.

The company has recorded substantial travel and entertainment expenses. Inspection of the company's paid bill file disclosed an invoice for airline tickets for a spouse. Although, due to unavailability of accounting records, it cannot be determined with certainty whether or not these expenses were included in the financial statements of the company, their presence in the "paid bill" files of the company raises in my mind a presumption that they were. Again, it is impossible to determine with great specificity the amount so expended. Unfortunately I cannot suggest a reasonable basis to calculate the total amount to be added back.

With regard to the issue of minority interest discount, let me make the following observation. It is true that the literature and cases are filled with support for minority interest discounts ranging from 10% to 40%. I agree that under circumstances where there is a potential transfer of interests between unrelated parties the transfer correctly takes this discount into consideration. However, in situations where there is no potential transfer, I believe that this forces an artificial and extremely speculative reduction in value on one of the parties. It is similar to valuing a company's assets at going concern (auction) values where there is no realistic potential that the company will be liquidated. In cases where there is in fact no buyer and no seller, but rather a sort of settling of accounts between parties, it seems unfair to reduce the overall family values based upon a speculative discount which would apply to circumstances which will likely not occur soon if at all.

Very truly yours,

The Accounting Firm
of the Wife

You will notice in the valuation above that there is no dollar amount which shows how much the company was worth. Our question is just what was the spouse paying for?

Benchmarking Competition

In the evaluations above, you probably noticed that one way of buttressing your argument is to benchmark the competition. What that means is to establish what is normal and reasonable in a business which is similar to yours. One reason you should take this step is to help explain the ups and downs in your sales and as a way to establish normal ways of operating a business in your industry or field. Consulting, for example, does not have large expenses for raw materials like a manufacturing company has, but it does have large entertainment and travel expenses. Benchmarking helps you discover and then defend what is normal for your field.

Records and Financial Data

Another area to which you will need to pay attention if you own a business and find yourself in the midst of a divorce is the keeping of records and financial data. Lawyers often like to ask for more than is possible in order to put you on the defensive. You don't necessarily have to comply with every harassing request. Certainly you should keep and hand over to your spouse's lawyer everything that is legally required and reasonable. But, remember that you can't supply what you don't have and that you do not have to answer what has not been asked. This is not meant to be construed as thwarting audit trails. You shouldn't, nor should you even look like you are attempting to stonewall. But that does not mean that you can't stand up for your rights.

For example, a corporation may own assets, such as cars, which are used by members of the corporation. If this is true, a court does not have power to control those assets unless the corporation is joined as a party to the divorce action. That means that if you are driving a car owned by your spouse's business, the court cannot give it to you in the divorce decree unless you are also suing the business. Instead, you are more likely to get half of your spouse's shares in the business or their value which will include the worth of the car you are now driving.

Salary and Personal Expenses

The last issue which will gain attention if you own a business and are getting a divorce is the area of personal expenses paid by the business plus your salary, bonus and perks. That means that you must state your income from the business as well as bonuses, perks, pension plans, insurance policies, IRAs, investments and bank accounts which are normally opened while doing business. Again, if you have done your homework and benchmarked other businesses, then you will be able to successfully defend what you earn and what you legitimately take out of your business.

As we mentioned earlier in this chapter, sometimes you will need the services of experts to help you gather this information and present it in a manner which reinforces your side of the story. In the next chapter, we will look at how a forensic accountant can help you in these areas.

Chapter 8

Hiring a Forensic Accountant

If you are asked by your attorney to hire a forensic accountant, you will undoubtedly have the following questions:

- **What is a forensic accountant?**
- **Why is it necessary to hire one?**
- **What do they charge?**
- **What do they do?**

First of all, a forensic accountant is a person who has learned through experience to expeditiously and cost effectively assemble the facts relating to the income, expenses, assets and liabilities of the parties to a divorce. Forensic accountants are experienced in assisting lawyers help their clients resolve and value the items that comprise the marital estate. (In our case, they verified our initial inputs.) In addition, these professionals look at the income and expenses of you and your spouse to determine what is commonly referred to as the parties' lifestyle during the marriage. A forensic accountant also assists you and your attorney in preparing the financial aspects of the case in order to achieve a settlement between the parties. Failing to achieve a settlement, the forensic accountant assists in the mediation process and/or the final hearing before a judge who will decide the couple's financial fate.

Characteristics of a Forensic Accountant

A forensic accountant must be sensitive to the emotional as well as the financial needs of the client. This is especially true in the beginning when the parties are often devastated by what is happening to their lives. That is part of the reason why a forensic accountant needs to be a good listener as well as honest. These characteristics are gained through experience and need to be augmented by imagination and creativity.

Forensic accountants should have the expertise necessary to help your lawyer prepare the case for trial. They should be instrumental in quickly identifying and evaluating assets, ferreting out hidden assets and determining you and your spouse's style of living. This will be done by analyzing the documents which your lawyer will have the other side produce under the discovery laws. As such, he or she should have read the case law and be current on developments as they effect the divorce process.

Why Should I Hire a Forensic Accountant?

Forensic accountants have the experience and ability to identify assets and evaluate them according to a methodology which has been found acceptable by the courts.

It is not in your best interest to use the accountant which you and your spouse have employed to help with personal income taxes or with the financial affairs of your business. The reason is that this person has been instrumental in advising you and/or your spouse in the management of your business with regard to its tax situation and financial planning. There quite simply is a conflict of interest here. Such an accountant will tend to favor the person who owns the business or who has the most money. That may be unfortunate, but it's human nature. Depending on the relationship, we would suggest reviewing your position with trusted advisors.

It is our belief that a small accounting firm which is primarily engaged in forensic accounting can best serve the needs of a client in need of divorce work. A smaller firm that serves clients referred by attorneys is apt to be more responsive to requests, to meeting deadlines and to having staff and principals available for conferences, depositions, mediation and courtroom appearances.

Forensic Accounting: Fees and Charges

The forensic accountant's fees are generally, if not always, less than the hourly fees charged by lawyers, so there is an economic benefit from having a forensic accountant employed to assist in the discovery process. When you make your first visit, you will generally be given an engagement letter which sets forth the terms and conditions and the scope of the employment. If you do not understand any part of it, ask for a complete explanation which you fully understand before you sign.

We asked Emanuel (Manny) Gerstein to work with us on this chapter. Manny has assisted numerous lawyers in preparing financial data. A copy of his engagement letter appears in Appendix C.

Although a forensic accountant's fees are generally less than a lawyer's, they are by no means inexpensive. In our area of the country, they run anywhere from $150 to $300 an hour. The median is somewhere between $150 and $200 an hour. The advantage in hiring a forensic accountant is that they often can speed the process along since they can be made fully aware of financial matters than most attorneys. The result is, of course, less money that you will have to spend.

A forensic accountant will bill you on a periodic basis which is usually set forth in the engagement letter. Make sure you examine and understand each and every invoice, just as you would do for your lawyer's bills. If you don't understand the invoice or you have a problem with billing, contact your forensic accountant immediately. Don't let a billing problem linger and fester into a bigger problem which can make the work suffer. Don't forget, either, that a substantial portion of the services you receive may be applied to tax matters or preservation of income and assets. That means that you may be able to deduct some of the fees on your IRS 1040 filing. Your forensic accountant will let you know what you can and can't do in this area since such determinations depend on the circumstances of each individual case.

What Does a Forensic Accountant Do?

Since forensic accountants are only brought into a divorce case to help determine an equitable distribution, there is no reason for them to play an advocate role as lawyers do. They assess the marital estate and the needs of the parties and then assist you in constructing plans for an equitable distribution of the marital estate, a reasonable amount of alimony, and a fair level of child support. They do this with the hope of reaching an equitable settlement on all matters through the negotiation of you and your spouse and your lawyers. Whatever is not settled will, as we have said before, be decided for you by a judge or other court-appointed official. It is not in your best interest to have someone else resolve your fate. A forensic accountant and a lawyer can help you gain financial control of your future and income by deciding who gets what and when, instead of leaving those decisions to somebody who can't possibly be as familiar with your lifestyle, needs and dreams.

When you first see a forensic accountant, you should have a good idea of that person's reputation and experience since you and your lawyer have discussed him or her and why you need to hire them. The forensic accountant, on the other hand, needs to learn a great deal from you. Most will have some type of checklist which they go through during an interview process.

In the early stages, a forensic accountant should be patient and explain the procedure he or she will be following from start to finish. Most people have never been through this experience before. He or she should also explain to you the importance of maintaining open lines of communication. Only when they know what you know can they determine your future financial security.

Your responses to their questions should be honest and fair. The worst thing that can happen to your case is to be caught in a lie when a truthful explanation of the causes of events and circumstances comes out in testimony from your spouse's side. You will immediately lose your credibility and that will hurt you at the cash register because a divorce is a procedure to divide money and property and that's the way that the courts will determine what is equitable. If you mislead your forensic accountant or your lawyers, you are the only one that will have to pay.

You should also be aware as well that any communications between you and the forensic accountant are strictly confidential.

None of the information you give will be discussed outside the parameters of the forensic accountant's office, your lawyer's office, the discovery process, mediation or court appearances. Keep in mind as well that both parties to a divorce should hire their own forensic accountant just as they hired their own lawyers.

The Services of the Forensic Accountant

In order to show the many activities that a forensic accountant will undertake, we have arranged them in chronological order below:

Assist client in preparation of his or her financial affidavit— A financial affidavit consists of two parts as shown in Chapter 2. The first part deals with the income, deductions and tax of the client and with how the client spends his or her money. The expenditures follow a structured format which has been adopted by the courts and includes such items as food, maid service, cable television, clothing, tuition, health care, vacations, charities, travel, automobile expense and the like which a person commonly incurs as a result of their standard of living. The second part deals with the record title of the parties' assets and liabilities.

Valuation dates—Establishing a valuation date is one of the first significant acts of a forensic accountant. It is usually one of three different dates. The first is the day of the filing of the cause. The second is the day the parties separated and no longer lived together. And the third date is made at the discretion of the judge.

Assets and liabilities—Forensic accountants are trained to look for the existence of assets which would not come to your mind. For instance, they will seek out any patents, copyrights or other intangible assets which will need to be valued. And, even though a forensic accountant is not employed to uncover fraud, they are often asked to find hidden assets. Unfortunately, they are often only discovered if the defrauding spouse has become careless in the implementation of his or her plan or they will be uncovered during the examination of records and data.

There are signals, however. It is the forensic accountant's experience which serves them best here. For example, if they find a number of telephone calls to a country where people often hide money (the Bahamas, Switzerland, or Liechtenstein) while examining telephone bills for the past three years, they can advise the lawyer to begin an investigation. Your lawyer, in such a circumstance, would use depositions and other legal methods to determine where such hidden assets are located and their extent.

Another way that hidden asset trails are uncovered is by looking at charge accounts. Charge accounts which show a number of alleged business trips to offshore places may turn out to be trips to hide money in foreign banks or in a company that has been created offshore specifically for the purpose of hiding money or other assets.

Analysis of production—In a divorce case, your lawyer will ask your spouse's lawyer to produce, or turn over, financial information. The forensic accountant then catalogues, inventories and analyzes this information. If your spouse has a forensic accountant, he or she will assist your spouse's lawyer in gathering the information so that it is complete. Your forensic accountant will do the same when you are asked to produce as well. It is very important to complete the requests since both sides are entitled to a fully complete, open and honest discovery. Even if their clients are reluctant to come forth with all the documents, a forensic accountant will urge the client to make a complete and open discovery. The role of the forensic accountant is not to be an advocate, but to be an expert. You already have an advocate, your lawyer, who will protect your rights. The forensic accountant's role is to assist the lawyers and the final trier of the facts in understanding the financial factors influencing your divorce case.

Interrogatories—Interrogatories are questions which one spouse's lawyer will serve on the other spouse. They require written responses to questions which deal with employment history, assets, income, liabilities and health and education. Their purpose is to get an overall understanding of the spouses involved in the divorce proceedings. As we have said on numerous occasions before, the most important thing to do is to be complete and honest in your responses. One small misstatement can undermine your whole case.

Whether the financial information has been gathered from Notices of Production, interrogatories, or depositions, the task before the forensic accountant is to analyze the information. Let's turn now to some of the areas they cover and how they determine their findings.

Gross income—When determining your gross income, a forensic accountant takes into consideration the benefits or perquisites paid to the self-employed person by his or her company: a company car, life insurance premiums, health insurance premiums, automobile allowances, and other items of this nature. These benefits are then added back to your gross income. When a forensic accountant looks at a company's financial statement, he or she must also determine what portion is taxable and what is non-taxable. On one occasion, an analysis of the repairs and maintenance accounts of a privately-held company revealed that all of the expenses charged to these accounts over the past two years were actually embellishments and improvements to a new home purchased by one spouse and paid for by the company. When these expenses were added back to the spouse's income, it quite obviously changed the final figure quite significantly.

Company loans—Many self-employed owners of businesses frequently borrow money from their company which they do not convert into income in order to diminish their income during a divorce. When discovered, these loans are added back by the forensic accountant to the spouse's income.

Thwarting discovery—Some spouses, in order to thwart the discovery process, decide not to file income tax returns or file incorrect ones. They may also keep their books and records in poor shape so that it is difficult to reassemble incomes and the value of assets. A forensic accountant can, however, reconstruct these records to show the true income and value which the spouse has tried to hide by maintaining poor records. They are able to do this by a combination of their experience uncovering paper trails and through the use of computers.

Accountability for cash—In a small, closely-held enterprise, accountability for cash can be a problem. Forensic accountants deal with this by doing an historical analysis of the gross profit margins of the business and a trend analysis of sales. If available, inventory records are used as well, but they are often poorly maintained in a small, closely-held company. In specific instances where a forensic accountant is dealing with jewelry, gold coins or objects of art, it is not very difficult to determine whether cash has evaded the tax collector's grasp. When it is determined how much such items are worth, that sum is simply added back to the income of the corporation or closely-held entity. The value is then based on actual performance rather than what is depicted on tax returns or financial statements.

Non-marital assets—After all the checks have been analyzed, the financial affidavit completed, the spouses' standard of living determined, the assets put on the books, the liabilities analyzed and the net worth of the spouses determined, the forensic accountant begins work on another factor. The assets and liabilities comprising the gross estate needs to be analyzed to determine what assets are non-marital assets. Non-marital assets are those assets which you and/or your spouse owned before you were married or which you brought into the marriage as a result of gifts or inheritances.

Non-marital assets may have increased in value over the years of a marriage and that increase in value, or appreciation, is either marital or non-marital. If the appreciation is due to market forces only, then the increase of the non-marital asset is considered to be non-marital as well. Let us give you an example. Say that you owned some IBM stock before you were married and, that at the time of valuation of the gross estate, the stock's value had doubled. Furthermore, assume that the increase in value was due to the workings of the stock exchange and not because you were an active investor. The appreciation of your original non-marital asset would be considered non-marital as well. In other words, it doesn't get thrown in the pot to be divided. It is yours alone.

However, let's assume the same set of circumstances and that you are an active investor. You were active as a trader and spent considerable or significant time dealing with your portfolio during the course of your marriage. Any appreciation in your stock portfolio is considered a marital asset because your participation was ongoing and active. However, the original invested amount would still be considered non-marital. If you started with a $20,000 investment before you were married and it appreciated to $30,000, then only $10,000 is considered a marital asset. The original $20,000 is non-marital. Because it can often get complicated about who owned what and when, we strongly advise couples about to be married to set forth and value those assets which they are bringing to the marriage. As we have said before, nobody foresees divorce, but it is unfortunately a fact of life.

If a couple sets down on paper their respective financial conditions before their marriage, it becomes easier to trace assets in order to establish if there is a non-marital asset or special equity arising from an asset brought to the marriage. The courts can decide to bifurcate the prenuptial agreement (if one exists) in a divorce proceeding. That means that the court assesses the validity of the prior agreement and decides whether to uphold it or not. If it does, the role of the forensic accountant is virtually over. Equitable distribution has, in effect, been already determined. We would strongly recommend that either a prenuptial or postnuptial agreement be drawn up in the situation where a substantial estate exists.

Another example of non-marital property is receiving an inheritance during the course of a marriage which you do not co-mingle with you and your spouse's savings. What are called special equities arise when you use non-marital money in whole or in part to purchase an asset. A special equity is a claim in which one party has a claim in excess of the other party's claim despite the record title. Some state courts, those in Florida particularly, have approved a formula called Landay which enables you to determine the special equity of you or your spouse.

One example of an item which is difficult to value is a country club bond and whether the former spouse can regain admittance to the club. This is often an enormous issue with people since it effects their social status in their community and thus gets exaggerated out of proportion. As we said earlier in this book, the argument is probably over something other than who gets to play tennis and golf where.

Plan of equitable distribution—A forensic accountant to this point has dealt with the gross marital estate, special equities and non-marital assets. He or she has then determined the total marital estate and how the record title is held. In addition, they should know the circumstances of the marriage: long-term or short-term, number of children, and style of living. Now, it is the job of the forensic accountant and your attorney to determine a plan of equitable distribution which is what is required by many states which are not community property settlement states. Remember that equitable distribution does not necessarily mean half, although recent case law in long-term marriages has established a pattern of fifty/fifty.

Discovery process—The discovery process continues even after the submission and receipt of interrogatories and the production of information through depositions. Here again, the forensic accountant has a specialized role. He or she has the role of bringing forth the financial questions which your lawyer will ask your spouse during the deposition. The forensic accountant can also participate in a deposition at the request of your lawyer to assist in deposing your regular accountant, your spouse's expert or forensic accountant and any other expert brought into the divorce proceedings such as appraisers of real property, personal property, intangible assets or closely-held businesses. But remember, all of these actions will cost you money.

In addition to depositions, the forensic accountant's review of the production may raise more questions which require additional production. He or she will then instruct your attorney to request the information from your spouse's attorney or to draw up more interrogatories to serve upon your spouse.

As mentioned before, your forensic accountant may be deposed by your spouse's lawyer in the presence of your spouse's forensic accountant. They will be asked to describe their work effort, the scope of their engagement and to detail what documents were produced at the request of your lawyer. The documents will generally be an historical analysis of you and your spouse's tax returns, an historical analysis of the closely-held business's tax returns and/or financial statements, checking account analyses and an historical analysis of financial statements prepared by you and your spouse or on your behalf by third parties. All of this historical information is used in predicting the future needs of you and your spouse after your divorce is final.

Alimony and child support—Further documentation deals with the issues of alimony and child support. Forensic accountants use studies which suggest levels of support based on historical data to determine what the taxable income will be of you and your spouse in the future. These levels are interpolated to show the annual, monthly and weekly net disposable income and cash flow of the parties to a divorce.

Alimony itself has three forms. The most common form is permanent periodic alimony in which money is paid to the spouse until death or remarriage of the payee or the death of the payor. Rehabilitative alimony is paid for a designated period of time so that the recipient can either enter the work force or start a new career. This type of alimony is generally taxable and given to young people who have had a relatively short marriage and who have good health. Lump sum alimony is not taxable and payment is either done in one amount or over a period of time with terms and conditions as well as security assurances that it will be paid.

In determining your earning capacity so that alimony can be reckoned, a forensic accountant takes a number of things into consideration:

- **The historical background of the person and whether he or she has worked.**

- **Education.**

- **Health.**

- **Presence of children who need the substantial or full-time care and guidance of a homemaking spouse.**

Child support payments are determined by the age and health of the children and the standard of living enjoyed by the parties during the marriage. This can be determined by running an analysis of you and your spouse's financial affidavits and by negotiating through your attorneys, a mediator or a judge. In Florida, the courts have established a schedule of child support payments and have incorporated it into the statutes.

One tactic that is often used during alimony negotiations is for the spouse who will be paying the alimony to offer all the marital assets to the other spouse to get off the alimony hook. If the assets are sufficient to maintain the receiving spouse's standard of living, then this proposition can work. More often than not, however, the assets will only cover an insufficient period of time and will soon be exhausted.

There are instances, and they are becoming more common, in which the husband obtains alimony. The circumstances leading to this situation are often the result of the fact that the wife has a large inheritance or makes a great deal of money, while the husband has been the homemaker. Another circumstance occurs when the husband has not been the homemaker, but has dedicated his net taxable income to family support while the wife has reinvested her inheritance income without spending much on family support.

Closely-held entities—Forensic accountants are better able to valuate interests in closely-held entities because they are experienced in using methods and technologies which can unravel who holds what and how much each asset is worth. When a professional practice becomes a question in a divorce proceeding, the problem of evaluating goodwill always arises. If the enterprise has goodwill, it is an asset that is subject to equitable distribution and will be dealt with by the courts. But, if it can be proven that the goodwill belongs to the individual, then it will not be distributed. It will, however, be a factor which will be used in determining that spouse's ability to pay alimony and child support.

Another difficult question that arises in a closely-held company is the determination of a non-marketable security. It is difficult precisely because of the fact that it is not marketable and the position is subject to a discount. Finding the proper discount is a matter of experience and of knowledge acquired over the years as they apply to current market or other determinable factors.

Another tricky area is pension plans which are often a substantial asset in the marital estate. In the case where some part of the plan was acquired prior to the marriage, that portion plus the income it has generated during the marriage is a non-marital asset and should be excluded from the marital estate. A spouse, however, by law has a joint and survivorship interest in the ex-spouse's pension plan unless he or she has specifically waived those rights. Divorcing couples can divide pension plans in a non-taxable fashion under the Internal Revenue Code by using what is called a Qualified Domestic Relations Order. Basically, it gives the recipient spouse a specified amount of time to reinvest the funds in a qualified roll-over plan, usually an individual retirement plan.

Mediation and the Forensic Accountant

Sometimes, the parties to a divorce cannot settle their differences and arrive at an agreement. An interim step can be taken which has proven to be very effective. That step is mediation which is discussed in Chapter 11. The forensic accountant in this case again plays the role of helping the mediator to try to settle the dispute by preparing exhibits commonly called demonstrative exhibits. They contain information about the assets of the parties, their income and expenses, any non-marital assets or special equities and the net worth of the marital estate. The mediator then rules on an equitable distribution.

Conclusion

The experienced forensic accountant uses techniques which enable him or her to help you and your spouse reach an agreement. Because they are experts in their field, they can often suggest equitable distributions more quickly than lawyers and that is why many attorneys hire them to help in their valuations of marital estates and businesses. And once again, we would like to thank Manny for his contributions to this chapter. As we have seen, forensic accountants are even helpful in the determination of alimony and child support which we will discuss in more detail in the next chapter.

Chapter 9

Alimony

Along with child support and property settlement, alimony is one of the most contentious areas of divorce. Much of this contention has to do with the anticipation of one spouse having to pay exorbitant sums of money to the other. These fears are fed by stories in the media about the dependent spouse (usually, even in the 1990s, the wife) who gets $300,000 a year in alimony like Ivana Trump. That is a lot of money, but it needs to be put in perspective. The average person is not going to pay anywhere near this amount. A rule of thumb is that you will have to pay 30% of your income for the duration of the alimony payments. The fact is that the granting of alimony follows fairly well-established guidelines as we shall see. And most of the figuring of alimony payments is based on the Financial Statements which we have repeatedly discussed throughout this book.

Our advice, as always, is to avoid paying the courts and lawyers in favor of working out a fair deal with your spouse. This does not mean that your lawyers are excluded. Lawyers and accountants who are well-versed in the financial ramifications of alimony can contribute to the process. They can provide you with data to make sure that you and your spouse arrive at a fair settlement. We are in favor of this type of legal and accounting help. We are not in favor of those lawyers who ask for alimony payments which are clearly impossible to meet as a method of negotiating. All too often, this is the norm. Nor do we think it is fair for a lawyer to continue dragging a couple into court when alimony could be negotiated between the parties themselves. The only person who wins in that situation is the lawyer who gets paid for more billable hours.

Alimony in the "Old Days"

Many of the fears about alimony are based on old definitions and applications of laws which have been replaced in recent decades. In the "old days," both spouses had to agree to a divorce unless fault could be proved. Fault was most often defined as adultery, abandoment or cruelty by one of the spouses. What usually happened is that the husband and principal wage-earner (and often, in those days, the only wage-earner) would ask for a divorce. His wife would eventually respond by saying that if he wants a divorce, he will have to support her. That support included alimony payments. No-fault divorces replaced this old practice with property settlement and what is called either spousal support, maintenance or rehabilitation.

In fact, no-fault divorce laws have changed the scene so much that wives are now ordered by the court to pay alimony to their ex-husbands. Such is the case with the well-publicized divorce of

ABC's *Good Morning America* co-host Joan Lunden and her husband Michael Krauss. Lunden had been ordered by the courts to pay Krauss temporary alimony of $18,000 a month. He claims that he was instrumental in helping her achieve the level of fame and income that she now enjoys. It is the same argument, of course, that spouses of professional people, such as lawyers or doctors, have used. They claim that by taking care of other matters while their spouses built up their practices, they deserve a share of what they have achieved. We say that all of this is fair game and should be brought to the negotiating table. What we think you need to remember is that both sides should try to avoid a long and messy battle in court.

A Definition of Alimony Today

The rationale behind alimony or spousal support today is to help the spouse who was dependent during the marriage become self-supporting as soon as possible. What happens in a divorce case is that the property is divided and then the courts decide on how much money the dependent ex-spouse needs in order to get back on his or her feet. In most marriages under ten years, the alimony is awarded for a fixed period of time. The court may also order a spouse to pay for the education of the other party so that he or she can eventually enter the job market. For marriages in which the dependent spouse has never worked during his or her married life and where the spouse is of an age where he or she cannot be expected to find a new career, the courts will award alimony for an indefinite period of time. In most states, however, alimony does end when the ex-spouse remarries or starts living with another person as man and wife.

What we have just described is referred to as permanent alimony, even though it does not mean that you have to pay forever. It is called permanent to distinguish it from temporary alimony which is the spousal support paid before the divorce is final. As we mentioned in Chapter 2, you need to be careful about what you offer or agree to as temporary support. Don't come up with an arbitrary number. Base the support on actual needs minus any earnings that the dependent spouse will be earning. Also be sure that you obtain "court-ordered" temporary alimony. The disadvantage of voluntary support is that it is not deductible when you file your income tax returns. In addition, do some research on other cases and learn what to expect.

The award of temporary alimony will be used by the court later when it awards permanent alimony. For example, if your spouse is getting $2,000 a month in temporary alimony and is doing fine, a court will be unlikely to increase the amount since it will determine that $2,000 is enough for your spouse to live on.

Palimony

Palimony refers to the alimony which is paid to a partner who lives with another partner, but who is not married to him or her. As most people know, palimony became a familiar concept after the Lee Marvin case in which his live-in lover and companion sued him for support when the couple split up. Years ago, of course, this never would have even entered a person's mind, but now that many couples live together without getting formally married, the issue is very important. Men and women are asking the courts to provide the same support to an unmarried partner who was, for all intents and purposes, fulfilling all the roles of a husband or wife. Such an unmarried person is looking, as would a married partner, for equitable distribution of property and wealth accumulated during the course of their relationship.

What the courts have usually decided over the ensuing years is that palimony is far easier to obtain if there was a written agreement between the two partners, sometimes known as a "nonmarital cohabitation" or "living together" agreement. Such an agreement would state when the nonmarital relationship began, the financial conditions of each partner at the beginning of the relationship and how each partner will contribute to the maintenance of the relationship and a home. There are other considerations which should be included as well, but they are best found out by negotiation between the partners. Separate lawyers should then look over any agreement which the partners have drawn up.

Although full palimony is obtainable only in the presence of an agreement as described above, an unmarried partner can still seek financial payments when the relationship splits up. In fact, the Lee Marvin case did not end up with the actor paying palimony since there was no contract between the two unmarried partners. Marvin, however, did have to pay $104,000 for rehabilitation purposes so that his former partner, Michele Triola, could resume the acting career she gave up or seek other employment. A man or woman can seek relief from the court in the absence of a contract but must meet certain criteria such as an express contract, implied contract, quasi-contract or a constructive trust. All of these legal terms designate that an unmarried couple living together implies some level of commitment and trust between the partners and thus can legitimize claims made by one partner or the other.

Gay Couples

One of the legal questions which has grown out of palimony is whether or not a partner in a same-sex relationship can seek financial recovery when a relationship ends. They do not have the protection awarded to partners in a marriage, but they can seek redress. If a home or other property, for example, is jointly owned by both partners, then the law will partition the assets. In the case of the home, of course, this often means selling the house and splitting the proceeds. Most experts agree that the best way to protect your interests in a same-sex relationship is to draw up an agreement beforehand, much like a prenuptial agreement. In the event of a "divorce," the agreement would state the conditions of the separation. In the event of the death of one partner, the agreement could state rights of survivorship in which the house will become the property of the surviving partner. As can be seen, the law does not automatically cover same-sex relationships. Special efforts must be made to ensure this protection through other legal agreements.

The Emotional Side of Money

Money and the division of property are very emotional issues. You should treat them objectively, but you can do so only after you understand the psychological undercurrents. Fights over alimony bring up all the old battles of a broken or failing marriage. Money comes to represent the love denied or taken away during those difficult times. So people often use the battle over alimony to play out the very problems which caused the split in the beginning.

This is why it is so important to learn how to negotiate a win/win agreement in the presence of emotional factors as we shall discuss in Chapter 11. Sometimes the desire for revenge makes people concentrate on alimony alone and the size of monthly payments when other solutions are possible which would be more beneficial to both sides. Again, don't stuff down the emotional issues or they will cloud your judgment in other areas.

A divorce will often seem to be proceeding smoothly until the issue of money comes up. Then, all the pent-up anger comes out in demands which are not practical or realizable. Unscrupulous lawyers take advantage of this situation to feed the fire. What is needed, instead, is to sort out the source of all these strong emotions, deal with them and then move on to the money issues. All too often in divorce cases, money equals self-esteem. The more I have, the better I am. But in the end, no amount of money is going to make somebody with deep resentments feel better.

How Alimony or Spousal Support is Determined

The way that alimony or spousal support is determined varies from state to state, so you need to be aware of your state's regulations and laws before you start negotiating with your spouse. Most states, however, do consider the items in the following list:

- **Standard of living enjoyed by the couple during the marriage.**

- **Earning ability of both spouses.**

- **Ability of spouse to make payments.**

- **Length of marriage.**

- **Job experience, age, health and level of education of dependent spouse.**

- **Number of children and their ages plus their effect on dependent spouse's ability to work.**

- **Any expected inheritances.**

- **Payment of education, training and counseling for dependent spouse.**

- **Assets and liabilities of both spouses.**

- **Property owned before marriage.**

- **Contribution of homemaker.**

- **Tax ramifications resulting from alimony payments.**

Much of this information comes from the Financial Statements of your net worth which you are required to fill out for the courts. Many of the other figures which need to be determined in the list above come about as the result of testimony by expert witnesses. For instance, a job counselor will testify that the dependent spouse has the skills to become a newspaper reporter with the proper education and training. Part of the alimony then would be payment toward tuition, books, etc. for the spouse to attend college. Alimony includes payments toward insurance, education and training as well as the more commonly known payment toward living expenses.

What Every Alimony Agreement Should Contain

We have found that it is advisable to try and include the following terms in any alimony agreement you may make. These items are designed to protect both parties and ensure a win/win situation:

- Method of payment—lump-sum or periodic. If periodic, are payments fixed or will they fluctuate with cost of living index or ability to pay.

- Open-ended—meaning it can change if desired or supported with information concerning a change in the supporter's income level.

- Date of payment.

- Penalty for late payments.

- Direct payments or payments through the court.

- Posting a bond to secure payment.

- State whether marriage or living with someone ends support or not.

If the agreement is detailed, then there will be no difficult questions in the future about whether or not alimony should end or be changed. Write into your agreement what will happen if there are any changes in economic conditions for good (windfalls like winning the lottery) or bad (a bankrupt business). Even if you don't write these conditions into your agreement, either spouse is eligible to petition the court for changes in the size of alimony payments or their duration.

The principal thrust of determining alimony should be to come up with a settlement before going to trial. This support can include insurance and money for education and training. Lastly, do both of yourselves one last favor and negotiate in good faith. Don't just ante up your demands in order to exact revenge. Only the lawyers win when that happens.

A word to those of you reading this book who will be receiving the alimony payment—be careful about taking lump sum alimony.

Certainly it appears that a lump sum check is the easiest and quickest way to end your relationship with your spouse. You get all of your money up front, you don't have to worry if your check is going to arrive on time and every time and you don't have to ever talk to your ex-spouse again. However, we have often found that it is not in your best interests to receive your money this way. All too often, the spouse receiving the money will spend it quickly and unwisely and soon be left with no money to live on and no more money coming in. For example, you may decide to go on a trip to forget your troubles and celebrate, you may buy back half of the furniture which your ex-spouse took, you may buy a house with a large down payment or you may decide to invest your money in a risky venture. Any and all of these actions can leave you with nothing. That is why we say that periodic payments may be, despite the emotional baggage attached, in your best interests. Periodic payments forces you to manage your money and it keeps a steady stream of income coming in for you over the years. That will be especially important if you have children to take care of as well, so let's now turn to the next chapter and another major area of contention—child support.

Keep in mind that no matter what happens, between the first and the tenth of each month, you will get a phone call which will undoubtedly contain the following words if you have not mailed the alimony check to your ex-spouse.

"By the way, did you mail my check yet?"

The only way to eliminate the call is to make sure the check gets there ahead of time or to have it directly deposited in your ex-spouse's bank account.

Chapter 10

What About the Kids?

A divorce does not necessarily have to be a disaster for the children. Unfortunately, the legal system is structured so that it often is. The courts and lawyers operate as an adversarial system where children can be relegated to the status of property in a battle between two adults. In such a system, children often have to watch or even participate in a custody battle where both parents must tear each other apart to prove that they are the best choice. This is made worse by lawyers who advocate using custody and child support battles as a way to win the war. When two parents battle over the children, only the children lose.

A lot of this sad situation could be alleviated if divorcing parents would recognize that they aren't ruining their children for the rest of their lives. It is not inevitable that your child will suffer from psychological problems for the rest of his or her life because you are getting divorced. And, any psychological difficulties which do arise can be handled. It is rarely, if ever, too late to try and make things right. Knowing this should take the burden off a parent who feels that he or she must battle for sole custody of the children in order to assure their best interests. That's not necessarily the case. Joint custody and shared custody are proving to be acceptable and, what is most important, they are proving to be a loving way of bringing up children of divorce.

One other topic needs to be discussed before we move on to the hows and whys of child custody and support. That topic is the question of who is the best custodial parent. Years ago, the courts and most people just assumed it would be the mother. That assumption doesn't always hold true and lately people are recognizing that fathers are loving, caring parents as well. Studies have shown that the children of divorce who do best are the children that have frequent and harmonious contact with both of their parents. There are even cases where the grandparents have been awarded custody. We are all in favor of society's move to reject stereotypes of men as somehow being deficient in the area of parenting.

Ages of Children

A major factor in how children will react to a divorce is their age. The major questions in a child's mind are whether you still love him or her and, "What's going to happen to me?" Divorce ruptures the structure that each child needs in order to maintain their stability, confidence and self-worth. Therefore, each stage of childhood presents unique problems and there are specific ways of dealing with them. Infants, for example, are very sensitive to how their parents are feeling. Children internalize these feelings. They become upset by changes in routine and by the presence of new people and places. Most often they react to these problems by regressing to patterns of sleeping, eating, or toilet training that they had when they were even younger. They may start talking like a baby or lash out when they are upset by kicking or biting. One- to three-year-olds will also display their feelings about a divorce by hanging on when a parent leaves the room. What should you do if your child starts acting in these ways? First of all, rule out physical causes of distress. If the distress is not physically related, then begin to make your child's daily schedule as routine as possible. Consistency and structure are essential in normalizing a child's life after divorce. Another essential rule is to have your battles outside of the infant's range. This does not mean that they will not sense your anger or unhappiness, but they will be spared from seeing their parents, both of whom they love, attacking each other. Children in such a situation often feel forced to take sides.

Preschoolers are most upset by a fear of abandonment, by being punished for "bad" feelings, and by a lack of security. They show these fears by withdrawing from normal activities, trying to stay up late and becoming "fussy" about what they eat. The best advice for what to do is to listen to their fears, their feelings of guilt or self-blame and reassure them that the divorce is not their fault. Experts also say that it may be a good idea to talk about their problems in a non-threatening manner, perhaps by reading or telling a story about another child facing the same problems.

Six- to eight-year-olds are most upset by depressed or needy parents, lack of support and the loss of a known and secure place in the world. They show their unhappiness by hoping that their parents will get back together and by exhibiting nervous habits, excessive crying, whining and complaining. If you are depressed about your divorce, the best thing you can do for your children is to get help for yourself. Then you will be able to help them by listening to their own feelings of loss. Feeling better about yourself will also allow you to spend quality time with them. As for the children's feelings about the parent out of the home, you can best assure them by letting your children see the noncustodial spouse on a regular and frequent schedule.

Nine- to twelve-year-olds become upset when they are forced to choose sides between their parents and when they feel that they are not able to cope with the sadness they are experiencing. Their hidden feelings most often get expressed as fighting with brothers and sisters or with classmates, constantly arguing and experiencing psychosomatic complaints like headaches or stomachaches. The solution to the anguish a child feels about choosing sides is *never* to use children as a conduit between you and your ex-spouse, either for information or to fight a battle. Experts also advise that you don't make your children into miniature adults and start discussing your personal problems with them on an adult level. It is also advisable not to go toe-to-toe with them when they are angry. Let the situation cool off and then try to find out what is fueling the anger. It will probably be one of the situations just mentioned or something closely related.

Teenagers are upset by having to reconcile the changes in their own lives and bodies with the changes in their family, by feeling a loss of stability in their lives, and by experiencing feelings associated with their parents' dating or remarrying. Teenagers demonstrate their problems with drug and alcohol abuse, poor grades, sexual promiscuity, and running away from home. What can you do when a teenager has a problem associated with your divorce? Probably the best advice is to be open about your own needs while reinforcing the importance of their feelings and lives. Now is the time that you can show your love by letting them grow up. Because the teenage years are often traumatic even in a normal family setting, the additional burden of divorce may be more than your teenager can handle alone. If you begin to lose control, we recommend that you immediately seek counseling help. It may be the best (and only) way of gaining control of the situation before you both lose your teenager for good.

There is another group which is often overlooked during a divorce. These are the children who are now young adults. The emotions of your sons and daughters in this age group are no less painful or critical. The sense of abandonment may not be as strong as in earlier years, but the anger is just as strong. Young adults of this age often feel that the person who precipitated the divorce deserves all the blame. They are doubly hurt because of the pain they are feeling and because of the pain they see their other parent going through. It then becomes extremely difficult for you to communicate with that child since they tend not to believe anything you might say.

There are only two pieces of advice that we can give you in this situation:

•   Keep trying to communicate why you wanted the divorce.

•   Be patient because the effort to communicate and the growing maturity of your adult child will heal all wounds eventually.

Saying Good-bye

There is no such thing as a clean break in a divorce, especially when children are involved. Letting one parent be the sole parent so as not to confuse the children by asking them to choose between the two of you is not the solution to this problem. Such a clean break often causes more problems. Children feel abandoned. Often, they feel that they were in some way deficient and that's why the other parent left and wants nothing to do with them. Studies show, time and time again, that the most well-adjusted children of divorce are those who have continuous contact with both parents. It is true that parents will often continue their battle in fights over the children when there is joint or shared custody, but then it is the responsibility of the parents to start acting like adults.

Telling the Children You are Getting a Divorce

The advice we have to give here is very simple. Explain everything they are capable of understanding. Above all, insist that the divorce is nobody's fault and certainly not the children's. The fact is that no matter how much you try to assure your children that they had nothing to do with you and your spouse splitting up, they will harbor some fears that they were the cause. This is actually quite normal and only patient and persistent assurances and love will eventually make your children feel free of guilt. During this difficult time, you must also assure the children that they will have contact with the parent who is moving out. This is important or else the children will feel that they are being abandoned. You may have a secret desire yourself to let the children think that way about "that rat" who just left you, but just remember that your children didn't ask for the divorce.

Maintaining and Building Love and Trust

The way to build love and trust is to show unconditional love and trust. Unconditional love, however, is not the same as being permissive or doing everything for the child or letting the child do everything. You must be firm, but not dictatorial. Many divorcing parents are so guilty about what is happening to their children that they let them have whatever they want. But this is not realistic. The other side of unconditional love is allowing the open communication of feelings between parent and child even if they are painful. Listen to the hurt and anger. Love them for who they are, not what they do or what you hope they will become. And one final word: Don't forget to take care of yourself. Show your children that you can handle hardships and move forward. Be a good role model by showing that love and trust is stronger than hate and revenge.

Continuing the Relationship

You can't fix the past, but you can influence the present and future. That's the best advice there is for continuing your relationship with your children. You should take responsibility for what has happened, but don't let guilt stop you from moving forward. Start now to establish a better relationship. Children are very forgiving.

When you are with your children, watch how you behave and don't transmit negative behaviors to your children. Try to see the world and the divorce through their eyes and allow them to have their feelings. Above all, don't say everything is OK when it isn't. Children are not stupid. Children are so sensitive, in fact, that they sometimes know there is trouble before the parents do.

As for your children's behavior, look upon any unusual behavior during or after the divorce as a plea for help. Children don't always have the vocabulary or sophistication to express what is bothering them, so they may act out what is bothering them. Read their behavior for clues. On the other hand, don't hover over them and evaluate everything they say or do. Remember that it will take time for them, as well as you, to heal.

It is also important that you don't convey the message that your children are somehow lacking or different just because they don't live in a two-parent family. It can become a self-fulfilling prophecy. A one-parent family is different than a two-parent family, but one is not necessarily better than the other. Again, the importance of allowing your children to maintain frequent and continuous contact with the other parent is probably one of the two most important factors in your children's happiness. Your children love both of you or, at least, want to. Therefore, don't undermine your children's love for your ex-spouse. Teaching your children to hate the other parent has a nasty way of eventually blowing up in your own face. The other important factor for ensuring your children's security and happiness is to continue to provide them with love without any conditions.

Will They Understand?

Some children are actually relieved when an abusive relationship ends by way of a divorce. Whether your children understand or not depends on whether the divorce is negative or positive. A negative divorce either brings the children right into the middle of the battle or totally excludes them from what is going on. A positive divorce allows for the honest sharing of feelings without overburdening children or making them take sides.

Your attorney's job is to help you to understand your choices and what their potential results could be. Since the laws vary from state to state, your attorney is an important part of your decision-making process and can substantially affect the outcome of your visitation rights. The few items we are discussing in this chapter are just the tip of the iceberg. Your attorney is there to help you based on your special circumstances.

Child Support

First of all, you need to know that child support can start as soon as the divorce process is set in motion. You don't have to wait until the divorce is final. The courts will grant temporary support while the divorce is in process. The purpose of this temporary support order is to help provide for housing, food, clothing, insurance, utilities, car expenses, medical bills and telephone for both the dependent spouse and the children. It is granted without prejudice, which means that the amounts are not binding on the final child support and alimony awards. However, you should be aware of the fact that a court will likely view the home of a parent who is supervising a child as the primary residence. As a result, the court will be reluctant to change the child's residence especially if the child appears to be well adjusted.

How Child Support Payments are Determined

Whether you are Ivana Trump who gets $300,000 annually to support her three children or just an average parent, the court will look at the same basic factors in determining how much child support could be provided. These are the five most common factors:

- Financial condition of each parent.
- Health and educational needs of the child.
- Support given by each parent which is not monetary.
- Family's standard of living prior to divorce.
- Tax consequences of support payments.

The actual guidelines for child support depend on the state in which you live. It can be based on everything from the income of the noncustodial parent, both incomes, a percentage of the gross income or a percentage of the net income. The three most common guidelines are as follows:

In the **Wisconsin formula**, child support is a percentage of the noncustodial parent's pretax income according to number of children. If there is one child, child support amounts to 17% of the noncustodial parent's income. For two children, the figure is 25%. For three children, the figure is 29%. For four children, the figure is 31%. For five or more children, the figure is 34%. This formula is often criticized because it does not factor in the income of the custodial parent or the debt burden of the noncustodial parent. It assumes that the more children, the lower the payment will be (as a percentage). For example, one child equals 17%, six children equals 5.6% each.

The **Delaware Melson formula** first sets subsistence levels for both parents. Then the difference between their combined income and the money they both need to live is considered for child support. The formula states that $180 a month is for the first child, $135 for the second and third and $90 for the fourth through sixth. Each parent is expected to meet their share of these amounts of money based on their income. If there is still money remaining after these payments have been met, certain percentages (again based on the number of children) are set aside for child support as well.

In the **Income Shares formula**, the amount of child

support is made equal to that percentage of family income which the children would have received if the parents remained married. As in the above formula, the proportion each parent pays is based on their respective incomes.

The duty to support the child exists at all times, from the time you are separated to the time you are divorced. And, both parents have the duty to support the children. You should also be aware of the fact that you cannot give away the duty to support your child, even if you give up the right to custody of that child.

What to Do

Whatever formula is used in your state, you can help your children best by doing some homework of your own and, if possible, with your spouse. First of all, make a list of all your children's present and future needs—medical/dental, allowances, hobbies, camps, lessons, education, etc. Child support is more than just food and shelter. Child support can even include entertainment and vacations. The court takes its actions based on what the child was accustomed to and what can be reasonably expected. Do this income and expense statement for each child from birth and calculate their percentage of household expenses.

Follow the court procedures in your state. Usually there is a hearing to see if the case can be easily settled. Otherwise, you must go to trial which can take months.

How to Get a Modification of a Support Order

A child support order can be modified at any time with no limit on the number of times either parent can take action. Modifications are usually granted when the courts find that new circumstances—pay raises, business losses, expensive medical treatment—warrant a change in the amount of money paid. It is strongly advised, however, that you don't use child support modifications as a weapon to get your ex-spouse to do something you want him or her to do. The courts are aware of these tactics and your harassment will probably backfire.

Who Gets the Deduction/Who Pays the Taxes

The spouse paying alimony can deduct the payments on his or her tax returns. As for the spouse who receives the alimony, he or she must include it on tax returns as reportable income. Child support, on the other hand, is not deductible by the spouse paying, nor is it considered taxable income for the spouse receiving it. That set of circumstances is behind a lot of the fights which occur over the size of child support relative to alimony. If you are the principal wage-earning spouse, it makes economic sense to want to pay more alimony since payment usually ends upon remarriage of your ex-spouse. Child support continues, in many cases, until the child reaches majority. And, if you include college expenses, it does not even necessarily end on the day they reach legal age.

The Child Support Crisis in this Country—the Husband's Fault or the Fault of the System?

First of all, some facts and figures about child support. A recent news story in *USA Today* reported that 49% of the single mothers who should get child support receive only a portion of it or none. Reports also claim that 30% of the families where one of the parents leaves end up in poverty. Family income, it is claimed, can decline by up to 37% even with child support. The average amount of child support was $2,995 in 1989, the most current year for these figures. In addition, only 15% of divorced or separated women are awarded alimony, so there aren't a lot of women getting rich or eating bon-bons while watching the soaps. These statistics are true for all ethnic groups and income levels.

Many people contend that there would be more responsibility about paying child support if there was more access to children by the noncustodial parent and if the courts were not prejudiced toward granting one parent sole custody. The way we see it is that we pay one way or another. The less child support that gets paid, the more children there will be who go on government programs. The facts say that 80% of fathers with visitation rights pay their child support and that the percentage increases to 90% for fathers with joint custody. It's clear to us that child support must be linked to fair custody and visitation rights.

If you are a father who does not pay his child support, you are not only faced with possible jail time but also with a mandatory income deduction order. This happens through a court order. As a result, the court takes the money for support, in addition to interest and costs, directly out of your pay.

Custody/Visitation

Try to avoid going to court about custody because not only will it cost you a great deal of money but it has the potential of upsetting your children by having to watch one parent tear the other one apart or by having to choose sides. You must be reasonable, otherwise your bitterness will only continue through the years and possibly adversely affect your children. Remember that you don't divorce your children, so you will always have some form of a relationship with your ex-spouse.

The next thing you must do is consider what you want in relation to the custody issue. Are you seeking custody as revenge? Asking for custody to get a concession somewhere else? Are you acting out of pride? Trying to prove that you love your child? The hardest question you may have to ask yourself is whether you are indeed the best parent. Don't feel guilty if you would rather not have sole custody of the children. This is especially true for women who are still looked upon as bad when they don't want sole custody. Again, we emphasize that some form of shared, or joint custody is best for all involved—parents and children.

During Divorce

The court will usually award temporary custody to one parent during divorce proceedings. Permanent custody is awarded after the divorce. Although all custody rulings by the court are open to modification, temporary custody does affect permanent custody since many courts are unwilling to uproot children. So, if you want your children, don't move out of your house unless ordered to do so or move out and take the children with you. Either way, expect a court battle if you and your spouse can't come to an agreement by yourselves. The court will make its decision based on what it deems to be in the best interests of the child.

Visitation

The best idea about visitation in our opinion is to work out a schedule and put it in the divorce decree. Be as detailed as possible and include written and telephone contact. Here are some guidelines for visitation that we suggest:

Infants—Children at this age need strong and almost constant attachment to one parent. The other parent should make brief and frequent visits.

Preschoolers—Children have a limited idea of what "see you in a week" means. More than one visit a week is best. Well-adjusted children may be able to spend a night away from the custodial home.

Six- to 12-year-olds—Noncustodial parent should make at least one visit a week. The regularity of visits is most important to children of this age. If you come every Saturday, expect to come every Saturday. Not every other Saturday or three Saturdays out of four. If something does come up which will prevent you from making a regular visit, explain the circumstances to the child in advance. If it keeps happening, then find another time you can make regular visits. Ask yourself what is more important, business or your children.

Teenagers—Our advice here is to arrange visitation in conjunction with them and the custodial parent. Let your teenagers have a greater say in when they want to see you. And again, make every effort to be there.

Adult children—Adult children in our opinion require the same attention and care as teenagers. They may know more about life and relationships, but they are still subject to very strong feelings. Many young adults of this age blame themselves for the collapse of the marriage.

What should you do if your ex-spouse refuses visitation rights? The first step is to get the court to issue an order which requires the custodial parent to allow visits. Then, if necessary, go to the police with the order and ask them to enforce it by accompanying you to your child's home. Be prepared, however, to encounter some foot-dragging on the part of the police. This is not a high priority for the police. The courts can stop child support if your ex-spouse continues not to comply or they can tie child support to your visitation rights. If the child doesn't want to see the noncustodial parent, the court will question the child for evidence of coercion or "brainwashing" by the custodial parent and ask for an examination by a psychologist. Although every charge of child abuse or molestation will be investigated, the courts are aware that one parent will falsely accuse the other.

Other areas which you will need to consider in a separation agreement concerning custody are whether you and your ex-spouse live in separate towns, who drives the child and where do you meet, who gets the child if your birthday falls on a holiday, etc.

Physical and Legal Custody

Physical custody defines the situation where a child lives with the parent. Legal custody defines a situation in which parents are allowed to have a say in how the children are raised, what schools they attend, what medical care they should receive and so on.

Joint custody is the situation in which both parents are responsible for determining how the child is raised. Both parents have equal responsibility for the children's care and equal or joint time with the children. This means that the children will live part of the time with each parent. There are many variations on joint custody from 50/50 to a plan where both parents have a say in raising the children, but one parent has physical custody. Although the reason behind joint custody is to allow children to have the maximum contact with both parents, joint custody sometimes only prolongs the battle which came to a head with the divorce. Nevertheless, most child experts agree that the children benefit the most when both parents have a say in the children's upbringing. It is the best insurance for continued support and psychological well-being.

What Does the Child Want—their Best Interests

The courts are paying increasing attention to the child's best interests. In fact, a Florida court recently ruled that a child can sue his or her parents for "divorce." The child in this case reportedly doesn't want to live with his natural parents who are divorced because he claims they abused and neglected him. The court ruled that the child has the same constitutional rights as an adult has to protect their interests in court.

In more typical cases, the court looks at the following factors to determine the child's best interests:

- **Age and sex—Young children often go to the wife; adolescents with parent of same sex.**

- **Parent's ability to meet the needs of a child.**

- **How a child will adjust to new surroundings.**

- **Physical and mental health of children and parents.**

- **Child's choice.**

The courts will also order social workers to report on suitability of each parent and their homes in order to help determine the child's best interests.

Shared Parental Responsibility

The courts have several options concerning the child. First, they may adopt the option of shared parental responsibility in which both parents retain full parental rights and responsibilities for the care of the child. On the other hand, the court may adopt the concept of sole parental responsibility in which the court orders one parent as responsible for the decisions concerning the child. Today, courts recognize that a parent is much more likely to pay child support if he or she has a continued interest in the care of the child. Below is a sample claim of shared parental responsibility:

> **"It is in the best interest of the child that both parents share parental responsibility. As a result, all decisions shall be made jointly. The child shall reside in both parents' homes and spend time with both parents equally."**

Whatever agreement you enter into concerning your child, here is a list of items for you to consider:

1. **Holidays**
   - **Christmas, Thanksgiving**
   - **Birthdays—yours and the child's**
   - **Where is the child dropped off**
   - **Who is responsible**
   - **Who pays**
2. **School**
   - **Who pays**
   - **Who makes sure homework is done**
   - **Who meets with the teacher**

- Who takes the child to extracurricular activities
- Who can see the child in extracurricular activities
- Who chooses the school
- Who saves for college

3. Medical and dental expenses, including insurance
   - Who pays
   - Who makes the decisions
   - Who is responsible for transportation

4. Grandparents
   - Who takes the child
   - Whose time does it count against

5. How much time will the child spend with each parent

6. Can one of the parents move at will?

Again, your attorney should have a more complete list. Use the above list to get you started thinking about what you need to discuss.

How to Get a Modification of a Custody Order

Like child support orders, the courts will modify custody decisions. Even after your divorce, the court will retain jurisdiction over the child. The overriding condition for obtaining a modification is what the court deems best for the child. There is no limit on the number of times you can seek a change. The following are some of the reasons why courts will consider modifications:

- **Interference with visitation rights of the noncustodial parent.**

- **Neglect.**

- **Emotional, physical or sexual abuse.**

- **"Brainwashing" a child to hate the noncustodial parent.**

- **At the child's request, especially if they are teenagers.**

Court Battles over Custody/Support

Court battles can get ugly like the recent story about a woman who was denied custody and normal visitation rights in part because she burned her husband's clothes, spray-painted their home and drove her car into the house where he was staying after he had moved out. The divorce began, in part, because her husband had left her for a younger woman. The case then got even more ugly. According to whether you believe the defense or prosecution, the woman cold-bloodedly murdered her ex-husband and his new wife or killed them in the heat of passion.

Of course, not all court battles are this tragic, but they all exact a heavy toll. Mike Termini knows firsthand just how heavy a toll. The following is his story of a custody battle for his child:

> Once the initial wounds of divorce heal and the settlements are reached, the downstream relationship of parents is key to the ability of children to cope with the situation. My wife and I divorced when our eldest child was barely three years old. At the time, the courts almost universally awarded custody of young children to the

mother. And the custody of the bills to the father. My
case was no different. In all honesty, I thought it was
more appropriate for my daughter at that age in her life to
be with her mother.

For awhile, the bitterness of the divorce continued.
Financial plans were made which were difficult to meet.
Like most fathers, meeting my child support payments
was my number one objective. It was, after all, not money
going to my ex-wife, but to the support of my daughter.
During the ten to twelve months after the divorce was
final, my God-given and court-approved rights to see my
daughter were slowly beginning to erode away. As in
most cases, I was given weekend visitation rights and one
night during the week to see my daughter.

As my ex-wife found companionship, it became increasingly more difficult for me to exercise my visitation
rights. I realized, of course, that the situation with a
newly-divorced woman with a child becomes sensitive
when there is a new man in her life and the old man is
still around. But that's not the issue. The issue is easing
the child through the transition without a significant
emotional scar. As the visitation rights were becoming
progressively more restrictive, the emotional impact on
my daughter and myself became increasingly more
heavy. Arguments between my ex-wife and I (and her
new companion) grew more intense and frequent which
only intensified the impact on my daughter.

As time went on, my visitation rights were reduced even
further to the point where, for a two-month period, I did
not see my daughter at all. I can't begin to explain the

emotional impact that absence had on me as it would have on any father. Or any mother. The separation of spouses is traumatic, but the separation of a parent (mother or father) from a child is an incredible loss, one that could drive a parent to seek some kind of irrational action. A rational parent, as I fortunately was in this case, will seek relief from the court. I can understand, however, how an irrational parent would be driven to kidnapping. The emotions are intense. The depression is so deep that you would go for days without even a smile. You would never feel happy. There would be no hope.

I found myself looking back through old scrapbooks and pictures and as a grown man, beginning to cry. Her birthday came and went. I called. I was not allowed to talk with her. I could hear her crying in the background, screaming for Daddy! It was almost as if my ex-wife was using this enforced separation as a form of punishment against me and my daughter.

After several months with no break in the circumstances, I was forced to go back to court. Even though I was financially strapped as a result of the divorce, I had no recourse. I retained a lawyer and initially sought the enforcement of my visitation rights. My attorney and others from whom I received counsel said that I had no chance to gain custody of my child. They said that it was unheard of and that was mostly true back in the late 1970s.

Back in court, the visitation rights were once again emphasized, but unfortunately to no avail. Three months later, after seeing my daughter only once, I again went back to court. This time, against all odds, I was seeking full custody. The next eighteen months were a time of bitter frustration, anger, anxiety and hope. The costs mounted. In addition to the legal fees, the first counter maneuver by my ex-wife's lawyer was to retain the services of a child psychologist. This person testified to the court that, in her professional opinion, it would be unhealthy for me to see my daughter until she reached the age of ten. In other words, six more years.

My attorney felt that we needed professional advice to counter that opinion, so I retained a well-renowned child psychologist to testify on my behalf. Obviously, his position was 180 degrees from that of the psychologist that testified on the behalf of my wife. At that point, the court saw fit to assign an attorney and a child psychologist to represent my three-year-old daughter. In retrospect, although the costs were extremely high, it was probably the wisest decision the court could have made from my child's standpoint. Her attorney and psychologist had no axe to grind. They carried no baggage, had no opinion pro or con relative to the father or the mother, but only for the well-being of the child. After all, that is exactly what we should have all been after.

After 18 months and many tens of thousands of dollars, I was awarded custody of my daughter. In the court's opinion, my wife had used my daughter in a vindictive manner to inflict pain upon me. Her actions were not in the best interests of the child.

At the time of the writing of this book, my daughter is 15. We've been through a lot together. I've been a single parent and I've remarried. We've moved, been through job changes, school changes. I've tried to be a good father, a good parent. And part of being a good parent is encouraging my daughter to have a positive relationship with her mother, including frequent visitations.

At the time of the divorce of Mark Grieco's parents, he was able to maintain an excellent relationship with both. His law background provided him with a view on the process that many adult children lack. This experience of having to live, or as we say, *walk the walk*, has helped develop him into an attorney with a real rapport with his clients. He can honestly say that he has been there.

Deciding on alimony, child support, custody and property settlements in a divorce requires a great deal of negotiating. In the next chapter, we will show you a method of negotiating which will help both parties come to a decision which makes both sides happy.

Chapter 11

Reaching an Agreement

The goals of a divorce are:

1) Termination of a legal relationship.
2) Attaining an equitable distribution of marital assets.
3) Continuing your relationship with your children.
4) Be happy with yourself.

The first goal is relatively easy. The next two get progressively harder. The last is the most important. Peter Grieco, for example, is now remarried to the most wonderful woman in the world. And what's more, his two sons support his new wife and understand that happiness is the most important consideration of all. That is why you need to know how to negotiate a fair divorce settlement.

There are many techniques we recommend. Some people want to use the approach of getting all you can and screwing the other person as much as possible. Others want to achieve a 50/50 split. The past relationship and what triggered the split have a lot to do with what method will be employed.

Even in the best of situations where one party hires a lawyer, the other side has no choice but to hire one too. This could turn the divorce into the most frustrating situation which you have ever been involved in. The court and both lawyers are in it to follow the legal process and receive payment for their services. They are not there to help because they feel sorry for you. Their task is to get a settlement at the expense of either or both parties. If you think otherwise, you're in for a big surprise.

Each side will request so much paperwork that it will take months to unravel. You have no control in scheduling the dates of various hearings. All offers go through a third party (one lawyer to the other). When you try a direct approach, the response is: "In your best interest, I advise you not to sign or do this." We must learn to manage the people we are paying. Remember that the lawyer works for you; you don't work for them.

A recent example from a friend comes to mind. He offered his ex-spouse a very good settlement early in the process. Her lawyer felt that it was too good to be true and that he must be trying to hide something, so he advised her to wait until he could review the whole case. When this case finally got settled, the settlement was far less than the first offer. Most of the money went to pay both attorneys and accountants. Even in community property states, each side does not present a worst or best case. What is required, we think, is a system that allows negotiation to take place so that a fair result can be achieved for both parties.

Divorce negotiation is always difficult because it violates the first rule of negotiating: Don't get emotionally involved! Since this relationship was once a partnership and is now being dissolved, people forget that the process still requires communication.

Most divorces are not win/win and that's why they cost a great deal in terms of money and pain. Only the lawyers win in those cases. Consider the case of the recent divorce battle between golf professional Fred Couples and his wife, Deborah. They are battling over what the courts call "Celebrity Goodwill," or the amount of money which Fred can be expected to make by lending his name to the endorsement of products. Deborah claims that she contributed to the making of Fred's career (which has become quite lucrative after winning the 1992 Masters) and deserves to join in the results of the work she did to make his success come about.

What about Mediation

One increasingly popular alternative to going to court is to negotiate some or all of the issues in the presence of a neutral mediator. In Florida, for example, it is usually ordered by the court. Mediators are facilitators. They try to create a nonconfrontational environment where you and your spouse can iron out your differences without attacking each other. Unlike arbitration in which both parties agree to what the arbitrator decides, the mediator makes no ruling. Instead, he or she helps the two spouses hammer out a settlement agreement which can be presented to the court without having to resort to the high costs of court and lawyers. Although a mediator's fee can be as much as $100 an hour or more, their work is often done in ten hours or less. That is considerably less money than what you would pay a lawyer.

There are some people, however, who claim that mediators do not protect rights of divorcing spouses because they don't understand all the legal or financial aspects of divorce. This may have been more true in the early years of this field, but probably is not true now. There are professional associations and professional training in the legal, financial, tax and psychological aspects of divorce for mediators. The emphasis of all this training and education is on establishing a win/win arrangement in an atmosphere of cooperation and creative problem-solving. Some of the activities of a mediator are listed below:

- Maintain open and honest discussion of issues.
- Keep the children's interests in view.
- Facilitate compromises and trade-offs.
- Make creative suggestions.
- Advise on legal, financial and emotional points.
- Write up the agreement.

It should be noted that lawyers are normally involved in the mediation process. They act as an advisor to both parties and the mediator or as a counsel to each spouse.

We believe that mediation often airs differences which might not get put on the table and which probably would cause one or both parties to be unhappy with their divorce. These unresolved matters usually lead to more court action and costs in the future. With mediators, you can save money now and save money later. Mediation fills the psychological need, mentioned earlier in this chapter, in which a person needs to feel like they have participated in the decision in order for them to have some future happiness.

Mediation links emotional issues with financial and legal ones in the sense that it doesn't act as though they are not related as is the case often in the legal profession. That can only lead to a more satisfying conclusion to the divorce process.

Preparing for the Mediation Process

Mediation is a process. It is not a static event, but a lively interchange between you and your soon to be ex-spouse. Preparing for mediation is like writing the script for a play. It is often necessary to develop several alternate scripts in order to find a scenario that makes all parties happy.

Planning for mediation should typically follow a strategy like the one outlined here:

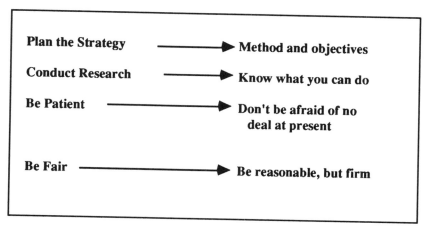

The predominant purpose of your negotiations during the divorce process is to reach an agreement to as much as possible before going to court. It not only costs much less, but it is your best insurance that you will achieve a fair position, especially if children are involved.

Types of Negotiations in Divorce (Mediation)

We have noticed four different ways that people handle negotiations in a divorce, whether it is mediated or not. How they handle the negotiations will play a large part in whether they view the results as successful or not. That is why it makes a great deal of sense to pay attention to how you and your spouse negotiate. So let's take a look at each of these four ways of negotiating:

See-saw—This type of divorce negotiation could also be called "Yes, we will! No, we won't!" A couple going through this type of negotiation is very ambivalent about divorce. First, they want to get divorced. Then they make up and try again, whereupon they end up back where they started and begin the cycle of fighting, asking for a divorce and making up all over again. When they are in the divorce phase of their cycle, they fight to the end over every detail and neither side is willing to budge. Such a couple is not emotionally ready for divorce. They haven't been able to accept breaking apart their marriage. It is probably best if couples in this pattern sought psychological counseling on how to say "good-bye" to a marriage that no longer works, before they try to negotiate.

Ostrich—This category is for the people who act as if their upcoming divorce doesn't bother them in the least. The husband and wife hardly talk to each other, let alone negotiate over custody, support, alimony, or settlements. They are content to let the lawyers or the courts do what they will. On the surface, this may appear better than ugly arguments, but it is not. Below the surface, the anger and hurt still simmers. Not having a chance to engage in negotiations and let off some of that pressure only hurts more in the long run when bitterness begins to rule over these people's lives. Do yourself and your spouse a favor. Get everything on the table and don't pretend you don't care what happens, because you do.

Cat and dog—Although there is a great deal of argument in this type of divorce, it usually ends with more satisfaction than the preceding two methods of negotiation. With a good mediator (as we shall discuss later in the chapter), this type of couple can end up with an agreement both sides feel is fair. The problem here is that sometimes the anger can get out of hand and cause damage. If you feel that you and your spouse fall into this category, it may be best that you don't attempt to negotiate without an impartial referee.

Fork in the road—In this last category go the couples who are able to disagree, but who realize that the marriage is over and that each will go their separate ways. There will still be points of contention in the negotiations, but the overall atmosphere is one of cooperation. People who want to avoid the adversarial nature of the legal system and the high costs of lawyers often choose this type of negotiation. Sometimes, these couples are able to do it on their own and other times, they seek professional help from a mediator. As you will see, this method is essentially the win/win approach to negotiations which we advocate.

Fulfilling Psychological Needs

In a win/win divorce, both sides need to feel like they have worked together to reach their goals. In divorce, there is a psychological need by both the parents and the children to be an active part of the process. Somebody who does not participate will probably become angry later on for being left out of the process. An agreement that is worked out together will feel more fair and will be more fair. Being constructive and cooperative will not only cost less in legal fees now, but it could save fees later on since there is less chance of retributive court action. Equally important are emotional costs. There are far fewer psychological problems in a win/win divorce and hence less money paid out to psychologists and other mental health professionals.

The process of working out an agreement can be therapeutic itself. Coming to an agreement makes you actively confront the changes in your life and the attendant emotions brought about by divorce, instead of burying them away, only to have them inevitably return later to wreak havoc in your life. Negotiating a win/win divorce will help you go through the stages of grief discussed in Chapter 5. The anger and hurt you may experience are actually the means whereby you can get better if we use this time to air the differences, find the common ground and come to an agreement. Most post-divorce problems, in our experiences, are directly related to the inability or reluctance of both spouses to work together one last time to find an agreement which will make both parties happy, now and in the future.

There will also be less bitterness as a result of a win/win divorce because you will not feel as though the decision was imposed on you by the courts and your lawyers. You and your spouse know yourselves and your family better than anyone else. The two of you owe it to yourselves to act like adults and come up with your agreement, not some legal boilerplate which doesn't take into account your special circumstances. The agreement begins with you.

Win/Win Negotiation

There are three types of negotiation philosophies of which you
should be aware, says Pete Grieco, in his book **The World of
Negotiations:** *Never Being a Loser* (PT Publications, Inc., Palm
Beach Gardens, FL). The first is cooperative, or win/win, negotiation. The second is competitive, or win/lose, negotiation. The
third is lose/lose, or no negotiation possible. Let's look at some
definitions:

> **Win/Win**—A philosophy and frame of mind that constantly
> seeks mutual benefit and interaction. This is not easily
> obtained in a divorce case.

> **Win/Lose**—This is an authoritarian approach in which I win,
> you lose. They simply want to succeed at all costs and to
> get even.

> **Lose/Lose**—This situation occurs when two stubborn, thick-
> headed people get together and let ego or individual
> interest override common sense in the search for a solu-
> tion. Normally, this person ends up with a judge deciding
> the case and who gets what.

Cooperative negotiation is easy. It says that there is always a better
situation if you take the time and the attorneys let you build a
relationship with your ex-spouse. This process of making the pie
big enough for everybody is a new trend in divorce negotiations,
but it is long overdue.

If your negotiation is competitive, you are not building a relationship for the future. We know you are saying "What relationship?
I'm getting divorced to end a relationship." But you would be

wrong to think this way. There will always be something that you will have to communicate about in the future. You or your spouse may believe that divorce negotiation is a one-shot deal. Despite what you may think, it is not. Alimony, support and custody are never fixed. They are subject to change and hence to negotiation. If you antagonize the other side so much during the initial divorce proceedings, they probably won't want to deal with you again.

Win/Win Approach to Mediation

If you know how to structure a mediation so that it's a win/win for both sides, so that each party gets some of what they want, the results will be successful. This success comes without the pressure, anxiety and tension that most feel is normal. Negotiation and mediation should be as free of revenge and hate as is possible. A hard goal to achieve, but worth the effort.

The approach for win/win requires establishing a trusting and cooperative attitude in order to achieve success. That's difficult, but you need to establish it in this forum by looking at the list below. A win/win divorce is based on a commitment to interaction. It is not a technique. It is a philosophy which consists of several dimensions:

<u>DIMENSIONS OF WIN/WIN</u>

Character—Build a foundation on high integrity, ethics and trust.

Relationship—Build on the trust which used to exist by being honest as you put your cards on the table.

Agreement—Shift the mediation to a strategy where both sides can be partners in success through the use of performance agreements. These are vehicles used to measure each other's post-divorce activity concerning such areas as joint custody, child support and alimony.

Trust and cooperation—Trust and cooperation are the foundations upon which everything else is built. Trust requires integrity and maturity. As the chart below shows, the closer we move to the high end of both axes, the closer we are to achieving win/win.

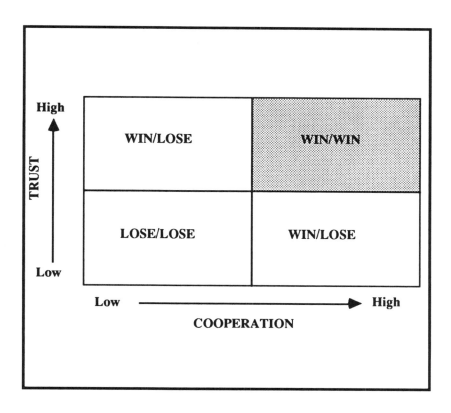

The Mediator's Role

The good mediator must be aware of each of the stages of the
negotiating process and their different strategies and approaches.
The stages of negotiating are:

---

1. Developing your Opening Position

2. Presenting the Opening Offer

3. Determining the Min-Max Range

4. Finding the Soft Ground

5. Getting to an Agreement

The basic tenet of negotiating is to give nothing away unless you
are completely aware of the implications of doing so and only if
you have balanced those implications against the reasons for
giving away the item being negotiated. You must always be on
your toes and keenly aware of your *self-interest* and the purpose
of the negotiations.

When you give something away, you should be aware of its value
because you want something of equal value in return. Unless you
communicate what you're giving to the other person at the
negotiating table, he or she may not be aware of its value to you.
If you allow your spouse to remain ignorant of that information,
your goodwill gesture is for nothing. In the eyes of your spouse,
you haven't given anything away. Let them know that you have.

Style

It is extremely important to show respect for the other person while establishing your own right to respect. The more we learn about the other person's requirements, the better equipped we are to satisfy their needs. Perhaps even more important, the better we know a person's needs, the less apt we are to offer more than is required or to offer them something which they will not consider valuable.

Despite these intentions, you may come up against lawyers who have negative negotiating styles. Here are some suggestions for how to deal with these situations:

Smoke screens—When you are in a negotiation with a lawyer or spouse who fights over every detail, you may also decide to fight over every detail. If you don't, they may think you are weak—a pushover—and you may wind up with a less than desirable settlement. Such a negotiating tactic clouds the air with trivial and unimportant issues. At times, you may need to take this approach in order to strengthen your position. But when somebody uses it on you, respond by keeping your major issues on the table. Sometimes you just have to set the other party straight. Tell them that you can see exactly what they are trying to do and that it is a waste of time. Then get back to the issues that you have decided are important and deal with them.

The key to success in negotiations depends upon your ability to focus on the issues and not the peripherals. Ignore the "smoke" and stick to the issues during negotiation. Make a statement, put your facts on the table and go with them. Don't defend them. Try to make the opposition tell you why they want their needs granted. You become the listener. If you're defending your position, then you aren't listening.

Unreasonable tactics—A negotiator who is unwilling to seek a win/win agreement is being unreasonable. Here are some ways to recognize this style:

- Attorney starts with ridiculous offers.
- They use emotional tactics.
- They view your concessions as signs of weakness.
- They act as if they have all the time in the world.
- They make you react emotionally.
- They break the rules without concern.
- Their desires know no limits.
- Winning is everything to them.

"Unreasonable" negotiators always start with an extreme opening position. For example, if your home is worth $150,000 on the market, your spouse's lawyer will claim it is worth $300,000. When you reply that this is unfair, they will flare up and say, "We have a written estimate stating that value." If you make a concession and come up to $175,000, they will either not budge or come down to $298,000. Our advice is to seek a professional who will value such large ticketed items before you proceed.

The most effective method for fighting this style of negotiating is to recognize the tactics and then let the other side know that *you know* what is going on. Don't respond to ridiculous offers and measly concessions as though they were realistic. Finally, if your spouse's lawyer is using your feelings or sentimental attachments to pets or property to pressure you, ask yourself if it is really worth it. Then, ask yourself if it is really the pet you are arguing over or some unresolved emotional issue with your spouse.

Presenting the Opening Offer

Your opening offer provides the other side with an understanding of your position on custody, child support, alimony and property settlements. You should start with a settlement or deal which permits response and is realistic enough to leave room for negotiation. You can always go up in cost, but it is difficult to go down. What you have to do is fall within an upper and lower limit, or planning range, in order to be successful.

Determining the Range

Certainly alimony, child support and property settlement have prices which can be negotiated. But even custody has high and low bids. You may want to see your children three times a week and your spouse may want you to see them only once a week. Every point in the divorce process is negotiable, so be aware of what your opening offer contains. If you start off with an opening offer that is already your highest acceptable price, there is no room for negotiation. Without a range, you have a non-negotiable offer in which your spouse, for example, informs you that "this is my offer and if you want a deal, then give me what I want." Either you or your spouse may think that your non-negotiable offer is fair, but remember that a fair offer is what both sides are willing to accept.

Use caution when finding the range of acceptability so that you don't work against yourself when you set your opening position. You want the attorney to come back with an offer. If you set your opening too high, you have given away negotiating space without getting anything in return.

Finding the Min-Max Range

Finding the min-max range between your spouse's offer and yours is the next task. You are looking for the point at which both of you will be satisfied. A large part of your strength as a negotiator comes from your command of information both prior to and during the bargaining period. If your spouse has less command of the pertinent information, then you have the advantage and vice versa. In negotiating, *knowledge is power*. You must have an intimate knowledge of your requirements.

In the book, *Managing Negotiations* (Prentice-Hall, Inc., NJ), the authors identify five steps in searching for the range:

1. Argue (Discuss).
2. Signal.
3. Propose.
4. Package.
5. Bargain.

Before entering into any mediation, we strongly suggest that you write down realistic objectives. Use a worksheet like the one below to make reasonable guesses about what you are looking for. Then, fill out another worksheet for what you think your spouse is looking for. Power in negotiation is the result of having completed your homework prior to negotiation.

Task	My Position	Their Position	Must Have	Min	Max	Final Results

In the first column, list the tasks which you will be required to complete for each of the key items that you need to accomplish. Put a check mark in the "Must Have" column if you cannot afford to compromise on a particular item. In the Min/Max columns, determine the limits of the range which you will find acceptable. In the last column, put in post-negotiation session results to be used as material for future mediation strategy.

Argue (Discuss)

The early stages of searching for the range typically includes some "feeling out" or actual sparring. At this time, both parties determine what each side is after and has to offer. In this "Argue" step, you and the other party both state what is necessary for a satisfactory agreement and why. You will start to find out if your assumptions about the other side were true and if you have entered negotiations with the correct strategy for a satisfactory settlement.

After you state your position, you should **listen** far more than you talk. Listening is where you gain the most information. It is the single most important thing to do during the mediation process. The better you have prepared for negotiation, the more you will be able to accomplish. If you are busy trying to remember information, your mind cannot be actively listening.

```
LISTEN

SILENT
```

You don't have to back down after you have made a reasonable offer which the other person has refused. What do you do then? You say, "That's not reasonable. I don't understand how you arrived at that position. It's beyond what I can afford and live with. It's time for me to go home." If your spouse's lawyer has been bluffing, you will be asked to "cool down and stay."

The Signal

Signaling moves negotiation along by ensuring that a movement towards the range by one side is matched by a movement from the other side. A good mediator starts that process and often begins his or her work by working at first with each side independently. At some point one of the negotiating parties will need to make concessions. A "signal" is a way to indicate your willingness to concede on a point, if the other side is also willing. You don't want your signal interpreted as surrender.

This is the way a signal works. Let's say that your spouse has just made an unreasonable offer. You have responded that the offer leaves you no room to make a deal and that you, unfortunately, will have to break off negotiations. The mediator has then asked you to reconsider your position. This is a signal that your spouse may be willing to move away from an extreme position. This tells you that perhaps they came on a little strong.

Now, what do you do once you have received this signal? Don't pull all of your options out of your briefcase and lay them on the table. Send out a signal of your own. Say something like this: "What kind of adjustments can we make in our offer to bring us closer together?" Or, "Are there parts of the offer or the alimony which are not acceptable to you?" Or, "Let's look at some of your major needs. Maybe we can save some dollars there."

The Proposal

Proposing is the stage where you move towards narrowing the gap between the two sides in a mediation. In negotiating, a proposal is a counteroffer which moves you from your original position, or opening offer. Early proposals should be tentative and concessions should be small. Avoid appearing too eager.

Your proposals should go something like this: "If we adjust the property settlement by this much, will you agree to our figure?"

Your spouse might say, "No, but I am willing to consider a new alimony payment to make a fairer deal."

Notice that neither of you have committed yourselves to a specific reduction, but you are agreeing on a way to narrow the gap. You are making a conditioned proposal. You should now be moving from generalities to specifics. Some words of advice here: Be firm on generalities. "You *must* increase your offer substantially!" But be flexible on specifics. "We *suggest* a figure of $30,000."

In **Getting to Yes**, authors Roger Fisher and William Ury suggest coming up with a BATNA (Best Alternative To a Negotiated Agreement) as a standard against which you test any proposed agreement. A BATNA stops you from accepting unfavorable terms or from rejecting favorable ones. It answers the question of what you will do if you can't reach a negotiated settlement. A BATNA prevents you from reaching an agreement at any cost.

If you get a "no" to your proposal, don't reward it with another proposal. Ask for alternatives to your proposal. You may need to coax a response from them at this point. While you are bantering back and forth about different proposals, you are identifying the parts of your proposal that can be adjusted to make both sides happy. By the end of this step, both parties to the negotiations should know what each other wants and what each is willing to live with.

Peter remembers a very emotional time when the final issue in his divorce was over lawyer fees. His ex-spouse's lawyer had a reputation for running up billable hours. During the mediation, this lawyer couldn't remember how much his bill was, but he had no trouble remembering all of Peter's data. The lawyer was attempting to get Peter to pay all of the fees, which were unknown at the time. The number would be filled in later. Our advice in this situation is to never walk away from the table without a written and signed agreement outlining everything which must be paid. With no signature, you just have to start all over again.

The Package

Your opening "package" was your most favored position. It set out your objectives for the ensuing discussion during the arguing step. The ultimate goal is to come up with a package that is agreeable to both of you by presenting various proposals. Packaging presents the pieces of your opening offer in a form which more closely matches the other side's interests and limitations. This is the place for some creative thinking.

Another way to be creative in packaging an offer is to ask yourself the following questions for each piece of your offer:

"Who gets how much of What? When? and Why?"

These questions will turn up the variables which can be adjusted to find the range. The more creative ideas you have available for exchange, the better the chances of finding the solution.

Bargaining

Now you find yourself in the position where, through bargaining, the value of every negotiating element will be established. Everything you give away is in exchange for something you get from the other side. Bargaining should be a collaborative act. Both sides should be trying to help the other side get what it wants—**without** giving up more than makes you comfortable.

The pivotal word at this point in negotiating is "if." For example: "if you will agree to two visits a week, I will agree to pay for you and the kids to go on a vacation." When you use "if," the other side is able to discern the value you place on a concession. This type of negotiating is often called *"quid pro quo"* (translated as "this for that"), a term used when making conditional concessions.

Besides always conditioning an offer with an "if," never negotiate the elements of your offer as individual items. Keep the pieces of your package linked. You want to agree on each element before you spend any real money. In this conditional situation, you have not yet agreed to or finalized any contract. You have simply indicated an area where the two parties can reach agreement.

Getting to an Agreement

When you sense that a reasonable agreement has occurred, you should push quickly for closure. The strategy at this point is to summarize where both sides stand and to craft an agreement which represents your positions. It is important when you have reached an agreement to close quickly, formally and legally. Always author the agreement yourself. We hate to write, but we will not let someone do us the favor of writing up our agreement. Once it is in writing, it becomes the completed deal. We all interpret things a little differently. Thus, if the agreement is not put in writing, there is the likelihood of a reversal later in the process.

Deadlines and Deadlocks

Power shifts quickly to the party that knows the other side's true deadline. All deadlines, however, are derived through some process of negotiation. When establishing a deadline in order to reach an agreement, be sure that you don't let deadlines force you to act. Try to remain cool under the pressure. If possible, try to avoid making any deadlines to begin with.

A deadlock occurs when a change of position is no longer possible. A deadlock, unlike a deadline which says this is the end of the negotiating process, is a situation in which both parties reach unacceptable positions. If the process ever does come to a stop, we recommend that each side summarize its position. We even suggest writing each side's summary on a white board or a flip chart.

Deadlocks occur when both parties dig in and won't budge. It's like trench warfare. You fight for weeks over a few yards of earth, often at tremendous costs. Here are some ways for you to break a deadlock:

• **Summarize**	**Find out what both of you do agree upon.**
• **Ask questions**	**Open up the discussion again by asking what the other party wants without reacting emotionally yourself.**
• **Use outside criteria**	**Compare the process of the negotiations against objective criteria, so you don't become entrenched again.**
• **Postpone**	**Agree to disagree later. Put off difficult parts of the negotiations until another time.**
• **Take a break**	**A shorter variation of the above. Come back and negotiate when tempers have died down.**
• **Split the difference**	**This often allows both sides to save face.**
• **Change partners**	**Have other people on both sides conclude the negotiations.**

Going to court

The last resort of a divorce process which cannot reach an agreement through negotiation is to go to trial. If you do, the judge will decide for you. You get to present your side of the case, but the negotiations are out of your hands. In the next chapter, we will look at what happens when you decide on this course of action.

Chapter 12

Deadlock—Going to Court

Going to court is the last stage in the divorce process. There is no longer any room to negotiate. But some still try. In a recent Florida case, for example, the husband's lawyer, in an attempt to settle, said his client was willing to pay for a monthly first class airplane ticket to New York City, including a limousine to and from the airport so his soon-to-be ex-spouse could visit her favorite beauty salon. She claimed that he took her to the city once a month when they were living together as husband and wife.

Most of the courtroom dramatics we read about are in the high-dollar income bracket. This is not to say that requests on a smaller scale do not come up in each and every case. In another divorce, for instance, the husband's attorney dumped a pile of shoes, makeup, bottles of perfumes and 200 pairs of pantyhose on the courtroom floor. He claimed this was just a sample of the over

$25,000 worth of personal items the wife had been accumulating when she began plotting to leave her husband.

The fact is, however, that most trial appearances are not as dramatic, even though the arguments are over the same issues—money, property, children and support.

Pretrial Hearings

A court appearance usually begins with a pretrial hearing of which there are two types. In the first type, the settlement or mediation conference, both sides try to reach a decision as we discussed in Chapter 11. In the second type, the pretrial conference, both sides meet before the trial starts and try to narrow down the issues so that the case will proceed as fast and smoothly as possible.

The settlement conference is like settling out of court before the trial begins. You, your spouse and your lawyers try for one last time to hammer out an agreement out of court. This is certainly an important time for you to use the techniques described in the previous chapter. A settlement conference is one or more informal negotiation sessions with a judge and your lawyers. Even though the judge has no legal standing to order a settlement at this point, their influence will often get the sides to come together. Judges will suggest what a court will and will not accept or whether they think a spouse's inability to pay will be thought reasonable by the court. Judges know what will happen during a court trial and they try to tell the couples what they see as a probable decision. Because of their impartiality, they are listened to and heeded more often by a spouse unwilling to settle.

In a typical settlement conference, the lawyers give the facts, the judge questions the lawyers and then the spouses. He or she does not try to come up with a solution, but tries to prod the spouses to negotiate on their own by suggesting what is and isn't in the range of court acceptance. If you are asking for $2000 a month in alimony and your spouse makes $30,000 a year, a judge is going to lean hard on you to come down to a more realistic level. That's the ideal settlement conference, of course. Often, even after several settlement conferences, the two sides are no closer to coming to an agreement. Then it's off to trial.

Pretrial Conference

The pretrial conference is the last time to reach a settlement before going to trial. A judge can't be as suggestive here since they can't prejudice the trial about to be heard. But often, the real fear of going into a courtroom makes people willing to compromise. Or, it smokes out the people who have been bluffing. The success or failure of a pretrial conference depends upon your trial judge in particular. Some judges are prepared to order the parties to settle.

The Trial

Divorce cases go to trial because you and your spouse cannot reach a settlement over the issues. Typically, less than 2% of divorce cases get to this point. There are several stages to this process:

- Pretrial conference—described above.
- Opening statements—long or short (or even waived) depending on complexity of trial. Summary of the case and what the lawyer intends to prove.
- Plaintiff's case—evidence presented by the lawyer representing the spouse who first filed for divorce.

- Defendant's case—evidence presented by the lawyer of the other spouse in response to plaintiff's evidence in order to deny or counter it.
- Rebuttals—each side has an opportunity to bring in new evidence or rebut the arguments of the other side. This stage is necessary only in the more complicated cases.
- Closing arguments—each side summarizes the case in a favorable light for his or her client.
- Judge's decision—not always made at time of the trial, but handed down later, if he or she wants to review the evidence.

Witnesses

As we noted in an earlier chapter, one of the reasons why a lawyer uses depositions and interrogatories is to find people who can attest to the facts of the case. Some of these people will become witnesses in your divorce process if you proceed to trial. Although it is not always necessary to have witnesses, they can help to give evidence which will persuade the judge. Character witnesses are generally not necessary except in cases where marital misconduct is at issue, such as spousal abuse and infidelity. Most witnesses are experts called upon to estimate the value of a business, real estate, personal property, psychological needs of the children and so on. Recognize that the testimony of each witness will have to be countered. You can help by providing information to your lawyer during the testimony which will aid them during cross-examination. Your best strategy is to help your lawyer find the most credible witnesses and let him or her prepare them to testify. Keep in mind that too many witnesses can be harmful. There is no guarantee that they will give their testimony in a convincing way.

One practiced witness who will not get ruffled by cross-examination is better than five witnesses who hem and haw and appear nervous.

You as a Witness

There are several points you need to know to be the most effective and convincing witness. The best character witness is yourself. If you are honest, straightforward, cooperative, you will get fair treatment. We have gathered these guidelines and put them in the following categories:

Dress—Dress appropriately, but not expensively. On the other hand, don't wear something you picked out this morning from the bottom of the closet in an attempt to look needy.

Conduct—You need to exert emotional control. Do not make snide comments under your breath or sneer when you disagree with something the other side says. You can communicate with your lawyer by whispering or by writing notes. Good manners count. Show respect for all officers of the court. Don't react to any of your spouse's attempts to rile you.

How to Answer Questions

- Answer the question as specifically as possible.

- If you get asked a complicated, three-part question, keep asking for it to be repeated or pared down until you understand it.

- Don't guess; if you don't know, say so. If you do know, don't start off by saying "I don't know, but I think ..."

- Don't get rattled by questions which are patently untrue or which try to get you to become emotional.

- Act cooperative even when you are being cross-examined by your spouse's lawyer.

- If you are confused, don't hesitate to ask for help from the judge, but don't overdo the "helpless" role.

- Don't be combative by adding statements like "I can prove it" or "That's the real truth." It only makes people doubt whether what you said was true.

- If you can't remember, you can't remember.

Preparation

- Get the facts straight. Review your literature (financials, settlement proposals and other pertinent reference materials).

- Don't memorize your testimony.

- Rehearse what you are going to say. There is nothing wrong with preparing a witness. Only on TV do they try to make it look bad. It would be negligent of your lawyer not to prepare you.

- Ask your lawyer the following questions:

  — What are we trying to prove?

  — If I forget something what should I do? (Your lawyer will be prepared to help you remember while you are on the stand. They will prompt you with a question or a statement to which you can respond with the needed information.)

  — If the other lawyer is badgering me while I'm being cross-examined, how will you help me?

  — What questions do you think my spouse's lawyer will ask me?

  — What should I say when he asks me about (fill in the question or questions you fear the most)?

After the Decision

Be forewarned—a 50/50 split is not always 50/50. Community property is property acquired after the marriage, including earnings. All community property is shared equally. Equitable distribution bases the division of marital property on the contribution of each spouse, the number of years you have been married as well as other factors. It is not necessarily an equal split right down the middle.

To give you an idea of how to reach a settlement agreement, we have included in Appendix B a copy of a package which can be obtained free of charge from the Clerk of the Court in every city and state. The final decree itself is written from the judge's final decision and whatever settlement agreement the divorcing couple had agreed upon before coming to trial. Either or both lawyers can write it and hand it to the other for approval. If lawyers can't agree, then the judge will write the final decree.

You have a certain amount of time, usually thirty days, to move to vacate the decree or petition for a new hearing if you are not satisfied with the results. If either of the motions is denied, you can appeal to a higher court. Your best chance of winning an appeal is if you have convincing new evidence or if you can prove that some legal error was committed in your trial. If you are appealing the judge's interpretation of the evidence, you will most likely be denied. Of course, you still have the options we have discussed earlier in which you can petition the court for changes in support payments, custody and visitation rights as circumstances change and dictate new agreements.

Aftermath

You're now divorced and it's time to pick up the pieces of your life and start over again. Even though it may appear that your divorce is final, it's not completely over. You will still have some type of relationship with your ex-spouse, even if it is only to send a check every month. And, in the case of children, it will be much more than that. The next chapter looks at what will happen when the divorce is final.

Chapter 13

It's Over

The legal battle of the divorce is finally over. The court has handed down its final decree and you and your former spouse have no legal relationship anymore. As we have tried to point out in this book, it's not quite that easy. There are still emotional, financial and legal issues which you will need to handle before you can finally say it is over. That does not mean that you can't get on with the rest of your life. In fact, just the opposite is true. One of the last acts of a divorce is getting on with the rest of your life, finding out what you truly want and eventually (believe us) finding somebody with whom to share your life. But first, there are still some things you need to do in order to bring your divorce to an end. In the next two chapters, we will discuss those issues.

Emotional Issues

We have dealt with emotional issues before when we talked about the feelings you were experiencing and would experience when you started the divorce process. It would be wise to review those pages again. In some respects, you are back where you began, although you have changed in many ways as well. In fact, right now, you are probably feeling a combination of relief and emptiness. You feel relief, of course, that the whole legal process is over. But you also feel emptiness because your relationships with your children, ex-spouse's family and with your friends have undoubtedly changed. There are probably friends and former in-laws that you liked, perhaps even loved, and now you are afraid that you will rarely see them. This only increases the sense of loneliness you may be feeling. But don't let happen to you what happened to one Boca Raton couple. The husband, Jose Habie, was upset over an article his wife put in the local newspaper. To retaliate, he distributed a flyer which contained the information shown on the following page to residents.

You are probably also feeling as though you have won your freedom from an unhappy marriage, but have lost your emotional anchor. Rest assured that all these feelings are normal. Your life is in the process of healing and rearranging itself. Look to other people for support and look inside yourself for the strength to enjoy your new life. Don't expect the courts or any other part of the legal system to give you advice or help in making your divorce work. That is your job. You must seek the help and comfort you need. Some people, unfortunately, use the courts to continue the battle long after the divorce is final. In effect, they are still hanging on to their marriages. Our advice is to let go, so that you can take the first step forward.

LOOK WHO'S POINTING FINGERS

AMY...

1. YOU WERE AN ADULTEROUS WIFE!

Have you forgotten your dalliances? Would you like the names of your lovers, their addresses, occupations and the times and places of your encounters?

I can also remind you of the name of your mother, who warned you on several occasions to clean up your act, or suffer the consequences.

2. YOU ARE A THIEF!

Have you forgotten the two million dollars ($2,000,000 plus) you embezzled from my family's corporations?

Would you like the names of your accomplices, bank name, bank account number and the name of the island outside of the United States of America where the stolen funds were deposited, and the written documentation of your scam done in your own handwriting?

3. YOU HAVE BEEN A DRUG USER!

If you have forgotten, would you like the name of the judge, the court and the date of your confession of drug use, after you presented seven (7) witnesses who claimed the opposite?

4. YOU ARE A COMPULSIVE LIAR!

If you have forgotten, would you like a detailed list of your lies in your personal life, your business life and in court under oath?

5. YOU ARE TRYING TO PRESENT AN IMAGE OF WHAT YOU WISH YOU HAD BEEN!

If you have forgotten, would you like to see a copy of the doctors reports suggesting that our children have been physically abused while under your "supervision"?

6. YOU CONTINUE TO BE A HOME WRECKER!

Have you forgotten that your thefts and infidelities were the cause of the destruction of our marriage and not the death of a blind Schnauzer? You have now also destroyed the marriage of your divorce attorney who had been happily married for over 20 years and had renewed his marital vows only one year ago. Since taking up with you, he has now left his respected wife, and his two minor children without sufficient financial support.

Would you like to be reminded of his name, address and telephone number? Did they also have a blind Schnauzer?

7. YOU CONSPIRED TO HAVE ME MURDERED!

If you have forgotten, would you like the name of your lover and a description by his own admission of the circumstances of your suggestion that he join you in having me killed?

For our children's sake, there are courts and judges both in Guatemala and the United States where your alleged grievances can be justly resolved. These Courts are where we should have these matters decided, not with public relations firms and their planted story in the Palm Beach Post.

Financial Factors

There are, of course, some financial matters which need to be wrapped up in the period just after a divorce is final. We have listed some of the areas which you may need to address:

- **Property and real estate transfers.**

- **Will revisions.**

- **Changing beneficiaries, insurance policies and/or releasing cash value in whole or part.**

- **Changing/canceling joint credit card accounts.**

- **Transferring automobiles.**

- **Stocks and bonds transfer.**

- **Division of pension, IRA and profit-sharing plans.**

- **Paying debts incurred while you were married.**

- **Paying off loans or transferring debt incurred while you were married.**

- **Closing bank accounts and transferring funds.**

- **Preparing income tax for year of divorce.**

- **Picking up your personal property.**

- **Updating your credit reports.**

Note that the transfer of any securities or funds requires copies of your divorce decree. Otherwise you will incur taxes. It is a good idea to complete the tasks above in as business-like a manner as you can. It's difficult enough without getting emotionally involved.

Was it Worth It?

The answer to this question is almost assuredly "yes," although you may have your doubts right now. It's normal to feel low after going through such a hard time, but keep in mind why you wanted a divorce in the first place. Were you happy then? Did your spouse provide you with the love and comfort that you wanted?

You started this process because you were unhappy. You wanted to live a more complete life than the one you were living with your ex-spouse. Remember these reasons when you are experiencing the inevitable low period which immediately follows the final granting of the divorce decree.

Letting Go and Letting Someone New into Your Life

Eventually, you will start to put your life back together and begin dating. It is quite probable that you will go through phases in this stage of regaining your balance. Many recently divorced people start going out with a great many people. This is often because they need to feel that they are attractive to the opposite sex. There is nothing wrong with this phase if you are not intentionally hurting others or doing it to get revenge against your ex-spouse. Most people move on from here to dating a few people and finally settling down with one person with whom they feel a mutual love. This process can take up to two years, so don't be impatient.

Of course, there are some people who swear that they will never marry again and some of you won't. Chances are, however, that you are saying this because you are hurt and afraid. In a way, then, it is good that you make this claim because it stops you from jumping into another marriage without finding out more about yourself first. Our advice is to take this initial post-divorce period and be good to yourself while you try to find out more about what you want.

Remarriage

For most of you reading this book, you will go on to remarry. The *Palm Beach Post* recently ran an article which described a study led by John Mordechai Gottman and other psychologists at the University of Washington in Seattle. The study had found that the most accurate predictors of whether a marriage would work are the intensity of the reasons behind a conflict and the skills used by couples to deal with these inevitable conflicts. The psychologists used an oral history questionnaire to gather answers and stories to a series of questions. The responses were then evaluated according to the factors below. It would be wise for you to look at them if you are considering remarriage as well.

- **Their level of affection toward each other.**

- **How negative or apathetic a spouse was in describing the other.**

- **The amount of expressiveness used while relating stories or feelings about the relationship.**

- **Togetherness—the sense of "we" versus "I."**

- **Whether either believed in stereotypes about men and women, husbands and wives.**

- **Intensity of feelings when there is a problem.**

- **How much control each spouse feels they have over their lives and external events.**

- **Pride in overcoming the tough times in a marriage.**

- **Disappointment or disillusionment in the marriage.**

We believe this a realistic appraisal since it clearly recognizes that there will be difficult times in any marriage. Whether it lasts depends a great deal on how the couple responds together and as individuals.

Prenuptial Agreements

If you are deciding on remarriage, then the issue of prenuptial agreements will undoubtedly come up. Instead of being afraid of them, think of them as a way to bring out issues that may affect you and your new partner in the future. Prenuptial agreements can be thought of as a tool you can use to bring up difficult issues like where you are going to live, how much of a stake will your new spouse have in your business or other economic affairs and how you will deal with the inheritance issues of children from your first marriage. Prenuptial agreements also spell out alimony and settlement issues prior to a divorce if there is one. Why should you enter a prenuptial agreement? For financial reasons, to clarify issues, or both.

Prenuptial agreements are considered enforceable if entered into voluntarily, if they contain nothing unlawful or grossly unfair and if both spouses fully revealed their finances and property. A prenuptial agreement, however, is not like a will. Both sides must agree to any changes. Below is a list of some of the items found in a prenuptial agreement:

- Summary of your financial positions at the start of the new marriage.

- Keeping maiden name.

- What surname any children might have.

- Who owned what property at time of marriage.

- Liabilities of both parties.

- Responsibility for purchasing personal belongings.

- Establishes income levels.

- How many children.

- How much the spouse will be paid in the event that this marriage terminates.

- The importance of each person's career and potential earning power.

- Visiting with children of previous marriage(s).

- Ownership of business(es).

As you can see, a prenuptial agreement is a matter of establishing the ground rules for the dissolution of the marriage. It may seem strange to plan for its end, but you don't want to go through another unprepared divorce.

The legal rules for such agreements vary from state to state. One rule that never varies is the children's rights to support. It can never be abridged in any manner or the agreement will be invalid. Prenuptial agreements can also be broken if they are unfair or signed under duress. Many couples now videotape the signing to show that it wasn't under duress. For example, you may have written a prenuptial agreement ten years ago and agreed to $5,000 a year in support when you were making $50,000 a year. But now you make three times as much money. The courts will not consider $5,000 as fair and will most likely modify the original prenuptial agreement.

Postnuptial Agreements

A postnuptial agreement is almost identical to a prenuptial agreement except that it is made after the marriage. For that reason, they are closely scrutinized by courts for any implicit coercion. Like a prenup, a postnup is a legal document which sets out what you bring to a marriage and what you intend to keep as your own if the marriage ends. This does not always work exactly as you may intend as seen in the discussion of the prenup agreement above. If the court does not feel that the distribution of assets after a divorce is equitable, they will amend the postnup agreement to make it fair. Still, a postnup agreement does indicate the intentions of both parties prior to a divorce.

Is it Over?

As we have said numerous time before, not if you have any

children and not if you are providing alimony or support. Mary Grieco recently purchased a book, *The Wife-in-Law Trap* by Ann Cryster that even addresses the issue of the wife-in-law and her effect on relationships in the future. And it is definitely not over if you are still emotionally tied to the other person especially if you are resentful or hateful. In the next chapter we will discuss these areas.

Chapter 14

You Thought It Was Over

Enjoying the New You

In the last chapter we briefly discussed the changes you would experience as you went through the emotional phases of the post-divorce stage. Let's look at them in more detail.

The end of your existing relationship is also the beginning of a new stage in your life. The first thing you need to do is accept that the marriage is over and that your bad feelings are actually helping you to disengage from the past. Once you have passed through the initial phase, begin to take pride in what makes you unique. You should also become more assertive without being aggressive. This is also the time in your life when you can take more risks in order to find out more about yourself. Sort out what you like in your life and what you don't. Then change what you can. The overall goal is to make friends with yourself and to trust yourself to be able to overcome adversity and the inevitable ups and downs of life. If you don't like yourself, then who will like you.

You should also use this new stage in your life to learn from the past in order to see that a relationship is multidimensional. It has physical, emotional and spiritual components. Learn from your "mistakes" and recognize that there is no such thing as a mistake if you have learned something about yourself in the process.

Some of the ways you can help yourself during this process are listed below:

- **Change your appearance—clothes, hair, dress, glasses, etc.**

- **Start exercising and get in shape—firm up, lose weight.**

- **Change your attitudes—say "hello" and smile, meditate, eat more healthy foods.**

- **Stop believing that all men or women are bad— there are many good people in the world. The right person is out there for you.**

- **Get rid of expectations and stereotypes which are harmful to yourself and others—be sure that people say, "He's changed!"**

- **Change your lifestyle—don't be a couch potato, listen to new kinds of music, buy a different brand** of car (new or used), change the time you go to sleep, join a club or church, do volunteer work for a charity, etc.

- Don't blame the world; change the way you perceive it. (Remember that the glass is half full, not half empty.)

- Take a vacation—go alone or with friends, plan day trips, take a cruise, visit old friends.

- Do something you never would have done before—dye or cut your hair, go on a safari, learn to ski, go snorkeling in Tahiti.

- Treat yourself to nice things, people and places—buy new furniture or a stereo, sit in a cafe all afternoon and read a good book, take a friend to the zoo, etc.

Remember, above all, that you deserve to be *happy*.

About Getting Mad

Do your best not to get mad or to seek revenge. You will only hurt yourself in the long run. Your ex-spouse could take legal action or could hurt your relationship with your children. But, most of all, it will poison your life and stop you from moving forward. It's time to let go of the anger and open up communications. Many divorced people have a better relationship with their ex-spouses now that they are divorced, but you have to work at it.

You need also to be aware that often a new spouse will harbor resentments toward the old spouse. They start to resent the support checks being sent out each month and sometimes pressure you to do crazy things. For example, a resentful new spouse may insist that they sign all the checks to the ex-spouse and thus set the stage for being late or falling behind in alimony checks. This, of course, only makes the ex-spouse angry and they take it out on you. Not exactly letting go of anger, is it? The old saying goes like this: Time heals all wounds. But wounds only heal if you put on a dressing and then leave them alone. The process of healing takes time. It is not easy. It requires balance and a vision for the future.

Being taken Back to Court

Sometimes it will be difficult not to get angry, especially if your ex-spouse doesn't abide by the terms of the settlement or court decree. Just remember that the court still has jurisdiction over the judgments, orders and decrees it has made. The court can attach your ex-spouse's wages or bank accounts, seize property, levy fines and even imprison. The first thing you should do when this happens is to recontact your lawyer. Don't try to take the law into your own hands or lash out at your ex-spouse. The bottom line is to be firm and hold your ground without causing a flare-up in anger.

Communication

The best way to solve problems is to leave channels of communication open between you and your ex-spouse. Be very careful, as well, about using kids as communication nodes. Sometimes it may be necessary to relay information but make sure the information is neutral not derogatory. *Don't* put your children in the middle.

If you remain in the same town or region, communication will be easier in some ways but it can make for some awkward moments. For example, meeting your ex-spouse in public. Our advice is to be polite and don't ignore him or her. It's probably more embarrassing and uncomfortable to pretend that he or she is not there. You may also be dealing with your ex-spouse's new partner during the times you communicate. You must respect the fact that your ex-spouse wants to get on with life by seeking adult companionship and intimate relations. You are *no longer married.* You have no control over that person anymore. He or she is free to do whatever they want. On the other hand, many divorced couples say that they finally can become friends again once they are divorced. Now that they are free of the issues and pressures which arose during their marriages, many couples find that they have renewed respect for their former mates and rely on their judgment.

Getting Support

Part of the process of paying attention to yourself and growing into a new life means finding support. There are a number of organizations or groups which can provide help. Parents Without Partners, for example, is a national organization. Other support groups are local and are often affiliated with a church, synagogue or social service agency. These groups are not therapy groups, but support groups. During their meetings, people with similar problems or from similar situations come together to share and support each other. It's free and nobody tells you what to do. More importantly, nobody judges you. The most precious gift is that you get reassured that you aren't alone or the only person that went through this process.

Many support groups also plan activities and social events for adults and for children, especially around holidays when many people feel particularly alone. Other groups offer workshops on coping with loneliness, filing income taxes, home budgeting, etc. There are also groups for children, especially teenagers, to help them cope with the changes in their lives. You can look for information about these groups in libraries, women's centers, your place of worship, colleges, hospitals or in the Yellow Pages under Social Services.

If a problem persists at an uncomfortable level for a long period of time, we would advise you to find professional support as we discussed in Chapter 5.

It Isn't So Bad

If you have taken a win/win approach and held your head up high, then you stand the best chance of picking yourself up and moving forward. If you have told the lawyers that you wanted a fair settlement, then your divorce will not have been a long drawn-out battle where everybody loses. Your aim in a divorce is to allow your ex-spouse to lead a happy life as well and to ensure that your children still have a loving environment in which both biological parents play a role. You can't erase the pain, traumas, feelings or anxiety, but you can control your future. You will soon realize that the material things really aren't that important. Being happy is all that really counts!

Whichever path you take, we hope that our book helps you to bridge the differences and heal the wounds and to provide a sound base for the decisions you will be called upon to make. But the process and the decision will be yours alone. We wish you the best of luck.

Epilogue

In the beginning, I thought the world was coming to an end, Pete says. All kinds of crazy thoughts came to mind. In the end, however, it was well worth the pain, anxiety and distress to arrive in a future that was better than I could imagine during those hard times. Time heals all wounds, they say, and I believe that we must learn to let go and go forward.

There is life after divorce. Peter is happy to report that he not only is very happily remarried but that he has achieved a respectful relationship with his ex-wife. Mike is also happily remarried and is busy raising two children. Mark is starting the third year of a budding career as an attorney helping people try to achieve happiness. He knows the type of attorney he wants to be.

Chapter 15

Checklist for Success

1. Work on your settlement:
   Child custody
   Child support
   Visitation
   Division of property
   Division of debts
   Alimony plus conditions of payment

2. Gather your financial records

3. Work out a budget for both households prior to divorce

4. Use experts, such as appraisers and accountants, when necessary to value your assets

5. What do you estimate your legal fees to be? Think of ways to decrease them.

6. Have you worked out a property and custody settlement with your spouse that meets state requirements?

7. Have you talked to a counselor or a religious figure for guidance in the dissolution of your marriage?

8. Have you looked into postdivorce counseling for your children?

9. Have you made a plan for your children's future needs?

10. Have you decided what you want from the rest of your life?

CREDITS

We would like to thank all the people who shared their stories, their pain and their joy with us in writing this book. They have helped to make this book what it is—a practical and compassionate guide to making it through tough times.

APPENDIX A:
DEPOSITION QUESTIONS

A.   Personal data
1.   Age.
2.   General health.
3.   Hospitalization or institutionalization.
4.   Medication.
5.   Doctors or psychiatrists treating deponent.
6.   Pre-existing health conditions at time of marriage.
7.   Aggravation of health condition since marriage.
8.   Hobbies.
9.   Outside interests.
10. Educational background.
11. Vocational training.
12. Family background.
13. Birthplace, geographical residences, and geographical moves.
14. Military service.
15. Religious affiliation.

B.   Marital information
1.   Date of marriage.
2.   Children born of marriage.
3.   Children adopted during marriage.
4.   Miscarriages.
5.   Separations.
6.   Incidents of marital misconduct.
7.   Marriage irretrievably broken and why.
8.   Past reconciliations.
9.   Marriage counseling.
10. Probability or possibility of reconciliation in this case.
11. Willingness and sincerity to seek marriage counseling.
12. Length of time spouse was known before marriage.
13. Written or oral contracts entered into before or during marriage.
14. Live-in situation before marriage.
15. Length of separation and acquisition of assets during separation.
16. Influence of family members on dissolution process.

C.   Custody, visitation, and shared parental responsibility issues
   1.   Sole or shared parental responsibility.
   2.   Mental and physical health of spouse.
   3.   Moral fitness of spouse.
   4.   Boyfriend or girlfriend problem now or in future.
   5.   Child(ren)'s physical and emotional well-being before and after separation of parties.
   6.   Child(ren)'s home, school, and outside activities before and after separation.
   7.   Reasonable preference of child(ren) to reside with either parent.
   8.   Grandparent visitation.
   9.   Emotional ties of child(ren) to one or both parents.
   10.   Disposition and ability of spouse to care for and support minor child(ren).
   11.   How spouse relates to child(ren) by a previous marriage, *i.e.*, support, visitation, moral, and emotional support.
   12.   Disposition and capacity of spouse to see that minor child(ren) receive(s) religious training, medical care, dental care, and other material needs.
   13.   Parent who is more likely to allow child(ren) frequent and continuing contact with other parent or parent's family.
   14.   All reasons why deponent should have residential custody of minor child(ren).
   15.   All reasons why spouse should have residential custody of minor child(ren).
   16.   All reasons why deponent will claim that deponent should not have residential custody of minor child(ren).
   17.   All reasons that deponent will admit or acknowledge or that others will claim spouse should have residential custody of minor child(ren).
   18.   Problems with visitation during separation.
   19.   Deponent's views on visitation during week, weekends, summer, spring, and winter school vacations, and each holiday.
   20.   Contemplated geographical moves by either or both parents.
   21.   Previous custody litigation by either deponent or spouse due to earlier marriage.
   22.   Ability of parents to communicate about child(ren).

23. Possible problem of stepfather or stepmother wanting custody of stepchild in initial dissolution action.
24. Possible problem of nonparent wanting custody of minor child(ren) in a dissolution proceeding.
25. Deponent's attitude toward "shared parental responsibility."
26. Present living conditions of minor child(ren) and other parent, such as cleanliness, sanitary conditions, alcohol or narcotics abuse, live-in lover, or overnight guests.
27. Current residence of child(ren) and effects on child(ren) by parent or nonparent.
28. Physical, mental, or sexual abuse of minor child(ren) by parent or nonparent.
29. Date and place of birth of minor child(ren).
30. General health history of minor child(ren).
31. Release of report cards and medical or dental reports.
32. Quality time or quality relationships of minor child(ren) with deponent or spouse.
33. Names and addresses of any potential custody witnesses.
34. Employment of expert or skilled witnesses.

D. Child support
1. Review of financial affidavit of both parties to determine true needs of child(ren) and ability of each party to pay for these needs.
2. Particular physical, emotional, or mental needs of minor child(ren) now and in future.
3. Special schooling.
4. Extraordinary anticipated expenses for minor child(ren).
5. Dependency exemption for federal income tax.
6. Life insurance for minor child(ren).
7. Hospitalization insurance for minor child(ren).
8. Transportation expenses for minor child(ren), including possible automobile at later date.
9. Consultation with physicians, psychologists, psychiatrists, school counselors, or others pertaining to any present or future changes as to child(ren)'s schooling, environment, or other related matters pertaining to additional support.
10. Termination or nontermination of child support during visitation.

11.   Possession or ownership of family furniture, furnishings, antiques, or other family personal property in trust for minor child(ren) or to be owned or possessed by minor child(ren) and kept in family.
12.   Past standard of living of family and minor child(ren).
13.   Sole and exclusive occupancy and possession of marital home as incident of child support.
14.   Neighborhood, schools, friends of minor child(ren), special housing, or other related matters pertaining to marital home.
15.   Possible college education or post high school vocational training for minor child(ren).
16.   Inter vivos trust for minor child(ren).
17.   Savings accounts for minor child(ren).
18.   Last will and testament designating minor child(ren) as a beneficiary.
19.   Declaration of intention from deponent or spouse as to devising undivided half interest in formerly jointly owned real property to minor child(ren).
20.   Possibility of annual gifts or trusts or other future contributions toward child(ren)'s support or education by deponent's family, spouse, or spouse's family.

E.   Assets
   1.   Real estate
      a.   Location.
      b.   Acquisition date.
      c.   Purchase price.
      d.   How purchase price was funded.
      e.   Separate or joint contributions toward purchase price, improvements, or refinancing.
      f.   Special labor and services as to building or improving real property.
      g.   Payment of mortgage, taxes, insurance, special assessments, or liens—joint or separate contributions or arrangements for financing.
      h.   Possible claim of special equity.
      i.   Pro tanto ownership interests to be claimed by deponent or spouse as to special equity.

j. Location of documentation for acquisition of title, loan, and payment of expenses.

k. Co-owner(s).

l. Examination of ownership documents as to alienating or encumbering the interest of either party without consent of co-owner(s).

m. Possible financial contribution or contribution of labor and services by third parties.

n. Present or future liens.

o. Unpaid federal income taxes—jeopardy assessment—federal tax lien.

p. Appreciation or depreciation in fair market value and reason—area development or rezoning, or valuable contribution by either or both parties.

q. Out-of-state interest in real estate.

r. Selling or refinancing of real estate and disposition of proceeds toward acquiring additional real estate.

s. Objection or lack of objection as to co-ownership after dissolution.

t. Rehabilitative or potential income-producing aspects of real property.

u. Possible "setoff" by way of lump sum alimony in equitable distribution of marital assets.

v. Desire of deponent or spouse to retain real property in joint or individual name after dissolution, and reasons why.

w. Repairs or expenditures, present and future, to be made.

x. Practicality of selling the real property at present time and comparable sales in area.

y. Possible witnesses or other persons who may testify to fair market value, special equity, enhancement of value, deteriorating condition, or any other matter pertaining to this asset.

z. Family funds by gift or by direct contribution as to purchase price, mortgages, improvements, or related matters pertaining to this asset.

aa. Equity that can be used to refinance mortgages, lower payments, pay off debts, or buy other party's interest.

F.   Banking records

G.   Retirement benefits, including pension, profit-sharing, and IRA

H.   Business or other income venture

I.   Separately owned assets of deponent or spouse—review of
      interrogatories

J.   Employment
      1.   Rate of pay.
      2.   Deductions.
      3.   Under- or over-withholding as to federal income tax and
            social security.
      4.   Reasons for business deductions.
      5.   Employment-related fringe benefits for employees.
      6.   Annual or periodic raises.
      7.   Possibility of being laid off.
      8.   Possibility of geographical move.
      9.   Possibility of advancement.
      10.   Past employment, rate of pay, advancement, and training.
      11.   Past present bosses or immediate supervisors.
      12.   Bonuses.
      13.   Deferred compensation.
      14.   Dividends.
      15.   Overtime pay.

K.   Alimony, equitable distribution, and other related matters
      1.   Sociological contribution of deponent or spouse to marriage
            and family.
      2.   Economic contribution of deponent or spouse to marriage
            and family.
      3.   Separately owned assets brought into marriage.
      4.   Assets acquired during marriage, in whole or in part,
            through separate funds or extraordinary labor or services of
            deponent or spouse.
      5.   Appreciation in value of separately owned property during
            marriage by joint efforts of parties or individual efforts of
            one party.

6.   Contribution of income during marriage derived from source unrelated to marital relationship, *i.e.*, inheritance, trust, or family.

7.   Financial contribution by one spouse to education, training, or advancement of other spouse.

8.   Disparity in earnings of spouses.

9.   Location, description, and valuation of all marital assets.

10.   Admissions made by deponent or spouse as to ownership or retention of assets after dissolution of marriage.

11.   Employment prospects of deponent or spouse after dissolution.

12.   "Fault" of either party, including, but not limited to, causing "economic hardship" that may take place on dissolution.

13.   Elements of "justification" and "financial ability" as to apportioning marital assets.

14.   Review of financial affidavits to determine true needs versus anticipatory needs.

15.   Review of financial affidavits to determine recurring and nonrecurring expenses.

16.   Past standard of living.

17.   Possibility of future rehabilitation, education, or vocational training.

18.   Actual expenses before and during separation, and projected expenses after dissolution process.

19.   Existence and effect of prior dissolutions or modification of dissolution judgments, as bearing on assets, income, and future or past expenses.

20.   Income tax audit, deficiencies, and tax refunds.

21.   Separately owned assets by one spouse that may "offset" interest in marital assets—question of valuation and other relevant factors.

22.   Names and addresses of expert witnesses, including up-to-date appraisal and methods.

23.   Liability that may be subject of equitable distribution, *e.g.*, unpaid loans, mortgages, or tax obligations.

L.   Predisposition review of records or review of records during deposition

1.   Individual and, if applicable, corporate income tax return.

2.   Profit and loss statements.
3.   Records pertaining to business or professional accounting systems, including accounts receivable, accounts payable, business income, and business expenses.
4.   Financial statements for any business.
5.   Partnership or joint venture agreement.
6.   Agreements pertaining to stock ownership in closely held corporation.
7.   Personal and business banking records, including bank statements, canceled checks, deposit slips, and any other banking records pertaining to transactions.
8.   Review of savings account books, certificates of deposit, liquid fund statements, or ready asset statements.
9.   Review of credit card statements and credit card invoices for each individual charge.

M.   Liabilities
1.   Current accounts.
2.   Unsecured loans.
3.   Secured obligations.
4.   Emergency loans.

N.   Other matters
1.   Life insurance.
2.   Safe deposit box.
   a.   Location of institution.
   b.   Persons authorized to enter.
   c.   Present and past contents of box.
   d.   Last entry to safe deposit box.
3.   Financial affidavit and related information.
   a.   Expenses before and after separation.
   b.   Mortgage payment or rent.
   c.   Electricity.
   d.   Water.
   e.   Telephone.
   f.   Garbage collection.
   g.   Lawn maintenance.
   h.   Gas for home.
   i.   Pest control.

j.   Taxes on home.
k.   Liability insurance on home.
l.   Homeowner's insurance—contents.
m.   Second mortgage or home improvement loans.
n.   Food.
o.   Newspapers, magazines, books.
p.   Recreation.
q.   Monthly loan installment payments, excluding automobile, airplane, boat, or furniture.
r.   Incidental expenses.
s.   Clothing.
t.   Life insurance premiums.
u.   Hospitalization and major medical premiums.
v.   Accident or disability insurance premiums.
w.   Dental expenses.
x.   Medical expenses.
y.   Drugs and medicine.
z.   Automobile insurance.
aa.   Boat loan installment payment.
bb.   Automobile or airplane loan payment.
cc.   Furniture loan installment payment.
dd.   Gas for automobile, airplane, or boat.
ee.   Maintenance for automobile, airplane, or boat.
ff.   Transportation expenses if other than personal automobile or motor vehicle.
gg.   Church contribution.
hh.   Other charitable contribution.
ii.   Babysitter.
jj.   Nursery for children.
kk.   School tuition for children.
ll.   Transportation to school for children.
mm.   School lunches for children.
nn.   Dry cleaning or laundry.
oo.   Personal necessities.
pp.   Fuel oil.
qq.   Average support paid.
rr.   Payments or bills.

4.   Unreported income and nonexistent or false expenses on federal income tax.

5.   Surveillance and witnesses.
    a.   Movies.
    b.   Written statements.
    c.   Electronic surveillance.
    d.   Photographs.
    e.   Private detectives.
6.   Possible use of mediator or general or special master.
7.   Repayment of family loan or restoration of personal property to family members.
8.   Existence of resulting or constructive trusts.
9.   Understanding of tax consequences or spousal support, child support, payment of marital obligations, or division of property.
10.   Witnesses for trial and location or identification of documentary trial evidence.
11.   Hidden income or assets.

(Used with permission of The Florida Bar: Continuing Legal Education Series, Florida Dissolution of Marriage.)

APPENDIX B:
SIMPLIFIED DISSOLUTION INFORMATION

(In Florida, the simple divorce kit shown on the following pages is available free of charge.)

Table of Contents

I. INTRODUCTION FOR
SIMPLIFIED DISSOLUTION OF MARRIAGE
(DIVORCE)

It is **important** that **both the husband and the wife** read and understand this entire appendix before using the Simplified Dissolution of Marriage (also known as divorce) procedures.

Please carefully follow the instructions. Both the husband and the wife should **read and understand** this appendix and its instructions before starting this procedure.

You should note that the clerk's office can **only** supply you with this booklet and the necessary forms. A clerk will **assist** you in the filling out of these forms; however, the clerk is **not permitted** to advise you of any **legal rights** you may have or the **legal consequences** of using this Simplified Dissolution of Marriage procedure.

The judge assigned to your case is **also prohibited** by law from giving you or your spouse any legal advice or assistance. The judge will **not explain** any legal consequences of using this Simplified Dissolution of Marriage procedure. Therefore, **do not ask** the clerk or the judge for any recommendations or advice.

This procedure is meant to provide a **simple, inexpensive** dissolution of marriage in **very limited circumstances** for persons who are eligible to use it. Part VI of this appendix will explain **who may use** the Simplified Dissolution of Marriage procedure.

You should fill out the forms **yourself.** If, however, someone helps you fill out the forms, that person should **not give you advice** on your rights or obligations **unless** he or she is a licensed Florida attorney. That is to **protect you** from getting bad advice from someone who is not trained in legal matters.

IF THERE IS ANY DOUBT IN YOUR MINDS OR YOUR SPOUSE'S CONCERNING A LEGAL QUESTION ABOUT EITHER YOUR RIGHT TO DIVORCE OR ANY PROPERTY RIGHTS OR TAX CONSEQUENCES, IT IS STRONGLY RECOMMENDED THAT THE SERVICES OF AN ATTORNEY BE OBTAINED. IF YOU DO NOT

KNOW AN ATTORNEY, YOU SHOULD CONTACT THE LAWYER REFERRAL SERVICE LISTED IN THE YELLOW PAGES OF THE TELEPHONE BOOK. IF YOU ARE FINANCIALLY UNABLE TO AFFORD THE SERVICES OF AN ATTORNEY, YOU SHOULD CONTACT THE LEGAL AID OFFICE IN YOUR AREA OR ASK YOUR LOCAL BAR ASSOCIATION FOR A REFERRAL TO AN APPROPRIATE PERSON OR AGENCY.

See Part X for more details about how a lawyer can help you.

II. WHAT IS THIS APPENDIX ABOUT?

This appendix describes a way to end a marriage through a divorce procedure called **Simplified Dissolution of Marriage**.

The official word for **divorce** in Florida is **dissolution**. There are two (2) ways of getting a divorce, or dissolution, in Florida. The usual way is called a **regular dissolution of marriage**. A shorter and easier way—what this appendix is about—is called a **Simplified Dissolution of Marriage**.

The second method is shorter and easier, but not everybody can use it.

Briefly, a Simplified Dissolution of Marriage is possible for couples:

(1)   Who both agree that their marriage is irretrievably broken and want to end their marriage because of serious permanent differences: **and**

(2)   Who must be able to appear before a circuit court clerk together to sign a petition for Simplified Dissolution of Marriage and, later, to appear before a judge together; **and**

(3)   Who have no minor (under 18) or dependent children together, and the wife is not pregnant; **and**

(4)   Who have no disagreements about how belongings, assets, and property, and their debts are going to be divided once they are no longer married to each other.

Both the husband and wife will have to appear in court before a judge who will consider their petition.

This dissolution procedure is started by preparing and filing a **Petition for Simplified Dissolution of Marriage** with the circuit court clerk in your county.

This booklet will tell you:

(1)   Where to turn for help if you want to save your marriage.
(2)   Who can use the Simplified Dissolution of Marriage procedure.
(3)   What steps you have to go through to get a Simplified Dissolution of Marriage.
(4)   When it would help to see a lawyer.
(5)   What risks you take when you use this simplified procedure rather than the regular dissolution of marriage procedure.

If you wish to use the Simplified Dissolution of Marriage procedure, it is important for you to read the **entire appendix** very carefully.

Save this appendix. If you decide to file a Simplified Dissolution of Marriage, it will tell you how to complete the procedure.

If you fail to complete the procedure the court may dismiss the action to clear its records.

III. ARE YOU SURE YOUR MARRIAGE CAN'T BE SAVED?

Before you take any legal steps to end your marriage you should make sure that you have thought of all possible ways of saving it.

Do you want professional help in working out ways to save your marriage?

Many communities and many social and religious organizations offer marriage counseling services.

If you believe your marriage can be saved, explore all possible steps for a reconciliation (getting back together) before beginning this Simplified Dissolution of Marriage.

You may wish to consult with a marriage counselor, psychologist, psychiatrist, minister, priest, rabbi, or other qualified person.

IV. SOME TERMS YOU NEED TO KNOW

In the following pages, you will often see the terms *marital assets, nonmarital assets, marital obligations,* and *equitable distribution.* Those terms are explained in this section.

As a married couple, you are, in the eyes of the law, a single unit. There are certain things which you own, together, rather than separately, and there may be debts which you owe together. If one of you buys something on credit, under certain circumstances the other one can be made to pay. If your marriage breaks up, you become two separate individuals again. Before that can happen, you will have to decide what to do with the things that you own as a couple and the debts that you owe as a couple.

The laws that cover these questions contain the terms marital assets, marital obligations, nonmarital assets, and nonmarital obligations. To understand what these terms mean, you should have a clear idea of the time you lived together as husband and wife. This is the period of time after you got married and before you separated.

It may not be easy to decide exactly when you separated. In most cases, the day of your separation was the day you stopped living together. You might want to choose the day when you definitely decided to get a divorce as your official date of separation.

(1)   Marital Asset: Everything that a husband and wife acquire during the marriage. In most cases it includes the following:

(a)   Money that you now have which either of you earned during the time you were living together as husband and wife.

(b)   Anything either of you bought with the money during that period.

(c)   Vested and nonvested benefits, rights, and funds during the marriage in a retirement pension, profit sharing, annuity, deferred compensation, and/or insurance plan and program.

(d)   Increase in value and appreciation of nonmarital assets resulting either from the efforts of either spouse or from the contribution of marital monies or other forms of marital assets.

(e)   Interspousal gifts (gifts from one of you to the other) during the marriage.

(f)   All real property (house, land) held as tenancy by entireties (held as husband and wife), whether obtained before or during the marriage.

(2)   Nonmarital Asset/Separate Property: Everything that a husband or wife owns separately, including:

(a)   Anything that you owned before you got married.

(b)   Anything that you earned or received after your separation.

(c)   Anything that either of you received, as a gift (other than from or to each other) or by inheritance, at any time.

(3)   Marital Obligation: Debts that a husband and wife took on during the time they were living together as husband and wife. (If you bought furniture on credit while you were married and living together, the unpaid balance is part of your marital obligations.)

(4)   Equitable Distribution: The husband's and wife's entitlement to each receiving a fair share of the marital property.

V. DIFFERENCES BETWEEN SIMPLIFIED AND REGULAR DISSOLUTION OF MARRIAGE

With a **regular dissolution** each spouse has the right to ask questions and obtain documents concerning the other spouse's income, expenses, assets, and liabilities before having a trial or settlement of their case. With a **Simplified Dissolution of Marriage** you may request financial information but it is not required.

With a **regular dissolution**, if there is no agreement about property or other matters, a judge conducts a trial or hearing. The judge listens to all the evidence and then makes a decision concerning the division of property and other matters. A husband or wife may ask for a new trial or appeal the judge's decision. **In a simplified dissolution, there is no trial and no appeal.**

With a **regular dissolution**, the judge may order one spouse to pay support (alimony) for the other—either for a period of time or permanently (until death or remarriage). **With a simplified dissolution neither husband nor wife can receive alimony** (support) from the other spouse regardless of how much income one person has and how much the other person may need support.

There are, however, some cases in which divorce agreements under a simplified dissolution can be challenged.

Correcting mistakes and unfairness in a simplified dissolution proceeding can be expensive, time consuming and difficult. It is **very important** for both spouses to be honest, cooperative, and careful when you or your lawyers do the paperwork for dissolution.

VI. WHO CAN USE THE SIMPLIFIED DISSOLUTION OF MARRIAGE PROCEDURE?

A husband and wife can get a divorce through the Simplified Dissolution of Marriage procedure only if ALL of the following statements are true about both spouses at the time they jointly file the petition for Simplified Dissolution of Marriage. Check this list very carefully. If even one of these statements is not true for you, you <u>CANNOT</u> use this way of getting a divorce.

____1.   We have no minor (under 18) children or dependent children.

____2.   We have no adopted children under 18 years of age.

____3.   The wife is not pregnant.

____4.   At least one of us has lived in Florida for the past six months.

____5.   We have made provisions for the division of our property and the payment of our obligations, and are satisfied with them.

____6.   We both will sign the joint petition and all other papers needed to carry out this procedure and pay the required fees to the clerk of the circuit court.

____7.   We both want to end the marriage because of serious permanent differences.

____8.   We have both agreed to use the Simplified Dissolution of Marriage procedure rather than a regular dissolution.

____9.   We both are aware of the following facts:

      (a)   That after the dissolution becomes final, neither of us has any right to expect money or support from the other, except for what is included in the property settlement agreement; and

      (b)   That by choosing the Simplified Dissolution of Marriage procedure we give up certain legal rights that we would have if we used the regular dissolution procedure. (These are explained in Part V.)

Appendix B   313

VII. WHAT STEPS DO YOU HAVE TO GO THROUGH TO GET A SIMPLIFIED DISSOLUTION OF MARRIAGE?

(1)   Both the husband and the wife must go to the office of the clerk of the circuit court in the county where they live.

(2)   Both the husband and the wife must read and sign before a clerk of the circuit court a joint petition for Simplified Dissolution of Marriage (Form 1).

(3)   A Certificate of Corroborating Witness (Form 6) must be prepared. THIS FORM MUST BE SIGNED BY A PERSON WHO KNOWS THAT EITHER THE HUSBAND OR THE WIFE HAS LIVED IN FLORIDA FOR MORE THAN SIX MONTHS BEFORE THE DATE THAT YOU SIGNED THE JOINT PETITION FOR SIMPLIFIED DISSOLUTION OF MARRIAGE.

This certificate may be signed in the presence of the clerk of the circuit court or you may take the certificate with you and have the corroborating witness (the person who knows that either you or your spouse has resided in Florida for more than six months) sign the certificate in the presence of a notary public who must affix his or her seal at the proper place on the certificate.

(4)   It is recommended, but not required, that you both prepare financial affidavits. If you choose to do so, fill out the Financial Affidavit for Simplified Dissolution of Marriage (Form 3).

(5)   It is also recommended that you fill out the Marital Settlement Agreement for Simplified Dissolution of Marriage (Form 5). It is not required that you do so. The financial affidavit and property agreement forms should be attached to the joint petition for dissolution of marriage.

(6)   You must pay the appropriate filing fee and costs to the clerk of the circuit court.

(7)   You or the clerk will need to complete a civil cover sheet found in Form 1.997 of the Florida Rules of Civil Procedure. The clerk's office can provide this form.

(8)   You must obtain a date for a court appearance from the clerk. On that date, you and your spouse must both appear before a judge. At that time, if all papers are in order, the judge may grant a final judgment dissolving marriage under Simplified Dissolution of Marriage procedures.

VIII. WHAT SHOULD BE INCLUDED IN THE FINANCIAL AFFIDAVIT?

A financial affidavit may not be necessary in every dissolution, especially if the husband and wife already have divided their property. A financial affidavit is recommended, however, if one or both spouses agree to some continuing financial obligation as part of their property settlement agreement.

Completion of the financial affidavit involves one or both spouses figuring out their income, the value of their property, and the amount of their debts.

A sample financial affidavit, filled out for an imaginary person, appears at the end of this section.

Income

Income is the average amount of money you receive from any source, usually calculated on a weekly, monthly, or yearly basis. When filling out the financial affidavit, you must specify on what basis you have calculated your income.

The financial affidavit includes a space for your average gross wage, which is the amount of money you would be paid without any deductions for taxes, social security, credit union, or other purposes. After listing all deductions from your gross wages, you then subtract your total deduction to calculate your average net wage.

The financial affidavit form also includes spaces for other income that you may receive from sources other than your employment. The total of your average net wage and other income equals your total net income.

Assets

Cash—Include all cash you have on hand and in all bank accounts (including savings accounts, checking accounts, credit unions, money market funds, etc.) on the day you sign the financial affidavit.

Stocks and Bonds—List all stocks and bonds. Call a stockbroker to determine their value or check the newspaper. If you own stock in a small corporation which is not traded, consult an accountant for value.

Real Estate—Your real property and buildings are worth what a buyer is willing to pay for them. Consult a realtor or appraiser to determine their value.

Automobiles and Other Personal Property—Things you own that have monetary value such as cars, furniture, jewelry, cameras, clothes, boats, etc. are personal property. The value of personal property is the fair market value of the items on the day you sign the financial affidavit. Fair market value means the amount of money you would receive if you sold that item (used or in its present condition) to a stranger. It does not mean the amount the item originally cost or the amount you would have to spend to replace the item. Count the full fair market value of the item even if you are still making payments on it. List the amount of money you still owe on the financial affidavit form under the columns marked "liabilities."

Pension, Profit Sharing, and Retirement Plans—Be sure to list all IRA accounts, Keogh plans, and other retirement plans.

Other Assets—Be sure to list all other assets, even if they do not fit into any category above.

Liabilities

Liabilities are debts, which means money you owe. These include mortgages, credit card bills, unpaid bills, loans, unpaid taxes, car loans, or anything you are purchasing "on time."

The amount of the liability is the "pay-off" amount you would have to pay the creditor to cancel the loan—not the total of all your payments. Check your last bill or payment coupon, or call your creditor and ask for a "pay-off" figure.

There may be taxes to pay on transfers of property. You may wish to consult an accountant or a lawyer.

Sample Financial Affidavit

Following is a sample form for an acceptable financial affidavit, prepared for an imaginary person. You may use it as a model for your own affidavit.

IN THE CIRCUIT COURT OF THE _____ JUDICIAL
CIRCUIT, IN AND FOR _____ COUNTY, FLORIDA

IN RE: The Marriage of   CASE NO: <u>XX-XXX-XX-XX-X</u>

<u>JOHN DOE</u>   ,
                            Husband,
                                      FINANCIAL STATEMENT FOR
and   **DISSOLUTION OF MARRIAGE**
                                            (DIVORCE)
<u>JANE DOE</u>   ,
                            Wife,

FINANCIAL AFFIDAVIT

STATE OF FLORIDA)
COUNTY OF   )

BEFORE ME, this day personally appeared ___<u>JOHN DOE</u>___, who being duly sworn, deposes and says that the following information is true and correct according to his/her best knowledge and belief:

ITEM 1: EMPLOYMENT AND INCOME

OCCUPATION:	Electrician's Helper
EMPLOYED BY:	Electric Works, Inc.
ADDRESS:	134 Electric Avenue
	Anywhere, Florida
SOC. SEC. #:	123-45-6789
PAY PERIOD:	Weekly
RATE OF PAY:	$7.00 per hour

AVERAGE GROSS MONTHLY INCOME FROM EMPLOYMENT	$ 1,204.00
Bonuses, commissions, allowances, overtime, tips and similar payments	$ -0-
Business income from sources such as self-employment, partnership, close corporations, and/or independent contracts (gross receipts minus ordinary and necessary expenses required to produce income)	$ -0-
Disability benefits	$ -0-
Workers' Compensation	$ -0-
Unemployment Compensation	$ -0-
Pension, retirement, or annuity payments	$ -0-
Social Security benefits	$ -0-
Spousal support received from previous marriage	$ -0-
Interest and dividends	$ -0-
Rental income (gross receipts minus ordinary and necessary expenses to produce income)	$ -0-
Income from royalties, trust, or estates	$ -0-
Reimbursed expenses and in-kind payments to the extent that they reduce personal living expenses	$ -0-
Gains derived from dealing in property (not including non-recurring gains)	$ -0-
Itemize any other income of a recurring nature	$ -0-
TOTAL MONTHLY INCOME	$ 1,204.00

LESS DEDUCTIONS:

Federal, state and local income taxes (corrected for filing
        status and actual number of withholding allowances) $___112.00
FICA or self-employment tax (annualized) $___92.10
Mandatory union dues $___-0-
Mandatory retirement $___-0-
Health insurance payments $___-0-
Court ordered support payments for the children actually paid $___-0-
TOTAL DEDUCTIONS $___204.10

ITEM 2: AVERAGE MONTHLY EXPENSES

HOUSEHOLD:

Mtg. or rent payments	400.00
Property taxes & insurance	-0-
Electricity	50.00
Water, garbage, & sewer	20.00
Telephone	20.00
Fuel oil or natural gas	-0-
Repairs and maintenance	-0-
Lawn and pool care	-0-
Pest control	-0-
Misc. household	20.00
Food and grocery items	200.00
Meals outside home	40.00
Other:	-0-
	-0-

AUTOMOBILE:

Gasoline and oil	30.00
Repairs	10.00
Auto tags and license	3.00
Insurance	20.00
Other:	-0-
	-0-

CHILDREN'S EXPENSES:

Nursery or babysitting	100.00
School tuition	-0-
School supplies	10.00
Lunch money	10.00
Allowance	5.00
Clothing	50.00
Medical, dental, prescription	-0-
Vitamins	-0-
Barber/beauty parlor	-0-
Cosmetics/toiletries	-0-
Gifts for special holidays	-0-
Other:	-0-
	-0-

INSURANCES:

Health	-0-
Life	-0-
Other:	-0-
	-0-

OTHER EXPENSES NOT LISTED ABOVE:

Dry cleaning and laundry	20.00
Affiant's clothing	50.00
Affiant's medical, dental, prescriptions	-0-
Affiant's beauty salon	5.00
Affiant's gifts (special holidays)	10.00

Pets:

Grooming	-0-
Veterinarian	-0-

Membership dues:

Professional dues	-0-
Social dues	-0-

Entertainment	10.00
Vacations	-0-
Publications	-0-
Religious organizations	-0-
Charities	-0-
Miscellaneous	-0-

OTHER EXPENSES:

_____	-0-
_____	-0-
_____	-0-
_____	-0-

TOTAL ABOVE EXPENSES

$1,083.00

PAYMENTS TO CREDITORS:

TO WHOM:	BALANCE DUE:	MONTHLY PAYMENTS:
VISA	300.00	20.00
Texaco	100.00	10.00
_____	_____	_____
_____	_____	_____
_____	_____	_____
_____	_____	_____

Total Monthly Payments to Creditors: $ 30.00

TOTAL MONTHLY EXPENSES: $1,113.00

ITEM 3: ASSETS (OWNERSHIP: IF JOINT, ALLOCATE EQUALLY)

Description	Value	Husband	Wife
Cash (on hand or in banks)	1,000	1,000	
Stocks/bonds/notes	2,000	1,000	1,000
Real Estate:			
Home:	100,000	50,000	50,000
Automobiles:			
1987 Nissan	6,000	6,000	
1988 GMC Van	7,000		7,000
Other personal property:			
Contents of home	8,000	4,000	4,000
Jewelry	1,000	1,000	
Life ins./cash surrender value	-0-		
Other assets:			
	-0-		
TOTAL ASSETS:	$125,000	$63,000	$62,000

ITEM 4: LIABILITIES

Creditor	Security	Value	Husband	Wife
VISA		300	150	150
Tex aco		100	100	
Mortgage Company		80,000	40,000	40,000
TOTAL LIABILITIES:		80,400	40,250	40,150

SWORN TO and signed before me
on _____, 19___.   _____
                                            Affiant

_____
NOTARY PUBLIC
My Commission Expires:

Approved for use under rule 10-1.1(b) of the Rules Regulating The Florida Bar.

IX. WHAT SHOULD BE INCLUDED IN THE PROPERTY SETTLEMENT AGREEMENT?

A property settlement should contain at least the following:

(a)   Preliminary Statement: This part identifies the husband and wife, states that the marriage is being ended, and states that both husband and wife agree on the details of the agreement.

(b)   Division of Property: This part has two sections. Part One is what the wife receives and Part Two is what the husband receives.

(c)   Division of Obligations: This part has two sections. Part One is the amount the wife must pay and to whom she must pay it. Part Two is the amount the husband must pay and to whom he must pay it.

(d)   Date and Signature: Both husband and wife must write in the date and sign the agreement.

Remember, you can divide the items any way you want. As long as you both agree, the court will accept it. If you cannot agree about the division of your property and debts, you should file a Regular Dissolution.

WARNING

In a number of circumstances, neither a written nor an oral property settlement agreement can, by itself, properly transfer ownership of property. Examples of property that require the preparation of additional transfer papers are real estate, automobiles, bank accounts, stocks, and bonds.

It is strongly recommended that you talk to an attorney before you sign an agreement. An attorney can tell you your specific legal rights in your case regarding marital assets, marital obligations, alimony, and other important rights.

X. SHOULD YOU SEE A LAWYER?

MUST YOU HAVE A LAWYER TO GET A DIVORCE WITH THE SIMPLIFIED DISSOLUTION OF MARRIAGE PROCEDURE?

No. You can do the whole thing by yourselves. But it would be wise to see an attorney before you decide to do it yourself. You should not rely on this appendix only. It is not intended to take the place of a lawyer.

IF YOU WANT LEGAL ADVICE, DOES THAT MEAN YOU HAVE TO HIRE A LAWYER?

No. You may hire a lawyer but you can also just visit a lawyer once or twice (at low cost) for advice on how to carry out the dissolution proceeding. Don't be afraid to ask the lawyer in advance what fee will be charged. It may be surprisingly inexpensive to have a lawyer handle your divorce.

DO YOU HAVE TO ACCEPT THE ATTORNEY'S ADVICE?

No, you don't. And if you are not pleased with what one attorney advises, you can feel free to go to another one.

HOW CAN AN ATTORNEY HELP YOU WITH THE SIMPLI-FIED DISSOLUTION OF MARRIAGE PROCEDURE?

First of all, an attorney can advise you, on the basis of your personal situation, whether you ought to use the regular dissolution rather than the simplified procedure.

Second, an attorney can check through your property settlement agreement to help you figure out if you've thought of everything you should have. (It is easy to forget things you don't see very often—savings bonds, safe deposit boxes, etc.)

Third, there are many situations in which it is not easy to figure out what should count as marital property and what should count as separate property. Suppose one of you had money before the marriage and put it into a joint bank account. It may not be easy to decide how the money that remains should be divided. An attorney can advise you on how to make these decisions.

Fourth, there may be special situations in which your property settlement is not covered by the form agreement.

An attorney can help you put the agreement in words that are legally precise and cannot be challenged or misinterpreted later on.

WHERE CAN YOU FIND AN ATTORNEY?

The yellow pages of your telephone directory will list, under "Attorney Referral Service," "Attorneys," or "Information Referral Service," organizations that can help you find a lawyer. In many cases you will be able to find an attorney who will charge only a small fee for your first visit. You can get information about free or low-cost legal services through the local bar association in your city or county.

XI. SOME GENERAL ADVICE

WHAT ABOUT INCOME TAXES?

If you or your spouse have filed a joint tax return, you both will still be responsible for paying any unpaid taxes even after your divorce.

If you are receiving a tax refund, you should agree in the property settlement agreement on how it should be divided.

The amount of money taken out of your paycheck for income taxes is going to be greater after you are single again, so you should be prepared for a bigger tax bite. It would be a good idea to consult the Internal Revenue Service or a tax expert on how the divorce is going to affect your taxes. You should probably do this before you make your property settlement agreement.

WHAT ABOUT BANK ACCOUNTS AND CREDIT CARDS?

If you have a joint bank account, it might be a good idea to close it and get two separate bank accounts. That way it will be easier to keep your money separate.

If you have credit card accounts that you have both been using, you should destroy the cards and apply for separate credit card accounts.

WHAT ABOUT REAL ESTATE?

Title to land or buildings cannot be changed by an agreement between the husband and wife alone. You may need to consult with a lawyer, title company, or other expert to help you.

WHAT ABOUT CARS?

If both your names are on a title to a car and you agree that one of you is going to own the car, you will need to change the ownership. You should call or visit the Division of Motor Vehicles to find out how to do that.

WHAT IF YOUR SPOUSE DOESN'T PAY HIS OR HER DEBTS?

If your spouse doesn't pay a debt, the person to whom the money is owed may still be able to collect it from you. However, later a court might order your spouse to pay to you the money you were forced to pay because of your spouse's failure to live up to your agreement.

CAN THE WIFE TAKE BACK HER FORMER NAME?

The wife in a dissolution has the right to give up her husband's name and get her former name back. You can do this by requesting it in the joint petition form.

WHEN YOUR DIVORCE IS FINAL, ALL YOUR RIGHTS AND DUTIES CONNECTED WITH YOUR MARRIAGE HAVE ENDED AND YOU CANNOT APPEAL. IF, HOWEVER, YOU DECIDE LATER THAT YOU WERE CHEATED OR PRESSURED BY YOUR SPOUSE, OR IF YOU BELIEVE THAT A MISTAKE WAS MADE IN THE PAPERWORK CONNECTED WITH THE DISSOLUTION THE COURT MAY BE ABLE TO SET ASIDE THE DIVORCE.

XII. SPECIAL INSTRUCTIONS
FOR _____ COUNTY

FEES:

FILING FEE: _____

Both **HUSBAND AND WIFE** should read and understand the informational booklet before starting the procedure.

Both **HUSBAND AND WIFE** must come into the office of the clerk of the circuit court in order to read and sign the petition for Simplified Dissolution of Marriage before the clerk of the court or a designated deputy clerk(s).

Both **HUSBAND'S AND WIFE'S** home and work telephone numbers must appear on the petition for Simplified Dissolution of Marriage.

Both **HUSBAND AND WIFE** must be present at the final hearing.

At the time the **petition for Simplified Dissolution of Marriage** is filed **AND**, again at the **final hearing, BOTH HUSBAND AND WIFE** must produce a(n):

    a.   Valid Florida Driver's License, or
    b.   Official Identification Card—Either will provide the picture identification necessary to file the petition and provide picture identification for the final hearing.

To obtain a Florida Driver's License or Official Identification Card contact the Florida Division of Motor Vehicles.

Identification Cards may be obtained if:

    a.   A person has never had a license, or
    b.   The license has been suspended

You cannot make application if you have a valid Florida Driver's License.

Persons applying for Identification Cards must produce:

    a.   Social Security Card—paper, no metal cards
    b.   Two (2) legal forms of identification. The Division will accept any two of the following; however, the identification must be the original or a certified copy.
        1.   Birth Certificate
        2.   Voter Registration Card
        3.   Marriage Certificate
        4.   Passport
        5.   Military Identification Card
        6.   Letter from last school with school seal verifying name and date of birth
        7.   Life Insurance Policy at least 2 years old containing name and date of birth of insured

The following forms should be filled out and filed with the court when using this Simplified Procedure:

1. Form 1—Petition/Request for Simplified Dissolution of Marriage (Divorce)
2. Form 3 or 4—Financial Affidavit
3. Form 5—Marital Settlement Agreement
4. Form 6—Certificate of Corroborating Witness
5. Form 34—Affidavit of Insolvency (should be completed and filed if you are requesting a waiver of filing fees because of financial reasons)
6. Civil Cover Sheet—available from the clerk of court's office.
7. Final Judgment Dissolving Marriage under Simplified Dissolution Procedure

FORM 1—PETITION FOR SIMPLIFIED DISSOLUTION OF MARRIAGE (DIVORCE)

You may use this form to request a Simplified Dissolution of Marriage (Divorce). This form is to be used only if <u>all</u> the following statements are true. If any one of the statements is not true, you cannot use this form.

1. We have no minor (under 18) children or dependent children.

2. We have no adopted children under 18 years of age.

3. The wife is not pregnant.

4. At least one of us has lived in Florida for the past six months.

5. We have made provisions for the division of our property and the payment of our obligations, and we are satisfied with them.

6. We have both signed the joint petition and all other papers needed to carry out this procedure and paid the required fees to the clerk of the circuit court.

7.   We both want to end the marriage because of serious permanent differences.

8.   We have both agreed to use the Simplified Dissolution of Marriage procedure rather than a regular dissolution.

9.   We both are aware of the following facts:

       (a)   That after the dissolution becomes final, neither of us has any right to expect money or support from the other, except for what is included in the Property Settlement Agreement; and

       (b)   That by choosing the Simplified Dissolution of Marriage procedure, we give up certain legal rights that we would have if we had used the regular dissolution procedure.

Please see Simplified Dissolution of Marriage (divorce), Appendix 1, for additional information on the use of this form. You also may read Chapter 61, Florida Statutes, for further information.

NOTE: You or the clerk will need to complete a Civil Cover Sheet (Form 1.997, Florida Rules of Civil Procedure) when this form is filed with the clerk of the court. The clerk's office can provide this form.

IN THE CIRCUIT COURT OF THE _____ JUDICIAL
CIRCUIT, IN AND FOR _____ COUNTY, FLORIDA

IN RE: The Marriage of   CASE NO: <u>XX-XXX-XX-XX-X</u>

_____.

             Husband,

                         PETITION BY HUSBAND
and   **AND WIFE FOR SIMPLIFIED**
                         DISSOLUTION OF MARRIAGE
                             (DIVORCE)

_____.

             Wife,

(NO CHILDREN OF THE MARRIAGE UNDER 18 YEARS OF AGE
AND PROPERTY AGREEMENT REACHED BY THE PARTIES)

The petition of the Husband and Wife says:

1.   This is a request for dissolution of marriage/divorce.

2.   The Husband and Wife or one of them is a resident of _____ County, Florida, and has been a resident of Florida for at least 6 months before filing this request.

3.   The Husband and Wife were married to each other on _____, 19___, in the City of _____, the County of _____, State or Country of _____.

4.   The marriage between the parties is irretrievably broken (We want to end our marriage because of serious permanent differences.)

5.   We do not have any children who were born or adopted by us who are under the age of 18, and the Wife is not pregnant.

6.   The Husband and Wife have made a Marital Settlement Agreement dividing their property and their bills. The Husband and Wife are satisfied with this agreement. The attached agreement was signed freely and voluntarily by the Husband and Wife, each intending to be bound by it.

7.   The Husband and Wife each have filled out and signed financial statements which are attached to the petition.

8.   The Wife wants to be called by her former name (yes ___ no ___). If "yes," state the Wife's former name: _____.

9.   Each party certifies that he/she has not been threatened or pressured into signing this request. Each understands that the result of signing this request may be a final dissolution of the marriage/divorce with no further relief.

10.   The parties understand that they both are required to appear before the judge to testify as to the matters contained in this request.

11.   The Husband and Wife understand that they may have legal rights against each other arising out of the marriage and that by signing this request they may be giving up those rights.

12.   The Husband and Wife ask the court to dissolve their marriage (grant a divorce) and to approve the Marital Settlement Agreement.

UNDER PENALTY OF PERJURY, WE STATE THE ABOVE FACTS ARE TRUE.

_____   _____
Wife's signature   Husband's signature

_____   _____
Wife's name   Husband's name
(please print or type)   (please print or type)

_____   _____
Wife's address   Husband's address

_____   _____

_____   _____

_____   _____
Wife's phone number   Husband's phone number

SWORN TO and signed before me on _____, 19_____

By: _____

<u>FORM 3—FINANCIAL AFFIDAVIT FOR DISSOLUTION OF MARRIAGE</u>

Completion of a financial affidavit involves figuring out your income, the values of your property, and your debts. A sample financial affidavit, filled out for an imaginary person, appears in Appendix 1. You may use it as a model for your own affidavit.

IN THE CIRCUIT COURT OF THE _____ JUDICIAL CIRCUIT, IN AND FOR _____ COUNTY, FLORIDA

IN RE: The Marriage of   CASE NO: _____

_____,
Husband,

and

FINANCIAL STATEMENT FOR DISSOLUTION OF MARRIAGE (DIVORCE)

_____,
Wife,

FINANCIAL AFFIDAVIT

STATE OF FLORIDA)
COUNTY OF   )

BEFORE ME, this day personally appeared _____, who being duly sworn, deposes and says that the following information is true and correct according to his/her best knowledge and belief:

ITEM 1: EMPLOYMENT AND INCOME

OCCUPATION:
EMPLOYED BY:
ADDRESS:

SOC. SEC. #:
PAY PERIOD:
RATE OF PAY:

AVERAGE GROSS MONTHLY INCOME
                    FROM EMPLOYMENT $
Bonuses, commissions, allowances, overtime, tips and
        similar payments $
Business income from sources such as self-employment,
        partnership, close corporations, and/or independent
        contracts (gross receipts minus ordinary and
        necessary expenses required to produce income) $
Disability benefits $
Workers' Compensation $
Unemployment Compensation $
Pension, retirement, or annuity payments $
Social Security benefits $
Spousal support received from previous marriage $
Interest and dividends $
Rental income (gross receipts minus ordinary and
        necessary expenses to produce income) $
Income from royalties, trust, or estates $
Reimbursed expenses and in-kind payments to the
        extent that they reduce personal living expenses $
Gains derived from dealing in property (not including
        non-recurring gains) $
Itemize any other income of a recurring nature $
TOTAL MONTHLY INCOME $

LESS DEDUCTIONS:
Federal, state and local income taxes (corrected for filing
        status and actual number of withholding allowances) $
FICA or self-employment tax (annualized) $
Mandatory union dues $
Mandatory retirement $
Health insurance payments $
Court ordered support payments for the children actually paid $
TOTAL DEDUCTIONS $

ITEM 2: AVERAGE MONTHLY EXPENSES

HOUSEHOLD:

Mtg. or rent payments
Property taxes &
        insurance
Electricity
Water, garbage, & sewer
Telephone
Fuel oil or natural gas
Repairs and maintenance
Lawn and pool care
Pest control
Misc. household
Food and grocery items
Meals outside home
Other: _____
        _____

AUTOMOBILE:

Gasoline and oil
Repairs
Auto tags and license
Insurance
Other: _____
        _____

CHILDREN'S EXPENSES:

Nursery or babysitting
School tuition
School supplies
Lunch money
Allowance
Clothing
Medical, dental,
        prescription
Vitamins
Barber/beauty parlor
Cosmetics/toiletries
Gifts for special holidays
Other: _____
        _____

INSURANCES:

Health
Life
Other: _____
        _____

OTHER EXPENSES NOT LISTED
ABOVE:

Dry cleaning and laundry
Affiant's clothing
Affiant's medical, dental,
        prescriptions
Affiant's beauty salon
Affiant's gifts (special
        holidays)

Pets:
Grooming
Veterinarian

Membership dues:
Professional dues
Social dues

Entertainment
Vacations
Publications
Religious organizations
Charities

Miscellaneous

OTHER EXPENSES:

_____
_____
_____

TOTAL ABOVE EXPENSES
                $

PAYMENTS TO CREDITORS:

TO WHOM:	BALANCE DUE:	MONTHLY PAYMENTS:
VISA	_____	_____
Texaco	_____	_____
_____	_____	_____
_____	_____	_____
_____	_____	_____
_____	_____	_____

Total Monthly Payments to Creditors: $
TOTAL MONTHLY EXPENSES: $

ITEM 3: ASSETS (OWNERSHIP: IF JOINT, ALLOCATE EQUALLY)

Description	Value	Husband	Wife
Cash (on hand or in banks)			
Stocks/bonds/notes			
Real Estate:			
Home:			
Automobiles:			
Other personal property:			
Contents of home			
Jewelry			
Life ins./cash surrender value			
Other assets:			
TOTAL ASSETS:	_____	_____	_____

ITEM 4: LIABILITIES

Creditor	Security	Value	Husband	Wife
VISA				
Texaco				
Mortgage Company				

TOTAL LIABILITIES: _____   _____   _____

SWORN TO and signed before me   _____
on _____, 19___.   Affiant

_____
NOTARY PUBLIC
My Commission Expires:

FORM 4—FINANCIAL AFFIDAVIT (FAMILY LAW)

See instructions for Form 3 and Appendix 1.

IN THE CIRCUIT COURT OF THE _____ JUDICIAL
CIRCUIT, IN AND FOR _____ COUNTY, FLORIDA

IN RE: The Marriage of   CASE NO: _____

_____,

Husband,   **FINANCIAL AFFIDAVIT**
                            (FAMILY LAW)
and

_____,

Wife,

FINANCIAL AFFIDAVIT

STATE OF FLORIDA)
COUNTY OF   )

        BEFORE ME, this day personally appeared _____, who being
duly sworn, deposes and says that the following information is true and correct
according to his/her best knowledge and belief:

ITEM 1: EMPLOYMENT AND INCOME

OCCUPATION:
EMPLOYED BY:
ADDRESS:

SOC. SEC. #:
PAY PERIOD:
RATE OF PAY:

AVERAGE GROSS MONTHLY INCOME
                 FROM EMPLOYMENT $

Bonuses, commissions, allowances, overtime, tips and
         similar payments $

Business income from sources such as self-employment,
         partnership, close corporations, and/or independent
         contracts (gross receipts minus ordinary and
         necessary expenses required to produce income) $

Disability benefits $

Workers' Compensation $

Unemployment Compensation $

Pension, retirement, or annuity payments $

Social Security benefits $

Spousal support received from previous marriage $

Interest and dividends $

Rental income (gross receipts minus ordinary and
         necessary expenses to produce income) $

Income from royalties, trust, or estates $

Reimbursed expenses and in-kind payments to the
         extent that they reduce personal living expenses $

Gains derived from dealing in property (not including
         non-recurring gains) $

Itemize any other income of a recurring nature $

TOTAL MONTHLY INCOME $

LESS DEDUCTIONS:

Federal, state and local income taxes (corrected for filing
         status and actual number of withholding allowances) $

FICA or self-employment tax (annualized) $

Mandatory union dues $

Mandatory retirement $

Health insurance payments $

Court ordered support payments for the children actually paid $

TOTAL DEDUCTIONS $

ITEM 2: AVERAGE MONTHLY EXPENSES

HOUSEHOLD:

Mtg. or rent payments
Property taxes &
      insurance
Electricity
Water, garbage, & sewer
Telephone
Fuel oil or natural gas
Repairs and maintenance
Lawn and pool care
Pest control
Misc. household
Food and grocery items
Meals outside home
Other: _____
      _____

AUTOMOBILE:

Gasoline and oil
Repairs
Auto tags and license
Insurance
Other: _____
      _____

CHILDREN'S EXPENSES:

Nursery or babysitting
School tuition
School supplies
Lunch money
Allowance
Clothing
Medical, dental,
      prescription
Vitamins
Barber/beauty parlor
Cosmetics/toiletries
Gifts for special holidays
Other: _____
      _____

INSURANCES:

Health
Life
Other: _____
      _____

OTHER EXPENSES NOT LISTED
ABOVE:

Dry cleaning and laundry
Affiant's clothing
Affiant's medical, dental,
      prescriptions
Affiant's beauty salon
Affiant's gifts (special
      holidays)

Pets:
Grooming
Veterinarian

Membership dues:
Professional dues
Social dues

Entertainment
Vacations
Publications
Religious organizations
Charities

Miscellaneous

OTHER EXPENSES:
_____
_____
_____
_____

TOTAL ABOVE EXPENSES

$

PAYMENTS TO CREDITORS:

TO WHOM:	BALANCE DUE:	MONTHLY PAYMENTS:
VISA		
Texaco		

Total Monthly Payments to Creditors: $
TOTAL MONTHLY EXPENSES: $

ITEM 3: ASSETS (OWNERSHIP: IF JOINT, ALLOCATE EQUALLY)

Description	Value	Husband	Wife
Cash (on hand or in banks)			
Stocks/bonds/notes			
Real Estate:			
Home:			
Automobiles:			
Other personal property:			
Contents of home			
Jewelry			
Life ins./cash			
surrender value			
Other assets:			
TOTAL ASSETS:	_____	_____	_____

ITEM 4: LIABILITIES

Creditor	Security	Value	Husband	Wife
VISA				
Texaco				
Mortgage Company				

TOTAL LIABILITIES:

SWORN TO and signed before me   _____
on _____, 19___.   Affiant

_____
NOTARY PUBLIC
My Commission Expires:

FORM 5—MARITAL SETTLEMENT AGREEMENT FOR DISSOLUTION OF MARRIAGE/DIVORCE

NOTE: This form is to be used:

(a) In a "Simplified Dissolution/Divorce Procedure" when (1) both parties agree to divorce; (2) there are no children under 18 years of age; (3) both parties have previously signed a "Petition/Request by Husband and Wife for Dissolution of Marriage/Divorce (No Children of the Marriage Under 18 Years of Age and Property Agreement Reached by the Parties)"; (4) there is no request for alimony; and (5) the parties have reached an agreement as to how all their property and bills are to be divided; or

(b) When both parties, although not initially agreeing to get a divorce, later do agree to a divorce, have worked out an agreement to split up property and responsibility for paying bills, there are no children under 18 years of age, and there is no request for alimony.

Other legal papers may need to be prepared, signed, witnessed, and recorded in order to give the title of certain belongings or possessions such as land, cars, boats, mobile homes, etc. For example, you may need to prepare a deed to give title of land or a house to the husband/wife, or you may need to sign a certificate of title to give a car to the husband/wife.

If additional space is needed, please use additional sheets of paper. Please sign and date any additional sheets of paper used and attach those sheets to this Marital Settlement Agreement for Divorce.

See Appendix 1 for more information.

IN THE CIRCUIT COURT OF THE _____ JUDICIAL CIRCUIT, IN AND FOR _____ COUNTY, FLORIDA

IN RE: The Marriage of   CASE NO: _____

_____,
Husband,

and

MARITAL SETTLEMENT AGREEMENT FOR DISSOLUTION OF MARRIAGE/DIVORCE

_____,
Wife,

We, _____, the Husband, and _____, the Wife, were married on _____, 19____. Because of irreconcilable differences in our marriage (no chance of staying together), we have made this agreement to settle once and for all what we owe to each other and what we can expect from each other. Each of us states that nothing has been held back, that we have honestly included everything we could think of in listing our assets (everything we own and that is owed to us), and our debts (everything we owe);

and each of us states that we believe the other one has been open and honest in writing this agreement. Each of us agrees to sign and exchange any papers that might be needed to complete this agreement. Each of us gives up any right to alimony that we may have.

DIVISION OF POSSESSIONS (EVERYTHING WE OWN)

We divide our possessions (everything we own) as follows:

    1.   The Husband gives to the Wife the following belongings:

A.

B.

C.

D.

E.

    2.   The Wife gives to the Husband the following belongings:

A.

B.

C.

D.

E.

DIVISION OF BILLS AND DEBTS (EVERYTHING WE OWE)

     1.   The Husband shall pay the following bills and will not ask at any time the Wife to pay these bills:

A.

B.

C.

D.

E.

     2.   The Wife shall pay the following bills and will not ask at any time the Husband to pay these bills:

A.

B.

C.

D.

E.

DATED: _____   DATED: _____

_____   _____
Husband's signature   Wife's signature
Name_____   Name_____
Address_____   Address_____
Telephone No._____   Telephone No._____

SWORN TO and signed before me
on _____, 19_____

_____
NOTARY PUBLIC
My Commission Expires:

FORM 6—CERTIFICATE OF CORROBORATING WITNESS

This form must be signed by a person who knows that either the husband or the wife has lived in the State of Florida for more than 6 months before the date you signed your Request for Dissolution of Marriage. The witness must be someone who can truthfully swear to your residence in Florida. This certificate must be signed in the presence of a notary public or the clerk of the circuit court, who must affix his or her seal at the proper place on the certificate. You file this document with the court when you file your Request for Dissolution of Marriage.

IN THE CIRCUIT COURT OF THE _____ JUDICIAL
CIRCUIT, IN AND FOR _____ COUNTY, FLORIDA

IN RE: The Marriage of   CASE NO: _____

_____.
                              Husband,

and   **CERTIFICATE OF
                                           CORROBORATING WITNESS**

_____.
                              Wife,

UNDER PENALTY OF PERJURY, I CERTIFY that I am a resident of the State of Florida; I have known _____ for more than 6 months before the date of filing the petition in this action and know of my own personal knowledge that this person has resided in the State of Florida for at least that period of time. I have attached a copy of Florida driver's license or Florida identification card to this certificate.

_____   _____
Witness' Signature   Witness Residence Address

_____   _____
Witness' Name (Typed or Printed)   City, State, Zip Code

SWORN TO and signed before me
on _____, 19_____

_____
NOTARY PUBLIC
My Commission Expires:

IN THE CIRCUIT COURT OF THE _____ JUDICIAL
CIRCUIT, IN AND FOR _____ COUNTY, FLORIDA

IN RE: The Marriage of   CASE NO: _____

_____,
                                                  Husband,
    and

_____,
                                                  Wife,

FINAL JUDGMENT DISSOLVING MARRIAGE
UNDER SIMPLIFIED DISSOLUTION PROCEDURE

This action came before the court upon the petition of the parties for dissolution of their marriage. Upon consideration thereof, it is

ADJUDGED that the bonds of marriage between _____
and _____ are dissolved.

(If Applicable) IT IS FURTHER ADJUDGED that the wife's former name is restored and she shall hereafter be known as
_____.

(If Applicable) IT IS FURTHER ADJUDGED that the property settlement agreement filed in this proceeding as Exhibit ___ was executed voluntarily, after full disclosure, and same is approved and incorporated in this judgment by reference and the parties are ordered to comply with it.

DONE AND ORDERED at West Palm Beach, Florida, on this _____ day of _____, 19___.

_____
Circuit Judge

(Used with permission of The Florida Bar: Continuing Legal Education Series, Florida Dissolution of Marriage.)

APPENDIX C:
Emanuel Gerstein Inc.
Forensic Accountants
44 COCOANUT ROW   PALM BEACH, FLORIDA
334800-4005
407/832-3060   Telex: 446140   Fax: 407/832-3224

AGREEMENT FOR PROFESSIONAL ENGAGEMENT
(Courtesy of Emanuel Gerstein Inc. Forensic Accountants)

AGREEMENT, made this _____ day of _____, 19___ between
_____, a _____ corporation with offices at
_____ (hereinafter referred to as the Firm), and
_____ (hereinafter referred
to as the Client).

IT IS AGREED AS FOLLOWS:

1.   SERVICES

The Firm will compile from information the Client provides, a financial affidavit containing among other terms, the Client's current income, current and/or prospective expenses, assets, and liabilities as at an appropriate date preceding the filing for the dissolution of marriage. Unless unusual circumstances not now foreseen make it impractical for us to do so, the Firm is available to assist the Client and the Client's counsel in the following areas:

- preparation of answers to interrogatories served upon the Client by the Client's spouse
- analysis of the Client's spouse's income, expenses, assets, and liabilities
- assistance rendered in producing items in response to a Notice to Produce
- review and analysis of the Client's spouse's production
- court appearances by the Firm on the Client's behalf pursuant to instruction by the Client's counsel
- attendance at depositions, as required by Client's counsel
- preparation of demonstrative exhibits

- attendance at settlement or mediation conferences as required by Client's counsel
- any other related functions pursuant to instructions by the Client's counsel

2.   POSSIBLE ADDITIONAL SERVICES

It is recognized by the parties that outside the terms of this Agreement, the Firm is available to provide other services upon request by the Client. Such services shall be provided under the same terms and conditions as those covered by this Agreement unless documented by a separate Agreement.

3.   FEES FOR PROFESSIONAL SERVICES

The Firm will keep records of the time it spends on these matters commencing with the initial contact on the above including time spent by the Principal, Manager, Senior Accountant, Semi-Senior Accountant, Computer Operator, and Clerical staff. The Firm shall be paid the hourly fee as set forth on the attached Fee Schedule. The hourly charge is specifically understood to include travel time. Furthermore, some duplication of time is necessary, for instance, accountants may consult from time to time regarding matters of discovery, research, document compilation, computations, and attendance at hearings. Duplication will be minimized consistent with proper representation of you.

4.   RETAINER, CHARGES, AND RESPONSIBILITIES

A. The Firm requires a non-refundable retainer of $_____ to be applied to the final billing.

B. It is impossible to determine in advance the amount of time that will be needed to complete your case. The Firm will use its best judgment to determine the amount of time, who is to perform the work, and the nature of the services to be performed in your best interests.

C. Invoices will be submitted monthly and are due upon presentation. Any balance unpaid after 30 days will bear interest at the rate of 18 percent per annum simple interest from the date of billing until paid in full. Failure by the Client to remit monthly charges and approved out-of-pocket costs in accordance with this Agreement may cause a delay in the Firm's ability to perform additional services until payment is received or other satisfactory arrangements in writing have been made. The balance of fees and out-of-pocket costs, if any, net of the retainer for our final bill is payable within ten (10) days from the date thereof.

D. In some instances, the Court will require an adverse party to pay a portion or all of the Firm's fees and costs incurred by the Client. Regardless of any such order of the Court, and regardless of whether or not any amount is or is not paid by any adverse party pursuant to Court order, the sole responsibility for payment of the Firm's fees and costs incurred in connection with the above-referenced matter will remain with the Client. Amounts received pursuant to Court orders will be credited to your account. The Court award of fees, if any, does not set or limit our fee in any way.

E. It is understood that the employment of the Firm for representation in the said matters is on an hourly basis, and no maximum fee has been quoted, and no guarantee of results has been or will be made.

F. The services described in paragraph one are not designed and cannot be relied upon to disclose errors, irregularities, or illegal acts, including fraud or defalcations that may exist; although their discovery may result from the Firm's engagement. However, the Firm will promptly inform the Client of any matters that come to the Firm's attention that appear to be unusual or abnormal.

5. CLIENT ASSISTANCE

In order for the Firm to work as effectively as possible, it is understood that the Client will provide information or documentation which shall be discussed with the client. The services will be completed in as timely a manner as possible consistent with the conditions of the engagement.

6. CONFIDENTIALITY

With respect to financial, statistical, and personal data relating to the Client which is confidential and which is submitted to or obtained by the Firm in order to carry out the Agreement, the Firm will instruct its personnel to keep such information confidential.

7.   RIGHT TO WITHDRAW

The Firm reserves the right to withdraw from this engagement upon notifying the Client of the Firm's intentions. In such an event, it is the policy of the Firm to bill the Client for services provided and charges incurred on the Client's behalf to the point of withdrawal.

8.   GOVERNING LAW

This Agreement shall be governed and its terms construed in accordance with the laws of the State of Florida applicable to contracts to be performed in that state. This Agreement supersedes all proposals, oral or written, and all other communications between the parties relating to the engagement subject matter.

9.   COSTS

You have agreed to pay this Firm, upon request, either by an advance which shall be retained by this Firm in its trust account, or promptly upon invoice, in addition to any fees incurred, all costs expended by this Firm which shall include, but not be limited to, such fees as may be charged by expert witnesses, photocopy expenses, long distance calls, and travel expenses, independently contracted research or investigation or similar items.

To protect the fees and costs until they are paid, you hereby grant to this Firm an accountants charging lien on the assets of any value whatsoever in connection with your interest in this litigation. In the event that this Firm is discharged or is required to withdraw as accountant for you or does withdraw as accountant for you, before completion of any of the above matters, prior to any substitution of accountant, this Firm shall be entitled to obtain an order protecting this Firm's right to a charging lien and to have the amount of accountants' fees determined in the same action before that suit is dismissed or concluded and before any distribution to you, if applicable.

10.   WORK PRODUCT

All papers, records, documents, exhibits, or other items delivered to this Firm by you shall be returned to you at the conclusion of the case and following the full payment of the fees and costs agreed to be paid, but may be retained by this Firm under a retaining lien which you hereby grant until full payment of all amounts agreed to be paid hereunder to this Firm. All papers produced by this Firm and all research and other work done by this Firm shall remain the confidential property of the Firm.

11.   ATTORNEY FEES

If it is necessary for either party to bring an action to enforce this Agreement or to collect any amount to be paid hereunder, the prevailing party shall be entitled to the payment of reasonable attorneys' fees, including those on appeal and all costs.

12.   RESPONSIBILITY

You are individually and personally liable for all amounts agreed to be paid to this Firm under this Agreement. By signing this letter, you hereby agree to the foregoing and consent to same, completely.

I HAVE READ AND UNDERSTOOD THIS AGREEMENT.

_____   _____
_____   _____
_____   _____

(Firm's name & address)   (Client's name & address)

BY: _____   BY: _____
TITLE: _____   TITLE: _____
DATE: _____   DATE: _____

BIBLIOGRAPHY

Florida Dissolution of Marriage, The Florida Bar: Continuing Legal Education Series.

The World of Negotiations: Never Being a Loser, Peter L. Grieco, Jr. and Paul G. Hine, PT Publications, Inc., Palm Beach Gardens, FL.

People Empowerment: Achieving Success from Involvement, Wayne L. Douchkoff and Michael W. Gozzo, PT Publications, Inc., Palm Beach Gardens, FL.

Getting to Yes, Roger Fisher and William Ury, Penguin Books, New York, NY.

The Wife-in-Law Trap, Ann Cryster, Pocket Books, New York, NY.

You're Entitled! A Divorce Lawyer Talks to Women, Sidney M. De Angelis, Contemporary Books, Chicago, IL.

Divorcing, Melvin M. Belli, Sr. and Mel Krantzler, Ph.D., St. Martin's Press, New York, NY.

The Custody Handbook, Persia Woolley, Summit Books, New York, NY.

Love and the Law: A Legal Guide to Relationships in the '90s, Gail J. Koff, Esq., Simon & Schuster Inc., New York, NY.

Men and Divorce: Coping, Learning, Starting Afresh, John Abulafia, Fontana Paperbacks, London, UK.

INDEX